WE ARE ANARCHISTS

Essays on Anarchism, Pacifism, and the
Indian Independence Movement, 1923–1953

M.P.T. ACHARYA

Edited and introduced by Ole Birk Laursen

We are Anarchists:
Essays on Anarchism, Pacifism, and the Indian Independence Movement, 1923–1953
Introduction and notes © 2019 Ole Birk Laursen
© 2019 AK Press (Chico, Edinburgh)

ISBN: 978-1-84935-342-7
E-ISBN: 978-1-84935-343-4
Library of Congress Control Number: 2018961759

AK Press   AK Press
370 Ryan Ave. #100   33 Tower St.
Chico, CA 95973   Edinburgh EH6 7BN
United States   Scotland
www.akpress.org   www.akuk.com
akpress@akpress.org   ak@akedin.demon.co.uk

The above addresses would be delighted to provide you with the latest
AK Press distribution catalog, which features books, pamphlets, zines, and
stylish apparel published and/or distributed by AK Press. Alternatively,
visit our websites for the complete catalog, latest news, and secure ordering

Cover illustration by Julia Simoniello
Cover design by Suzanne Shaffer
Layout and typesetting by Morgan Buck

Printed in the USA

Contents

Abbreviations

AINTUC	All India National Trade Union Congress
AITUC	All India Trade Union Congress
CPI	Communist Party of India
DCI	Department of Criminal Intelligence at Scotland Yard
FAUD	Freie Arbeiter Union Deutschlands
IIC	Indian Independence Committee
IIS	Indian Institute of Sociology
INC	Indian National Congress
INTUC	Indian National Trade Union Congress
IRA	Indian Revolutionary Association
IWA	International Workingmen's Association
IWMA	International Working Men's Association
IWW	Industrial Workers of the World
LAI	League against Imperialism
LSI	Libertarian Socialist Institute
PAICRC	Provisional All-India Central Revolutionary Committee
WRI	War Resisters' International

Acknowledgments

EDITING THIS BOOK HAS BEEN a labor of love, but I could not have done it alone. I would like to thank Andrew Zonneveld, Charles Weigl, and AK Press for taking on the project, and for their advice, help, and constant support throughout the writing process. I am very grateful to Julia Simoniello for bringing Acharya to life with the beautiful cover image. I am also indebted to Lina Bernstein, Jesse Cohn, Vadim Damier, Andrew Davies, Stephen Legg, Sara Legrandjacques, Pavan Malreddy, and Alex Tickell for their comments and clarifications as well.

M. P. T. Acharya wrote in numerous languages, and one of the greatest tasks has been to find and translate his writings. I am hugely grateful to Sarah Arens, Constance Bantman, Enrique Galvan-Alvarez, and Julia Scheib for their invaluable help with those translations.

Any historian relies on archives, and archivists and librarians are key to unlocking those archives. I am particularly thankful to Stefan Dickers at the Bishopsgate Institute, London; Jacques Gillen at Mundaneum, Centre d'archives de la Fédération Wallonie-Bruxelles & Espace d'expositions temporaries; Katherine Schmelling at Walter P. Reuther Library, Wayne State University; Carol Stewart at the Anderson Library, University of Strathclyde; the staff at the British Library, London; the International Institute of Social History, Amsterdam; and the Bibliothèque nationale de France, Paris.

Lastly, I could not have done this without Ariane Mildenberg, who patiently listened to many of my stories about Acharya, gave feedback, and offered advice without hesitation.

M. P. T. Acharya:
A Revolutionary, an Agitator, a Writer

BORN IN MADRAS (NOW CHENNAI), India, on April 15, 1887, the Indian revolutionary Mandayam Prativadi Bhayankaram Tirumal "M. P. T." Acharya had a three-decade career in the international anarchist movement from 1923 until his death in 1954. Throughout those years, this Indian anarchist—who was "striving on his own in the whole sub-continent to establish a movement," as Albert Meltzer recalled—mapped new conceptual territories as he straddled both anti-imperial and anarchist circles.[1] At a time when the Russian Revolution set in motion new hopes for colonized nations and their revolutionaries, Acharya's turn to anarchism is remarkable and stands out against more well-known contemporaries—and former comrades—such as Virendranath "Chatto" Chattopadhyaya and M. N. Roy as well as the Tolstoyan anarcho-pacifist tendencies of Mohandas K. Gandhi. Indeed, in a fitting testimony to Acharya, Meltzer wrote in his obituary:

> [I]t was impossible to comprehend the difficulty in standing out against the tide so completely as was necessary in a country like India. It was easy for former "nationalist revolutionaries" to assert their claims to the positions left vacant by the old "imperialist oppressors." This Acharya would not do. He remained an uncompromising rebel, and when age prevented him

---

1. Albert Meltzer, *I Couldn't Paint Golden Angels: Sixty Years of Commonplace Life and Anarchist Agitation* (Edinburgh: AK Press, 1996), 127.

from speaking, he continued writing right up to the time of his death.[2]

Echoing Meltzer, Vladimir Muños said that Acharya was "incorruptible," Victor Garcia called Acharya "the most prominent figure among Indian libertarians," and Hem Day summed up: "he is not well known to all, even to our own people, for he has neither the fame of Gandhi, nor the fame of Nehru, nor the popularity of Vinoba, nor the notoriety of Kumarapa, nor the dignity of Tagore. He is Acharya, a revolutionary, an agitator, a writer."[3] A prolific writer, Acharya's essays are testimony to a tireless agitator and intellectual within the international anarchist movement, often giving a unique perspective on anarchism, pacifism, and the Indian independence movement. Collected here for the first time, Acharya's essays open a window onto the global reach of anarchism in this period and enables a more nuanced understanding of Indian anti-colonial struggles against oppressive state power, be it imperialist, Bolshevik, or capitalist.

Acharya's wandering movements across India, Europe, the Middle East, the United States, and Russia during the early twentieth century has made it difficult for historians to trace his personal and political development from anti-colonial nationalist to co-founder of the Communist Party of India (CPI) in October 1920 and then, lastly, to international anarchist, as the archives housing his works are scattered across three continents. Aside from Maia Ramnath's acknowledgment that "among radical nationalist revolutionaries, none made their identification with the international anarchist movement more explicit than Acharya," there has been no sustained

---

2. Internationalist [Albert Meltzer], "M. P. T. Acharya," *Freedom: The Anarchist Weekly*, 15:33 (August 14, 1954), 3.

3. Vladimir Muñoz, "Filosofemas la Masculinocracia," *Cenit: Revista de Sociologia, Ciencia y Literatura*, October 1955, 1678; Victor Garcia, "Mandyam Acharya," in *Les Cahiers de Contre-Courant: Pionniers et Militants d-Avant-Garde*, ed. Louis Louvet (Paris: Contre-Courant, 1960), 219; Hem Day, "Voici Un Agitateur Indou: M. P. Acharya," *Inde: Social-Philosophie, Impressions, Essais* (Paris, Bruxelles: Pensée et Action, 1962); "Mandyam Acharya, révolutionnaire agitateur indou," correspondence with Hem Day, MUND ARCH 15 ANAR 3F 01 30, Mundaneum Archives, Belgium.

attempt to understand Acharya's anarchist philosophy as both a logical extension of and departure from his anti-colonial revolutionary activities.[4] Vadim Damier briefly discusses Acharya's work within the International Working Men's Association (IWMA) milieu of the 1920s, while Lina Bernstein has done a commendable job of tracing his activities in Russia during the revolutionary years.[5] C. S. Subramanyam's biography does not include any detailed examination of Acharya's anarchist activities, focusing instead almost exclusively on his anti-colonial and Bolshevik work. In fact, Subramanyam even notes that, after Acharya's turn to anarchism, "he seems to have come back [to India] having lost faith in political organization and political parties. That probably accounts for the lack of any significant political activity of his that could be traced or any activity that had any relevance to the events and movements of this period 1935–1954."[6] Subramanyam's suggestion that Acharya disappeared from politics in India signals, of course, the relatively minor influence of anarchism in India, but at the same time it also reveals a significant omission in Subramanyam's own critical historiography as Subramanyam was one of the founding members of the CPI in the south of India. While skeptics might object that Acharya's writings had little impact in India, his place within the international anarchist scene compels us to think more carefully about the global reach of anarchism and, at the

---

4. Maia Ramnath, *Decolonizing Anarchism: An Antiauthoritarian History of India's Liberation Struggle* (Oakland: AK Press, 2011), 125.

5. Vadim Damier, *The Forgotten International: The International Anarcho-Syndicalist Movement Between the Two World Wars, Vol. 1: From Revolutionary Syndicalism to Anarcho-Syndicalism, 1918–1930* (Moscow: Novoe literaturnoe obozrenie, 2006), 336–337; Lina Bernstein, "Indian Nationalists' Cooperation with Soviet Russia in Central Asia: The Case of M.P.T. Acharya," in *Personal Narratives, Peripheral Theatres: Essays on the Great War (1914–18)*, eds. Anthony Barker, et al. (Cham, Switzerland: Springer International Publishing, 2018), 201–214; see also Vadim Damier, "Мандьяма Пративади Бхаянкара Тирумала Ачарья: от большевизма к анархизму," НЕПРИКОСНОВЕННЫЙ ЗАПАС, https://www.nlobooks.ru/magazines/neprikosnovennyy_zapas/115_nz_5_2017/article/19413/.

6. C. S. Subramanyam, *M. P. T. Acharya, His Life and Times: Revolutionary Trends in the Early Anti-Imperialist Movements in South India and Abroad* (Madras: Institute of South Indian Studies, 1995), 176–177.

same time, to acknowledge the limits of anarchist thought and praxis in the colonial Indian context, where the project of national liberation backed by the Communist International often held greater sway. Instead, working toward "imaginary futures," Acharya's anarchist writings signal a decidedly international approach to the question of freedom that extended beyond the immediate concerns of the establishment of an independent Indian nation-state.[7] Therefore, to understand Acharya's turn to anarchism and writings on pacifism and the Indian independence movement, it is useful to provide a biographical sketch of his revolutionary activities from 1907 until 1922.

Indian anti-colonial nationalism and the communist turn, 1907–1922

In the first installment of his "Reminiscences of a Revolutionary" (serialized from July to October, 1937 in *The Mahratta*), entitled "Why I Left India and How?," Acharya describes his flight from India, activities in London and Paris, and his attempt to go to Morocco to join the Rifs against Spain.[8] As it happened, before turning to anarchism, Acharya was already an experienced revolutionary anti-colonial agitator. In collaboration with C. Subramania Bharati, he edited the nationalist paper *India* in the French-Tamil city of Pondicherry from August to November 1907. When the British Government put pressure on the French authorities in Pondicherry to suppress the Indian revolutionaries in the province, Acharya decided to leave for Europe in November 1908. Arriving in Paris in early 1909, and proceeding to London a week later, he quickly became involved with the nationalists at India House, a hostel set up by Shyamaji Krishnavarma for Indian students and hub for revolutionary activity in the first decade of the twentieth century, then under leadership of the militant nationalist Vinayak Damodar Savarkar. After the Indian

---

7. Manu Goswami, "Imaginary Futures and Colonial Internationalisms," *AHR Forum*, 117:5 (December, 2012): 1463.

8. M. P. T. Acharya, "Reminiscences of a Revolutionary," *The Mahratta*, July 23, 1937, 5.

nationalist Madan Lal Dhingra assassinated political assistant Sir William Hutt Curzon Wyllie in London on July 1, 1909, the India House group came under heavy surveillance by the Department of Criminal Intelligence (DCI) at Scotland Yard, and many of the Indians left London for Paris.

In an effort to learn armed warfare, Acharya and his friend Sukh Sagar Dutt instead decided to leave for Morocco to join the Rifs in their fight against Spain.[9] Acharya only made it to Gibraltar, and returned to Paris, where he joined the Paris Indian Society, led by Madame Bhikaiji Cama, editor of *The Bande Mataram*, S. R. Rana, a pearl merchant and financier of the Indians in Paris, Chatto, and Lala Har Dayal. Alongside Cama, Rana, Chatto, Har Dayal, V. V. S. Aiyar, Madhav Rao, Govind Amin, and other Indian revolutionaries in Paris, Acharya associated with French socialists such as Jean Jaurès and Jean Longuet, Russian revolutionaries like Charles Rappoport, Ilya Rubanovich, and Mikhail Pavlovich, as well as Turkish, Persian, and Egyptian anti-colonial nationalists, notably Mansour Rifaat, who became a long-standing friend of Acharya. Additionally, according to Bhupendranath Dutta's recollections, Chatto and Acharya also associated with anarchists in Paris, although it is uncertain who these may have been.[10]

Acharya moved to Berlin in November 1910 to foment revolt among the Indians in the city, and then to Munich a few months later, where he first met Walter Strickland, a staunch supporter of the Indian revolutionaries in Europe and "the most anti-British Englishman," as he later recalled.[11] At the suggestion of Ajit Singh and Chatto, and with a letter of introduction in hand from

---

9. "Movements of M. P. Tirumalachari, formerly proprietor, publisher and editor of a Tamil newspaper called *India*, and Sakkagar Dutt; extradition of M. P. Tirumalachari," PR_000001028100, file 37; National Archives of India (NAI), New Delhi.

10. Ole Birk Laursen, "Anti-Colonialism, Terrorism, and the 'Politics of Friendship': Virendranath Chattopadhyaya and the European Anarchist Movement, 1910–1927," *Anarchist Studies*, 27:1 (Spring, 2019).

11. M. P. T. Acharya, "The Most Anti-British Englishman: Walter Strickland," *The Mahratta*, September 9, 1938, 3.

Strickland, Acharya moved to Constantinople (now Istanbul) in November 1911. There he made contact with the Committee of Union and Progress in an effort to secure the support of Muslims against British interests in the region, but no substantial connections were established.

Acharya proceeded to the United States in July 1912, where he lived with Chandra Kanta Chakravarti in New York City. As Acharya later wrote to Boris Yelensky, in New York he first met both Alexander Berkman and Hippolyte Havel.[12] In 1914, he joined the Yugantar Ashram in San Francisco where he translated for the Tamil edition of the *Ghadar*, the organ of the Hindustan Association of the Pacific Coast (Ghadar Party). Because of his involvement with the Ghadar Party, he was later sentenced in absentia in the Ghadar Conspiracy Trial of 1917–1918.[13]

Shortly after the First World War broke out in August 1914, Acharya's old comrade Chatto set up the Berlin-based Indian Independence Committee (IIC), located at Wielandstrasse 38. The IIC was formally attached to the Nachrichtenstelle für den Orient (Intelligence Bureau for the East), a branch of the German Foreign Office. Among the other founding members were Chempakaraman Pillai, Abdul Hafiz, and Moreshwar Prabhakar, while Har Dayal, Tarakhnath Das, Mohamed Barkatullah, and Harish Chandra soon joined. Acharya also soon returned from the U.S. to Berlin, and under the auspices of the IIC he led missions to the Middle East to secure the help of the Muslim world against Britain. Spending considerable time in Constantinople again, Acharya made little progress, though, and as the tides of the war were turning, he and Chatto relocated to Stockholm in May 1917, where a socialist peace conference was in the planning. As European socialists from the divided Second International debated over the

---

12. Acharya to Boris Yelensky, May 22, 1947, ARCH01674.46, Boris Yelensky Papers, IISH.
13. "Application of Mr M P T Acharya for a British Passport," British Library, London, India Office Records (IOR), L/E/7/1439, file 721; Weekly Report of the Director of Criminal Intelligence, IOR, November 10, 1914.

next six months, Acharya and Chatto tried to bring the question of Indian independence into the peace negotiations. Meanwhile, the Russian Revolution set other aspirations in motion. Acharya and Chatto attended the third Zimmerwald conference in Stockholm in September 1917, making contact with Konstantin Troyanovsky and Angelica Balabanoff, which led to a turn to communism after the Russian Revolution.[14] Many years later, in one of his Letters to the Editor of the periodical *Thought* (Chapter 48), Acharya described Balabanoff as "the mentor of Lenin and Mussolini whom she later quit." Perhaps still hopeful of assistance from the international socialist movement, Acharya attended the International Socialist Congress in Bern, Switzerland, in February 1919, but is not known to have addressed the audience. He did, however, discuss Madame Cama's ailing health with Jean Longuet.[15]

After more than a decade of revolutionary activities across India, Europe, the Middle East, and the United States, Acharya spent three years in Russia during the revolutionary years. In May 1919, he and a group of Indians led by Mahendra Pratap met Lenin in Moscow, before they proceeded to Kabul (now in Afghanistan), where they set up the Indian Revolutionary Association (IRA). Congratulating them, Lenin wrote: "I am glad to greet the young union of Muslim and Hindu revolutionaries and sincerely wish that this Association will extend its activities among all workmen of the East."[16] Perhaps encouraged by Lenin's support, Acharya responded to Lenin's request for comments on his thesis on colonial and national problems, including the rise of pan-Islamism: "Is it necessary to fight it?," Acharya asked, and concluded:

---

14. For Acharya's own account of his activities in Sweden, see "Indian Propaganda During the Great War," *The Mahratta*, October 21, 1938, 3; "Traitor Turned Out: Indian Propaganda in The Great War," *The Mahratta*, November 4, 1938, 2.

15. Acharya, "Madame Cama," *The Mahratta*, August 12, 1938, 3.

16. "Wireless message of greetings dated 14.5.1920 from V. I. Lenin to Abdur Rabb Barq, Chairman, Indian Revolutionary Association," in *Indo-Russian Relations, 1917–1947: Select Documents from the Archives of the Russian Federation*, eds. Purabi Roy, Sobhanlal Datta Gupta, and Hari Vasudevan (Calcutta: Asiatic Society, 1999), 6.

"pan-Islamism, like all similar other –isms—pan-Germanism, pan-Slavism, and so on—is now a Utopia which exists only in the brains of a few perhaps idealist but misguided, unpractical but harmless people, however persistent their efforts may be."[17] However, despite Lenin's backing of the IRA, the Emir of Afghanistan, supported by Britain after the third Anglo-Afghan War (1919), soon expelled Acharya and his comrade Abdur Rabb for anti-British activities. They instead relocated to Tashkent (now in Uzbekistan) where they formed the Provisional All-India Central Revolutionary Committee (PAICRC) in August 1920. The PAICRC was supplemented by the formation of the CPI in October 1920, with Acharya as Chairman and M. N. Roy as Secretary. However, Acharya soon disagreed with Roy over the direction of the CPI, unhappy to subordinate the project of Indian national liberation to the Comintern, and he was subsequently expelled from the CPI in January 1921 "on account of actively supporting people engaged in frankly anticommunist propaganda."[18] Signaling Acharya's turn to anarchism, a couple of weeks later, he attended Peter Kropotkin's funeral in Moscow.[19] Acharya stayed in Moscow and took up work for the American Relief Administration, where he worked with the Russian anarchist Abba Gordin, and he most likely met his wife, the Russian artist Magda Nachman (1889–1951), around this time.[20] During his sojourn in Moscow, Acharya also met Rose Witkop, Guy Aldred's partner and sister to Milly Witkop, Rudolf Rocker's partner, as well as Alexander Berkman again.[21]

17. M. Acharya to V. I. Lenin, July 24, 1920, Russian State Archives of Socio-Political History (RGASPI), 2-1-24686-012:014. I am grateful to Lina Bernstein for sharing this letter with me.

18. "Copy of letter dated 30.1.21 from Secretary, Indian Communist Party, to M.P.B.T. Acharya criticising his activities and informing him of his removal from the Chairmanship of the Central Committee," in *Indo-Russian Relations*, eds. Roy, et al., 58–59.

19. Acharya to Yelensky, April 28, 1947, Boris Yelensky Papers, IISH.

20. Acharya to Yelensky, July 24, 1947, Boris Yelensky Papers, IISH.

21. M. P. T. Acharya, "Request from India," *The Word*, March, 1946, 95; Acharya to Yelensky, May 22, 1947, Boris Yelensky Papers, IISH.

From Indian nationalist to international anarchist, 1923–1935

In late 1922, Acharya and Nachman returned to Berlin, where they first lived at Leibnizstrasse 42, in the Charlottenburg district, the same address where he had also lived with Chatto, Har Dayal, and Abdul Hafiz during the First World War, around the corner from the former IIC. Acharya and Nachman were then at Bochumer Strasse 5 in July 1923, and in September 1923 they moved to Kantstrasse 90. Acharya struggled to survive, often destitute and reliant on Nachman's income, and he distanced himself from many of the other Indians in Berlin, especially his former IIC collaborator Pillai, "whom I never respected and respect now less," as he wrote to his friend P. Parthasarathy in Bangalore (now Bengaluru), India, in early September 1923.[22] Furthermore, he confessed: "I go to very few Indians and very few come to me—as all are busy enjoying themselves with those who can afford to pay for enjoyment and have a mind to do so." He did, however, remain close friends with Chatto and Chatto's partner in early 1920s Berlin, the American author and Ghadar-sympathizer Agnes Smedley, as well as Chatto's brother-in-law A. C. N. Nambiar. Acharya was so destitute that Smedley appealed to the Indian National Congress (INC) for help on behalf of Acharya, but the INC does not appear to have offered any assistance.[23]

While Acharya became a recluse and withdrew from most of the Indians in Berlin, Nachman traveled among Berlin's Russian émigré artists and authors such as Marina Tsvetaeva and Vladimir Nabokov—one of Nachman's paintings graces the back cover of Nabokov's *Glory: A Novel* (1972)—and Acharya also met Nabokov.[24]

22. "Orientals in Berlin and Munich: S I S and D I B reports," IOR/L/PJ/12/102, file 6303/22.

23. "Mandayam P Tirumal Acharya, anarchist; activities and passport application," IOR/L/PJ/12/174, file 7997/23; "Agnes SMEDLEY," KV 2/2207, The National Archives, Kew.

24. Vladimir Nabokov, *Letters to Vera*, translated and edited by Olga Voronina and Brian Boyd (London: Penguin, 2014), 193; Lina Bernstein, "The Great Little Lady of the Bombay Art World," in *Transcending the Borders of Countries, Languages, and Disciplines in Russian Émigré Culture*, eds. Christoph Flamm, Roland Marti, and Ada Raev,

However, aside from these figures, Acharya seems to have been closest to Chatto and his old friend Rifaat, the "former Secretary of the Egyptian National Congress whom I [have] known since my Paris days when I used to help them in their National Congress affairs—once held in Brussels," he wrote. Indeed, Acharya had attended the Egyptian National Congress in Brussels in September 1910 under the name Bhayankaram, and he describes in the letter to Parthasarathy how "at that time they took me and Madam Cama, Chattopadhyaya, [Mrs. Naidu's brother here], and Asaf Ali, Barrister now released from Prison and President of Delhi Provincial Congress Committee" to the congress. Moreover, according to Acharya, "Dr. Rifaat was also with me for some time in Stockholm. He is here in much straitened circumstances but certainly not so bad as I am." To earn a living, Acharya also typed and translated literature for Rifaat, including some letters to the Egyptian Prime Minister Zaghloul Pasha, the British Prime Minister Ramsay MacDonald, and officials in Cairo, and helped Rifaat publish the anti-Ahmadiya pamphlet *Die Ahmadia-Sekte* (1923).[25]

Acharya also instead sought out new political collaborators. In late December 1922, Acharya and a group of Indians attended the founding meeting of the revived anarcho-syndicalist IWMA, with Rudolf Rocker, Augustin Souchy, and Alexander Schapiro as secretaries.[26] At the suggestion of the IWMA secretariat, a committee of Indians in Europe was subsequently set up with the aim to send anarchist literature to India. While working in complete accordance with the IWMA, the committee was not formally attached to the IWMA.[27] Among the other delegates at the founding meeting was the Japanese anarchist Yamaga Taiji, with whom Acharya remained

(Cambridge: Cambridge Scholars Publishing, 2018), 143–158.

25. "Orientals in Berlin and Munich," Home Political NA 1925 NA F-139-Kw, NAI.

26. Wayne Thorpe, *The Workers Themselves: Revolutionary Syndicalism and International Labour, 1913–1923* (Dordrecht; Boston: Kluwer Academic and International Institute of Social History, 1989), 267.

27. "Die Propaganda des revolutionären Syndikalismus in Indien," *Der Syndikalist*, 5:4 (1923), Beilage.

in touch throughout his life.[28] The Indians' first "success," the secretariat noted sarcastically, was to get IWMA literature banned from import into India.[29] Indeed, under the Sea Customs Act of 1878, the Government of India prohibited "the bringing by sea or by land into British India of any publications issued by the International Working Men's Association (Internationale Arbeiter Assoziation), Berlin, in whatever language they may be printed."[30] Shortly after the meeting, writing under his middle name Bhayankar, Acharya offered a scathing critique of Roy's "Program for the Indian National Congress" from December 1922 (Chapter 1).[31] A few months later, Acharya wrote to Chittaranjan "C. R." Das, editor of the radical Bengali paper *Forward*, that his political belief was now "anarchism, pure and simple." During this transition period from communism to anarchism, he contributed to Sylvia Pankhurst's *The Workers' Dreadnought*, and the Berlin-based Russian anarcho-syndicalist IWMA paper *Rabochii put'*, edited by Grigori Maximoff and Schapiro, and sent his articles to India.[32]

Throughout 1924 and 1925, Chatto, Smedley, and Nambiar associated closely with Alexander Berkman and Emma Goldman, reportedly even attending a reading group with Berkman, Goldman, Rudolf Rocker, and Armando Borghi. Furthermore, Chatto translated for *Der Syndikalist*, the organ of the Freie Arbeiter Union Deutschlands (FAUD), edited by Souchy.[33] If Acharya remained

---

28. Victor Garcia, *Three Japanese Anarchists: Kotoku, Osugi, and Yamaga* (London: Kate Sharpley Library, 2000), 23.

29. "Bericht des Sekretariats der IAA über 1923–1924," IWMA Archives, International Institute of Social History (IISH), Amsterdam.

30. "Prohibition of the bringing by sea or by land into British India of any copy of any publication issued by the International Working Men's Association Berlin," PR_000000192248, file 22-23, NAI.

31. I am grateful to Vadim Damier for sharing this article with me.

32. IOR/L/PJ/12/174, file 7997/23. Acharya's articles for *The Workers' Dreadnought* and *Rabochii put'* have not been traced for this collection.

33. Janice MacKinnon and Stephen MacKinnon, *Agnes Smedley: The Life and Times of an American Radical* (London: Virago, 1988), 70–74; Laursen, "Anti-Colonialism, Terrorism, and the 'Politics of Friendship.'"

close friends with Chatto, Smedley, and Nambiar, it is likely that he was also introduced to these other well-known anarchists. Around the same time, the British Government put pressure on the German Government to deport Acharya, Chatto, Pillai, and some former members of the IIC and the CPI now residing in Berlin. The British authorities considered Acharya more dangerous than Pillai and concluded that: "it would be very dangerous to have him at large."[34] However, despite lumping Acharya in with the other Indian Bolsheviks in Berlin, they also noted that: "he has for some time been discredited in Soviet circles and is in the habit of writing tirades against Roy and the Bolsheviks. Being a good steno-typist, he is now reported to be employed not only by Indian revolutionaries in Berlin but by Egyptian and other extremist groups."[35] In another report from that period, the British authorities noted that: "though he is now ostensibly a member of the Fourth International, Acharya is of course purely personally interested in Eastern unrest. This is recognized by the Third International authorities in Berlin, who treat him accordingly and do not consider him an enemy as they do other definite members of the Fourth International."[36] Providing information about these figures to the British authorities, the German Foreign Office noted that Chatto "appears to be no longer engaged with political but only with economic questions" and wrote about Acharya that: "it is not possible to discover any activities of the person named." Despite having little information about Acharya from the Germans, the British authorities decided to issue a warrant for his arrest should he return to India.[37]

Probably aware of this, Acharya applied for a passport in January 1926, claiming that his passport had been stolen, and was asked to give an account of his activities. Perhaps in an effort to

---

34. "Proposed deportation of certain Indian seditionists from Germany," PR_000003031407, Home Political NA 1925 NA F-139-I, NAI.

35. Ibid.

36. Kw file no. 139.

37. "Indian political activity in Germany; deportation requests," IOR/L/PJ/12/223, file 1387(a)/24.

distance himself from the Indian Communists in Berlin, and what the British Foreign Office perceived to be the "Bolshevik danger," he stated: "I have been doing propaganda against English rule in India," but "I am also a convinced anti-Bolshevik." The British Foreign Office offered him an Emergency Certificate valid for a single journey to India on the most direct route. However, as a warrant was still out for his arrest, the British Consul in Berlin also made it clear that there was no guarantee that no action would be taken against him upon arrival in India.[38] Acharya must have considered the prospect of return too dangerous, as he did not accept the offer of an Emergency Certificate, but instead remained in Berlin and immersed himself further in the international anarchist movement.

In August 1925, Acharya contacted Thomas Keell, editor of *Freedom*, in London, and asked for copies of *Freedom* and other anarchist literature to be sent to India for propaganda purposes. He also claimed that he knew Berkman, Goldman, and Havel from Berlin, and asked Keell if he knew of anyone in Berlin who could lend him Berkman's *The Bolshevik Myth* (1925) and Goldman's work on Russia.[39] Keell found this request strange and checked in with Berkman, who "made inquiries about M. Acharya and [was] told that he is OK," and he outlined a list of publications to be sent to Acharya.[40] Upon receipt of these, Acharya wrote to Berkman and asked for advertising bills for Berkman's *Prison Memoirs of an Anarchist* (1912) and *The Bolshevik Myth*, some of them intended for Souchy, but most of them to be included in correspondence to India, Turkey, and South Africa.[41]

---

38. IOR/L/E/7/1439, file 721.

39. Thomas Keell to Alexander Berkman, August 7, 1925, ARCH00040.42, Alexander Berkman Papers, IISH.

40. Alexander Berkman (Berlin, Germany) to [Thomas H.] Keell (n.p.), August 26, 1925, Emma Goldman Papers, David M. Rubinstein Rare Book & Manuscript Library, Duke University.

41. M. Acharya to Alexander Berkman, August 29, 1925, ARCH00040.7, Alexander Berkman Papers, IISH.

In the summer of 1926, Acharya moved to Landgrafenstraße 3A, Berlin, and then the next month to Ringbahnstraße 4 in the Halensee area of Berlin. In October 1926, he contacted Guy Aldred, a long-time supporter of the Indian freedom struggle, asking for Aldred's pamphlet *Socialism and Parliament* (1923) to be sent to India.[42] What is more, in January 1927, Souchy wrote to Berkman that Acharya had translated some texts for him that were to be sent to Asia and India.[43] Testifying to the "success" of Acharya and the IWMA, Keell later wrote to Berkman that the Indian Government had seized a consignment of literature he had sent to Calcutta (now Kolkata) in 1929.[44]

However, Souchy was not always satisfied with the quality of Acharya's translations. In February 1931, Souchy complained to Berkman: "Acharya is not a conscientious translator, so there were errors in his translations."[45] Despite such errors, Acharya also translated for Berkman's Relief Fund of the International Working Men's Association for Anarchists and Anarcho-Syndicalists Imprisoned and Exiled in Russia.[46]

Meanwhile, Acharya was still friends with Chatto, who had abandoned his anarchist leanings and set up the Comintern-backed League against Imperialism (LAI) in February 1927 with the German Communist Willi Münzenberg.[47] According to the DCI, Acharya assisted Chatto at the founding meeting of the LAI

---

42. IOR/L/PJ/12/174, file 7997/23; for more on Aldred and the Indian revolutionaries, see Ole Birk Laursen, "Anarchist Anti-Imperialism: Guy Aldred and the Indian Revolutionary Movement, 1909–1914," *Journal of Imperial and Commonwealth History* 46:2 (2018): 286–303.

43. Augustin Souchy to Alexander Berkman, January 31, 1927, ARCH00040.54, Alexander Berkman Papers, IISH.

44. Thomas Keell to Alexander Berkman, January 6, 1930, ARCH00040.42, Alexander Berkman Papers, IISH.

45. Augustin Souchy to Alexander Berkman, February 31, 1931, ARCH00040.140, Alexander Berkman Papers, IISH.

46. Acharya to Yelensky, May 22, 1947, ARCH01674.46, Boris Yelensky Papers, IISH.

47. Fredrik Petersson, "Hub of the Anti-Imperialist Movement: The League against Imperialism and Berlin, 1927–1933," *Interventions: The International Journal of Postcolonial Studies* 16:1 (2014): 49–71.

in Brussels, which was also attended by the future Indian Prime Minister Jawaharlal Nehru. However, Acharya was skeptical of the organization's methods and objects, and was reportedly "convinced that the organization is run from Moscow and that its main object is pro-Communist propaganda."[48] Given Acharya's anti-Communist stance, it was perhaps not surprising that, when he asked Chatto for work with the LAI in December 1928, Chatto refused his request.[49] At that time, Acharya had moved again and now lived at Kaiser Platz 17 in Berlin.

Inspired by the literature sent to him by Berkman, Keell, Aldred, Souchy, and others, Acharya soon articulated his own perspectives on anarchism, often renouncing Bolshevism and the Comintern, commenting on the Indian independence struggle, particularly Gandhian pacifism, as well as developing an anarchist economic critique of state capitalism. Throughout the late 1920s, he regularly sent his own writings and other anarchist literature to communist organizations in India such as the Labour Kisan Party of Hindustan, a workers' party formed in Madras in May 1923 that was formally attached the to CPI; and the Shiromani Gurdwara Parbandhak Committee, a Sikh organization responsible for gurdwaras and supportive of the non-violence campaigns in India. Acharya also sent material to Satya Bhakta, editor of *The Socialist* and founder of the CPI in Cawnpore (now Kanpur), who had supported Acharya against Roy in *The Masses of India* (September 1926); J. P. Begerhotta, Secretary of the CPI; Feroze Chand, editor of *The People* (Lahore); G. S. Dara, Honorary Secretary of the London Indian Association and INC Secretary, and he sent "15 pamphlets published by the IWW to the Editor of the *Volunteer*, Hubli, South India." Reflecting on his literary and political career, K. Shivaram Karanth, editor of *Vasantha*, also later recalled how "M. Acharya sent articles on anarchism from Germany."[50]

---

48. *Indian Political Intelligence (IPI) Files, 1912–1950*, microfiche (Leiden: IDC Publishers, 2000).

49. IOR/L/PJ/12/174, file 7997/23.

50. IOR/L/PJ/12/174, file 7997/23; Shivaram Karanth, "I Do My Bit," *Indian*

Through and beyond anarchism

In a Letter to the Editor of *The Mahratta* from 1926 (Chapter 2), with reference to the German-American manufacturer and socialist Eugene Dietzgen, Acharya asserted: *"Communism can come only through and beyond Anarchism* not before and behind it, as Lenin predicted and died broken-hearted and mad."* In other words, Acharya saw the Bolshevik understanding of communism as false, and instead argued that the only path to liberty was through anarchism. Indeed, drawing on his experiences in Russia, in his review of Angelica Balabanoff's memoirs *Erinnerungen und Erlebnisse* (1927) (transl. *My Life as a Rebel*), published in this collection as "From a Bolshevik" (Chapter 7), Acharya critiqued: "We are Anarchists, because we do not want authoritarianism outside or inside, because to us anti-Marxists, life and society must be, immanently one indivisible whole impossible of mechanical separation—as the Marxists inorganically think and believe." This was central to Acharya's vision of anarchism. For instance, in his essay "Dans L'Inde" (translated here as "In India," Chapter 5) from the IWMA-affiliated *La Voix du Travail*, edited by Pierre Besnard and Schapiro in Paris, he warned of the dangers of communism making its way to India through the likes of the British-based Indian Communist MP Shapurji Saklatvala and Roy. To counter the communist threat, he argued: "What is needed for the Indian proletariat is new workers' organizations, of a revolutionary syndicalist character, which alone can tear it out of the misery in which it grows. Only federalist organizations, given their complete in-dependence, can create a solid foundation for class struggle in India." Many of the essays collected here revolve around these themes, giv-ing us a unique insight into Acharya's thoughts on anarchism as the only viable alternative to imperialism, communism, and capitalism.

In August 1929, Acharya again contacted the British Consul in Berlin and asked for a passport. Giving a statement again, he asserted: "since 1922, having seen the uselessness of politics and

---

Literature XXXIV:3 (May–June 1991): 54.

danger of agitators who want to preach violence, I have become a convinced and logical pacifist and want to have nothing to do with any Government or politics, directly or indirectly, nor with any individual acting with them."[51] In their internal correspondence, the British authorities noted: "it is more than doubtful whether he has any clear-cut political ideas: he claims to be an Anarchist ... but as an extremist may be regarded as a spent force." "The general impression, which is borne out by his writing," they noted further, "is that owing to ill-health, undernourishment and isolation, he is definitely a mental case." The British Labour MP Fenner Brockway, whom Acharya probably knew through the LAI, wrote to Labour MP Hugh Dalton, who was the Under-Secretary of State for Foreign Affairs, the department responsible for the issue of passports, in support of Acharya's application: "from his letters he appears to be a pacifist Anarchist, quite a harmless sort of person."[52] Nevertheless, despite being labeled "a mental case" and "harmless," the British Government wanted more information from Acharya, and he seems to have abandoned the plan to obtain a passport once again.[53]

Contrary to the view of the British Government, Acharya indeed had clear-cut political ideas and was not a spent force. In fact, given that Acharya knew Havel and Souchy, it was perhaps not surprising that he published regularly in Havel's New York-based *Road to Freedom* between 1926 and 1929. His essay "Mother India" (Chapter 8) from that journal was originally published in *Forward* and re-printed in the FAUD's paper *Die Internationale*, the successor to *Der Syndikalist*, also edited by Souchy, as "Der Antimilitarismus in Indien" in May 1928. In the Editor's Note, Souchy wrote that the essay was also submitted to the Internationale der Kriegsdienstgegner, the German section of the War Resisters' International (WRI). Charting a different path toward independence than Gandhi, Acharya's writings on pacifism and

---

51. "Passports: grant of facilities for Mr Lakshman P Varma and his wife and to Mr M P Tirumal Acharya," IOR/L/PJ/6/1968, file 3981.

52. IOR/L/PJ/6/1968, file 3981.

53. IOR/L/PJ/12/174, file 7997/23.

non-violence challenged the Tolstoyan anarcho-pacifist tendencies of Gandhi and his followers. Indeed, in many of his essays, Acharya engaged critically with anarchists and anti-imperialists fawning over Gandhi's nonviolence (*ahimsa*) campaign against the British in India. Whereas Havel and Bart de Ligt, for instance, admired Gandhi's tactics of civil disobedience, Acharya remarked: "without being a follower of Gandhi I am and admirer of Gandhism as practiced today in India" (Chapter 15).[54] For Acharya, the principles of civil disobedience and nonviolence, as practiced by Gandhi, had taught people to resist state-led provocations and exposed the hypocrisy of the British Government in India. Comparing Gandhi's Salt March in 1930 to Makhnovism (Chapter 22), Acharya called Gandhi "an Anarchist tactician of first magnitude," but he was also critical of Gandhi's failure to distinguish between the "mass liberation from violence" and the "violence of Governments."[55]

From the late 1920s until the mid-1930s, Acharya wrote extensively for E. Armand's *L'en dehors*, focusing particularly on issues of sex, free love, and jealousy between men and women. In his essay "De la Jalousie," translated here as "On Jealousy" (Chapter 12), Acharya argued that men have acquired and oppressed women much like cattle or material objects, and that women have become accustomed to the enslavement of their bodies. Jealousy, he noted, reduces human beings to objects of possession. His article found its way to Japan, where it was reprinted in *Fujin sensen* in 1931, and triggered a response from Takamure Itsue, who denounced Acharya's essay as "just another male view on sexuality," according to Andrea Germer.[56]

---

54. M. Acharya, "Gandhi and Non-Violence," *Road to Freedom*, September, 1930, 1; Hippolyte Havel, "Gandhi's Ideal," *Road to Freedom*, June, 1930, 1, 8; Bart de Ligt, *The Conquest of Violence: An Essay on War and Revolution* (New York: Dutton, 1938).

55. M. Acharya, "Nationalism in India," *Man! A Journal of the Anarchist Ideal and Movement*, July, 1933, 2; M. Acharya, "Mother India," *Road to Freedom*, April, 1928, 7.

56. Andrea Germer, "Continuity and Change in Japanese Feminist Magazines: *Fujin Sensen* (1930–31) and *Onna Erosu* (1973–82)," in *Gender and Modernity: Rereading Japanese Women's Magazines*, eds. Ulrike Wöhr, Barbara Hamill Sato, and Suzuki Sadamo (Kyoto: International Research Center for Japanese Studies, 2000), 125; M. Acharya, "Shittoshin no mondai ni tsuite," *Fujin sensen*, February, 1931, 14–17.

Acharya was a committed anarchist by then, but he still maintained contact with well-known communists and old friends. In 1931, Acharya assisted the Indian communist Indulal Yajnik setting up the Indian Press Service as well as translated for him. According to Yajnik, Acharya was "an old but poor patriot of south India," and yet he assisted Yajnik without any remuneration, causing Nachman to object to "his doing such work for free."[57] What is more, around this time, Acharya briefly served on the Executive Committee of Chatto's short-lived Indian Independence Union in Berlin.[58] In January 1932, Acharya wrote to Leon Trotsky, then in exile in Turkey, to offer evidence against Roy, Mikhail Borodin, Georgy Chicherin, Santeri Nuorteva, and Lev Karakhan as English agents and provocateurs who would "turn the Chinese revolution into counter-revolution." Acharya had sent some of his articles to Trotsky and offered to write more articles to prove his claims, but whether Trotsky accepted Acharya's offer is unknown.[59]

In 1933, Acharya became the tutor of the Indian communist Ranchoddas Bhavan Lotvala's son, Nitisen, and through Lotvala met the later Indian National Army leader and Nazi-collaborator Subhas Chandra Bose.[60] However, he avoided any further contact with Bose, and when Adolf Hitler came to power in 1933, life became difficult for many Indians in Germany. Furthermore, the Nazis banned both the FAUD and the IWMA, which subsequently moved its headquarters from Berlin to Madrid, causing the Government of India to amend its prohibition of entry of IWMA literature into India.[61] In one of his best essays on race and anarchism, "Sur la

---

57. Indulal Yagnik, *The Autobiography of Indulal Yagnik, Vol. 2* (New Delhi: Manohar Publishers, 2011), 440–441.

58. IOR/L/PJ/12/174, file 7997/23.

59. M. Acharya to Leon Trotsky, January 7, 1932, (95), Leon Trotsky Exile Papers (MS Russ 13.1), Houghton Library, Harvard University.

60. IOR/L/PJ/12/174, file 7997/23.

61. "Amendment to notification, no. 1702, dated the 24th March 1923, in regard to action under the Sea Customs Act, in respect of all publications issued by the International Working Men's Association, Berlin," PR_000003034354, Home Political NA 1934 NA F-35-7, NAI.

Question de Race" (translated here as "On the Question of Race," Chapter 23), Acharya pointed out the madness of Hitler's race project sweeping across Germany and compared it to the brutality of the caste system in India.

Finally granted a passport in February 1934, and guaranteed that he would not be prosecuted if he ended his political activities, Acharya and Nachman left for Switzerland in 1934 to live with some of her relatives. In preparation for his return, he donated all of his books to the Sino-International Library in Geneva, an organization set up by the Chinese anarchist Li Shizeng in 1932. In August 1934, Acharya and Nachman left for Paris, finding Zurich too expensive, and settled on Rue Parmentier in the Neuilly-sur-Seine area.[62] Acharya often visited the aging Madame Cama during his sojourn in Paris and later recalled: "sometimes I had to help [Cama] to walk in the Champs Elysees where every café knew her as their long years' customer, for she was always going to the nearest cafés around her house on the *Rue de Ponthieu*."[63] Acharya returned to Bombay (now Mumbai) in April 1935, and Nachman followed a year later.[64] Throughout this period, Acharya kept writing articles for numerous anarchist periodicals, including *Man!*, *Orto*, and *L'en dehors*, many of which are reprinted in this collection. What is more, his 1935 tribute to Max Nettlau in *La Revista Blanca* (Chapter 28) was later reprinted as the Introduction to Nettlau's *El lugar de las ideas anarquistas en la serie de las liberaciones humanas*, republished by *Le Combat Syndicaliste* in 1970.[65]

An Indian anarchist in India, 1935–1951

In Bombay, Acharya started writing more articles for Indian magazines, publishing his "Reminiscences of a Revolutionary" in *The*

62. IOR/L/PJ/12/174, file 7997/23.

63. M. P. T. Acharya, "Madame Cama: A Rebel Throughout Her Life," *The Mahratta*, August 12, 1938, 5.

64. IOR/L/PJ/12/174, file 7997/23.

65. Max Nettlau, *El lugar de las ideas anarquistas en la serie de las liberaciones humanas* (Paris: Le Combat Syndicaliste, 1970).

Mahratta as well as many shorter articles on Savarkar, Madame Cama, Walter Strickland, and the disappearance of Chatto in Russia (Chatto was executed in Stalin's purges in September 1937).[66] In the late 1930s and into the early years of the Second World War, *The Mahratta* veered strongly towards the politics of Hindu nationalism, and Acharya consequently severed his ties with this publication. He did, however, resume contact with Ranchoddas Lotvala. By then a Trotskyist and critical of Gandhi's politics, and influenced by Acharya's philosophical anarchism, Lotvala had set up the Indian Institute of Sociology (IIS) in the 1930s and overseen the publication of Rocker's *Anarcho-Syndicalism* in India in 1938, as well as later published several anarchist publications such as Rocker's *Socialism and the State* (1946) and Clarence Lee Swartz's *What is Mutualism?* (1927).[67]

Meanwhile, in his essay "Is War Inevitable?" (Chapter 31) from 1938, Acharya wrongly predicted: "a large scale war is becoming more and more difficult." When the Second World War broke out in 1939, Acharya lost touch with the international anarchist scene and little is known of his activities during the war. However, he joined the Managing Committee of the IIS in late 1945 and its successor, the Libertarian Socialist Institute (LSI), in 1947, then managed by Lotvala's daughter, Kusum. According to Garcia, the LSI had six objectives: 1) to encourage people's interest in libertarian socialism;

---

66. M. P. T. Acharya, "Reminiscences of a Revolutionary," *The Mahratta*, July 23, 1937; July 30, 1937; August 20, 1937; August 27, 1937; September 3, 1937; September 10, 1937; September 17, 1937; October 0, 1937); M. P. T. Acharya, "Savarkar in London," *The Mahratta*, May 27, 1938; M. P. T. Acharya, "What is the Fact? Fate of Viren Chattopadhyay," *The Mahratta*, June 3, 1938, 3; M. P. T. Acharya, "Viren Chattopadhyaya: A Chequered Career," *The Mahratta*, June 10, 1938, 7; M. P. T. Acharya, "Viren Chattopadhyaya Trapped by a British Spy," *The Mahratta*, June 17, 1938, 3; M. P. T. Acharya, "Swiss Attempts to Trap Chatto," *The Mahratta*, June 24, 1938, 3; Acharya, "Madame Cama," *The Mahratta*, August 12, 1938, 3, 5; M. P. T. Acharya, "The Most Anti-British Englishman," *The Mahratta*, September 9, 1938, 3.
67. Ramnath, *Decolonizing Anarchism*, 139–142; Nicolas Walter, Introduction, *Anarcho-Syndicalism: Theory and Practice*, by Rudolf Rocker (London: Pluto Press, 1989), xvi. Note that in most correspondence, Lotvala signs himself as R. Bhavan; M. P. T. Acharya, "What is Anarchism," in *Whither India?: Socio-Politico Analyses*, eds. Iqbal Singh and Raja Rao (Baroda: Padmaja Publications, 1948), 140.

2) to collect and spread information about libertarian thought and activities; 3) to facilitate the study of natural and social sciences; 4) to bring together different points of view of the libertarian movement; 5) to establish a library and publish a libertarian periodical; and 6) adopt all means necessary to achieve these objectives.[68] However, according to Maia Ramnath, Lotvala steered the new Institute more toward libertarian individualism than the logic of libertarian socialism, and the extent of Acharya's involvement with the LSI towards the end of his life remains unclear.[69] Around this time, Acharya is also believed to have written a book entitled *Mutualism*, "possibly his most important work," as Garcia noted, which delved into libertarian thoughts and debates between the United States and England.[70]

After the war, Acharya quickly resumed contact with the international anarchist movement. In 1945, together with Yamaga Taiji and the Chinese anarchist Lu Chien Bo, Acharya made contact with the Commission de Relations l'Internationale Anarchiste, but little is known about their relations with the organization.[71] As Acharya had donated all of his books to the Sino-International Library when he left Europe, he was in need of anarchist literature for the LSI's library. Consequently, Acharya asked Aldred in a letter from December 21, 1945, to send him Bakunin's "God and the State" (1882), the volumes of Proudhon's "What is Property?" (1840), and all of Aldred's literature. The Libertarian Book House, the publishing wing of the LSI, published Aldred's *Bakunin's Writing* in 1948. Furthermore, in a note published in *The Word*, Acharya asked Aldred to put him in touch with Souchy, who, he believed, could be reached through the Swedish anarchist Albert Jensen in Stockholm, and he wanted to "get in touch with all resurrected comrades and thinkers

---

68. Garcia, "Mandyam Acharya," 222–223.

69. Ramnath, *Decolonizing Anarchism*, 144–145.

70. Free Society Group of Chicago, *The World Scene from the Libertarian Point of View* (Chicago: Free Society Group of Chicago, 1951), 95; Garcia, "El Anarquismo en la India," *Tierra y Libertad*, February, 1960, 4.

71. *Dictionnaire des militants anarchistes*, Acharya entry, http://militants-anarchistes.info/spip.php?article75.

in Europe."[72] Acharya must have resumed contact with Souchy quite quickly, since by May 1947 Souchy wrote to Acharya that he would publish one of Acharya's articles on the labor movement in India in the *Freie Arbeiter Zeitung*. This article, Acharya wrote to Boris Yelensky, could be obtained from Souchy and reprinted in Russian, in case Yelensky wanted to.[73]

Perhaps responding to Acharya's note in *The Word*, the Russian-German anti-Stalinist communist Basil Ruminov, then living in exile in New York, sent his greetings to Acharya and Armand through Aldred's paper.[74] Acharya and Ruminov had met in Moscow in 1921 and resumed correspondence again now. Acharya explained to Yelensky: "he is a Marxian, never learns anything. But I like him: He is a sincere fanatic."[75] In another letter to Aldred from May 1946, Acharya warned against Roy's paper *The Marxian Way*, "which smacks of the old German social-democratic publications of the last century," and Roy's Radical Democratic Party's influence in India: "Thanks to the Communists' and Royists' tactics, the Congress leaders are growing Fascist—that is the only achievement of theirs."[76]

But it was not just European comrades whom Acharya wanted to contact. In late 1946 or early 1947, he contacted the anti-Stalinist German communist Ruth Fischer, then living in exile in the U.S., and sent her some of his essays. By then, Fischer had turned informant for the House Un-American Activities Committee and was embroiled in exposing communists in the Western hemisphere. In lieu of Fischer, her secretary (possibly Käthe Friedländer, Ruminov's wife, who worked for Fischer) wrote back to Acharya, sent him Fischer's *Newsletter* and encouraged him to "write an analytical survey on India, the Indian CP and Stalinist influence."[77] Whether

---

72. Acharya, "Request from India," 95.
73. Acharya to Yelensky, May 22, 1947, Boris Yelensky Papers, IISH.
74. Basil Ruminov, "Communist Workers' Opposition," *The Word*, November, 1946, 35.
75. Acharya to Yelensky, May 22, 1947, Boris Yelensky Papers, IISH.
76. M. P. T. Acharya, "The Indian Struggle," *The Word*, August, 1946, 11.
77. Acharya, recipient. 1 letter; 1947; Ruth Fischer Papers (MS Ger 204), Houghton

Friedländer referred to Fischer's paper *The Network* or the anti-communist newsletter *The Russian State Party* is unclear, and it is uncertain if Acharya did contribute anything to Fischer's paper. What is more, Fischer seems to have known Nachman, and asked Acharya to send photos of her paintings. Acharya later wrote to Yelensky: "My wife who is a painter earns now and then, but there is not much chance for a painter in this country."[78]

Throughout the 1930s, Acharya had contributed regularly to Armand's *L'en dehors*, which ceased publication when the Second World War broke out, and now he wrote for Armand's *L'Unique* (Chapter 32). Continuing his explorations of pacifism, he also contributed to Louis Louvet's *Etudes Anarchistes* (Chapter 39) and *Les Nouvelles Pacifistes* (Chapter 40), signaling his strong connections with the French anarchist movement. Even further, in 1952 he wrote to Louvet that: "society and state cannot co-exist. An anarchist economy will eradicate parasitism."[79] By the time of India's independence in August 1947, Acharya was a well-known international figure. Acharya's voice was also heard in international circles in May 1948, when anarchists from across the world gathered in Paris for the European Anarchist Congress to plan a world conference to be held in 1949. While Acharya did not attend this meeting, he and another "Bombay group" sent their apologies.[80] What is more, while he was fluent in English, German, and French, his essays were now also translated into Spanish for the Mexican paper *Tierra y Libertad* and the Uruguayan *Inquietud*. His essay "El Pensamiento libertario en la India" ("Libertarian Thought in India," Chapter 37) was published in *Inquietud* first and then reprinted in *Tierra y Libertad* in September 1948.

Although Tom Keell was no longer editor of *Freedom* in London, Acharya also contributed several essays to this journal after the war.

Library, Harvard University.

78. Acharya to Yelensky, May 22, 1947, Boris Yelensky Papers, IISH.

79. *Dictionnaire des militants anarchistes*, Acharya entry.

80. Gregorio Quintana, "Preparacion de un Congreso: Contribución Cordial," *Le Combat Syndicaliste*, March 30, 1967, 3; Ildefenso Gonzales, *El Movimiento Anarquista Español (F.A.I.) en el Exilio* (Paris: Frente Libertario, 1974), 11.

What is more, it was probably through Albert Meltzer, a regular contributor to *Freedom* in those days (often writing under the pseudonym "Internationalist"), that Acharya also came into contact with the North East London Anarchist Group in the late 1940s.[81] With Meltzer, too, Acharya formed the Asian Prisoners Aid committee to help political prisoners in India, extending it to cover Chinese as well as Indian prisoners.[82] Writing in the context of post-war, newly independent India, Acharya criticized the labor movement in India for following the line of the communists and the INC (see Chapters 34, 38, 42, 43). He was particularly critical of the INC's efforts to support peaceful nation building after the war (Chapter 47).

In the late 1940s, Acharya contributed to the Chicago-based Free Society Group's book *The World Scene from the Libertarian Point of View* (1951) (Chapter 45). The Group had been set up by Grigori Maximoff and Boris Yelensky in 1923, and to mark its 25th anniversary they invited Acharya, alongside old friends such as Rocker, Souchy, Meltzer, and Yamaga, to comment on the post-WWII world scene "as viewed in the light of libertarian philosophy."[83] Acharya regularly corresponded with Yelensky from early 1947 until the summer of 1953, when his health had deteriorated severely, and their exchange reveals much about Acharya's place within the international anarchist movement and the state of anarchism in India. As Acharya had donated his copy of Peter Arshinov's *History of the Makhnovist Movement* (1923) to the Sino-International Library in 1935, he needed that book and new material for the LSI library. Acharya had received Maximoff's journal *Dielo Trouda-Probuzhdenie* through a friend of Aldred, and asked Yelensky to send him copies

---

81. A. W. Smith, "Reviews," *East London Papers: A Journal of History, Social Studies and the Arts*, 8:2 (1965): 126.

82. Meltzer, *I Couldn't Paint Golden Angels*, 127; Meltzer, "Ongoing Anarchist Movements (1)," *KSL Bulletin*, 3 (1992), 6; Vadim Damier, *The Forgotten International: The International Anarcho-Syndicalist Movement Between the Two World Wars, Vol. 2: International Anarcho-Syndicalism during the "Great Crisis" and the Fascist Offensive, 1930–1939* (Moscow: Novoe literaturnoe obozrenie, 2007), 584.

83. Free Society Group, *The World Scene from the Libertarian Point of View*, 3.

of it, too. "My wife is Russian and can tell me what is in it," he wrote. A couple of months later, however, Acharya had to ask Yelensky to stop sending the publication to the LSI library, as no one there could read Russian.[84]

They were also interested in all books by or about Bakunin, Kropotkin, and Nestor Makhno, as well as James Guillaume's *L'Internationale* (1905–1910). The University of Bombay also wanted to stock anarchist literature, the librarian had told Acharya, but Acharya lamented: "There are no syndicalists or anarchists here: The result of foreign rule." However, his friend Lotvala, he wrote, was interested in publishing anarchist literature, and he might even contribute to the Alexander Berkman Aid Fund.[85] Acharya warned, though, that it might be difficult to donate to the Berkman Aid Fund: "It is difficult to get money for anarchism. Communists are still respectable!" He eventually suggested that it was probably better if Rocker wrote directly to Lotvala about money for the Berkman Aid Fund, "for Rocker is respected and is a foreigner."[86] Yelensky arranged to send Acharya the requested literature, and he asked friends in Paris to send on Sébastien Faure's *Encyclopédie Anarchiste* (1925–1934) for the LSI library. In case Acharya did not hear from them or receive this literature, Yelensky suggested that Acharya write directly to the Ukrainian Jewish anarchist Jacques Doubinsky in Paris and gave him his address.

Yelensky's friend Maximoff had suffered from heart trouble for some time, and he struggled to finish his book *The Political Philosophy of Bakunin: Scientific Anarchism* (1953). Acharya and Lotvala were interested in publishing a cheaper edition of it in India, and Yelensky seems to have obliged. However, Maximoff passed away on March 16, 1950, and the idea of bringing out a cheaper version in India never materialized, but Yelensky sent them Maximoff's work on

84. Acharya to Yelensky, July 24, 1947, Boris Yelensky Papers, IISH.
85. Acharya to Yelensky, April 28, 1947, Boris Yelensky Papers, IISH.
86. Acharya to Yelensky, May 22, 1947, and June 23, 1947, Boris Yelensky Papers, IISH.

Kropotkin as well as *The Guillotine at Work* (1940). In return, Acharya also sent some of his writings to Yelensky, noting that "We must meet—smash—the arguments of non-anarchists," but Yelensky suggested that he send them directly the *Freie Arbeiter Stimme* in New York. Whether Acharya actually did so is uncertain.[87]

It is clear from their correspondence, too, that Acharya was keen to reconnect with the international anarchist movement, and he inquired about several mutual old friends such as the Russian Bolshevik Gavril Myasnikov, whom Acharya had known in Berlin, but also Voline and Havel, as well as Alexander Schapiro and Luigi Bertoni, whose recent deaths he lamented. Acharya also wanted to resume contact with both Armando Borghi and Abba Gordin. Borghi, he wrote, "must be able to write English. Otherwise I cannot write him," and Gordin, Acharya noted, "will be surprised to hear that I am in Bombay." Yelensky also put Acharya in touch with the U.S.-based Russian anarchist John Cherney, and he asked Cherney to send him Berkman's *The Bolshevik Myth*, with the supplement on the Kronstadt Rebellion, a book that Acharya had acquired from Kœll twenty-five years earlier and probably donated when he left Europe.[88]

Many years of starvation and bad health caught up with Acharya in early 1948. "I have been ordered rest since 10 months owing to T.B.," he wrote to Yelensky, but Nachman had translated Maximoff's article on Russia for him.[89] In fact, as he wrote to the Dutch-American wobbly Nicolaas Steelink: "one month ago I became ill. I began to spit blood and the doctor advised me to keep to bed. He has stopped me spitting blood but he thinks I have T.B. and must go to a sanatorium for some months."[90] Nevertheless, Acharya distributed Steelink's package of the IWW paper *Industrial Worker*

---

87. Yelensky to Acharya, August 21, 1947; Acharya to Yelensky, November 30, 1948, Boris Yelensky Papers, IISH.

88. Acharya to Yelensky, July 24, 1947, Boris Yelensky Papers, IISH.

89. Acharya to Yelensky, November 30, 1948, Boris Yelensky Papers, IISH.

90. M. P. T. Acharya to Nicolaas Steelink, March 7, 1948, Nicolaas Steelink Papers, box 3, folder no. 6, Walter P. Reuther Library, Wayne State University.

and James Dawson's paper *Southern Advocate for Workers' Councils* to the Bombay Union of Journalists, the Royal Asiatic Society Library, the AITUC, and the library at the LSI, as well as "some to editors who are interested." After sending some of his essays to Dawson, Acharya received the *Southern Advocate for Workers' Councils* directly and hoped to distribute the journal "into proper hands." By spreading anarchist literature in libraries, he hoped that "the ideas will enter some heads sooner or later." Furthermore, Steelink had apparently suggested to Acharya that he should establish a local IWW branch, but Acharya admitted that "it is very difficult to one accustomed to a small way of thinking to give up [the wage-system], but many will in India even among the petty leaders." Acharya had no hope that the Indian Labour Minister Jagjivan Ram would be sympathetic, though, but concluded that: "the days are bad for all governments—that is the only relieving feature. Fascism in 1948 will be more bankrupt than when Hitler or Mussolini established it. I think even Bolshevism is impossible now. There may be chaos but not centralism."[91]

However, Acharya's tireless agitation and prolific intellectual output reached some of India's most prominent political authors. Shortly after independence in August 1947, Iqbal Singh and Raja Rao invited Acharya to contribute an essay "What is Anarchism?" (Chapter 35) to the collection *Whither India?* (1948). "We are to-day passing through a phase of extreme intellectual confusion and disor- der," they note in the Introduction. "In so far as Indian politics has evolved an ideological basis," they continue, "it can be claimed that this has resulted in the emergence of two major trends. These are Gandhism and Marxism." To the editors, Gandhism was "a com- plex and synthetic philosophy which has its roots in the tradition of moral humanism of the Indian thought, but at the same time draws liberally from European Utopian Reformism ranging from Rousseau through Proudhon and Kropotkin to Ruskin and Tolstoy."[92] Appearing alongside prominent figures such as Jawaharlal Nehru,

---

91. Ibid.
92. Iqbal Singh, Raja Rao, Introduction, *Whither India?*, ix.

Nirmal Kumar Bose, V. S. Srinivasa Sastri, Jayaprakash Narayan, K. S. Shelvankar, and Muhammad Ali Jinnah, Acharya's essay put forth the case for anarchism's relevance within India's political environment at the cusp of independence. Acharya sent a copy of the collection to Yelensky, noting that: "There are more books published here on anarchism than there are readers."[93]

While Acharya's ideas were somewhat redeemed with this essay, he did not let up the fight for anarchism against state communism, and in the early 1950s he published several shorter pieces in *Harijan*, a journal founded by Gandhi in 1932. At a time when even his brother in Bombay had abandoned him, to make ends meet, the editor K. G. Mashruwala helped Acharya, giving him a platform for his writings, and when Mashruwala died in 1952 his successor, Maganbhai P. Desai, continued to engage Acharya for the publication.[94] Responding to Mashruwala's article "In Regard to Communism," and a polemical exchange between Dange and Vinoba Bhave in *Harijan* (August 18, 1951), Acharya reiterated: "what the Bolsheviks do in Russia and try to do elsewhere is just Capitalism of another type and the quarrel between Capitalists and Communists is not about Communism but about the type of Capitalism which should prevail" (Chapter 46). In another short piece on the early 1951 unrest in Punjab, Acharya argued that it was necessary to organize villages across the country, because "it is not enough to appeal to the high ideals of past times. Nothing less than social solidarity will help in times of peace or turmoil."[95] Acharya later wrote to Yelensky that: "The only people who are nearest to anarchism are the Gandhians of the *Harijan* group. They are near-anarchists because they want decentralization (independent village communes), production for use and direct action." Even further, according to Acharya, Mashruwala had written to him that "the more he thinks, the more he feels converted to

93. Acharya to Yelensky, November 30, 1948, Boris Yelensky Papers, IISH.
94. Maganbhai P. Desai, "M. P. T. Acharya," *Harijan*, May 1, 1954, 73.
95. M. P. T. Acharya, "Protection of Women," *Harijan*, July 7, 1951, 165–166.

anarchist ideology."[96] Meltzer remarked about Acharya's articles from *Harijan* that they were "a striking success" that greatly influenced many other people's writings in that paper.[97]

At the same time, it was not just the communist influence in India that Acharya was worried about. In September 1950, Acharya wrote to Guy Aldred and warned against the rise of Hindu nationalism in India:

> It is regrettable that the Hindu Sabha has a good number of rich persons as its members, but they are very stingy, and it is therefore that this organization cannot fight the totalitarian and reactionary Congress Organization. Some of them control English Dailies, but they do not realize the necessity of organizing propaganda; especially in England and U.S.A., a good deal of propaganda is carried out against India.[98]

Aldred had been a long-time supporter of Savarkar and carried extensive coverage of the trial against Savarkar for his alleged involvement in the murder of Gandhi.[99] Acharya had written a more appreciative essay on Savarkar in *The Mahratta* in 1938, but in his essay "Savarkar: A Criticism" (Chapter 44) for Aldred's *The Word*, he warned against Aldred's admiration for Savarkar, because of the association with the nationalist Hindu Mahasabha movement: "What an end for a man who sacrificed his youth; he has ended politically nowhere. Others are much blacker reactionaries than Savarkar. I

96. Acharya to Yelensky, May 27, 1953, Boris Yelensky Papers, IISH.

97. Internationalist, "Anarchist Ideas in India," *Freedom: The Anarchist Weekly*, August 1, 1953, 4; for more on the politics of the *Harijan* group, see Taylor C. Sherman, "A Gandhian Answer to the Threat of Communism? Sarvodaya and Postcolonial Nationalism in India," *The Indian Economic and Social History Review*, 53:2 (2016): 249–270.

98. Letter to Guy Aldred from the Libertarian Socialist Institute, Bombay, September 10, 1950; Guy Aldred Collection, item 39; Mitchell Library, Glasgow, Scotland.

99. Laursen, "Anarchist Anti-Imperialism," 13; Guy Aldred, *Gandhi Murder Trial. Official Account of the Trial Godse, Apte, and Others for Murder and Conspiracy* (Glasgow: Strickland Press, 1950).

mean those who conduct the Hindu Mahasabha. Savarkar is now old and too decrepit to do anything."[100]

In May 1947, Acharya wrote to Yelensky: "I have to write for a larger public than anarchists. But I think anarchists have to do likewise to appeal to all readers, otherwise it would be like propaganda, which people of all shades do not like to read."[101] In fact, Acharya wrote for more mainstream magazines such as *Thought* and *The Economic Weekly* in the 1950s. In a series of Letters to the Editor of the Indian paper *Thought* published between 1950 and 1952 (Chapter 48), Acharya returned to his experiences in Russia and wrote about Lenin, Kollontai, Balabanoff, and the failure of the Russian Revolution. In an earlier letter to Yelensky, Acharya wrote: "I hear Balabanova is in [the] U.S.A. I knew her since Sweden in 1917. Pity she will die Marxian. A kind of Marxian ascetic. I read her books here."[102] In another Letter to the Editor of *The Economic Weekly* (Chapter 50), Acharya criticized the Indians in East Africa for repeating the oppressive and exploitative rhetoric of the British colonial masters, and referenced a conversation he had had with the East Africa-based Indian capitalist Kareem Jivanjee in Berlin in 1923. In fact, in his letter to Parthasarathy from September 1923, Acharya mentioned that "Jivanjee is an ignorant poor workman who has raised himself to the position of millionaire."[103] In addition to a series of essays in *Harijan*, these letters remain some of Acharya's last writings and are a fitting testimony to the long political career of this Indian anarchist, connecting the past to the present, never relenting in the struggle against imperialism, capitalism, and Communism.

On February 12, 1951, Magda Nachman died in Bombay.[104] Three months later, Acharya wrote to Hem Day: "I have been ill for the last three years and postponed writing to a large number of

---

100. M. P. T. Acharya, "Savarkar: A Criticism," *The Word*, 12:2 (December, 1950), p. 24.
101. Acharya to Yelensky, May 22, 1947, Boris Yelensky Papers, IISH.
102. Acharya to Yelensky, May 22, 1947, Boris Yelensky Papers, IISH.
103. "Orientals in Berlin and Munich."
104. Bernstein, "The Great Little Lady of the Bombay Art World," 143.

friends abroad. Recently my wife and breadwinner also died, and I feel like a baby without anyone to take care of me. I am now 65 years old."[105] Acharya regretted not contacting Day earlier, although he knew of him through *L'en dehors* and Armand, and commented on the present situation in India: "It is not the high ideals of anarchism which require the abolition of the state but the necessity to live, for states mean parasitism of workers."[106] In May 1953, Acharya wrote a heartbreaking letter to Yelensky:

> Dear Com. Yelensky,
> I have been confined to bed all these 5 years and [espe-cially] during the last year I have been worse off. You probably know that my Russian wife died over 2 years ago. She was earning and I am not earning anything since 1939. I am ill, alone and without money and I find I will die of malnutrition v. gradually. I have let two rooms—keeping a small one for myself—but that is not enough to give me food. I must have at least 20 dollars more a month if I must get enough nourishment.[107]

Yelensky replied a couple of months later: "We took up your appeal for help, so enclosed you will find a check for $15 from A. Berkman Aid Fund."[108] This carried Acharya through a few months, but in an effort to raise more money, he contacted Meltzer in London and asked him to help stage an exhibition of Nachman's artwork. However, the process dragged on and just as Meltzer had found a gallery prepared to stage the exhibition, news reached him of Acharya's death from tuberculosis on March 20, 1954.[109]

---

105. Acharya to Hem Day, May 15, 1951, MUND ARCH 15 ANAR 3F 01 30, correspondence with Hem Day, "Mandyam Acharya, révolutionnaire agitateur indou," Mundaneum Archives, Belgium.

106. Ibid.

107. Acharya to Yelensky, May 27, 1953, Boris Yelensky Papers, IISH.

108. Yelensky to Acharya, July 18, 1953, Boris Yelensky Papers, IISH.

109. Meltzer, *I Couldn't Paint Golden Angels*, 128–130.

Although the LSI had veered towards libertarian individualism under the management of Kusum Lotvala, in the Institute's journal *The Indian Libertarian*, J. Mazumdar mourned that "his passing away was so singularly record-breaking in its tragedy. [...] Though India attained Independence this veteran freedom fighter breathed his last in utter poverty, unsung, unwept, and unhonoured."[110] Acharya's friend Vasant Paranjape wrote to Aldred: "It is very sad to think that such a great patriot died like a beggar in a charitable hospital. The press of India, with only two exceptions, ignored his passing."[111] Meltzer later remarked in *The Anarchists in London*:

> [T]he new sahibs of India have forgotten the penniless militants who helped them out with one campaign after another to save political prisoners. [...] For years there was in the whole continent only one active militant. Like "Chummy" Flemming in Australia, my old friend M.P.T. Acharya plugged away on his own. [...] With a growing interest in anarchism among Indian students, a Bombay publishing house reprinted many classical Anarchist works, but Acharya did not succeed in building a movement before his death, nor do I think one exists yet.[112]

While Acharya never succeeded in establishing an anarchist movement in India, his tireless work within the international anarchist scene should not be underestimated. Ultimately, for Acharya, the question of Indian independence was connected to greater questions about individual freedom through anarchist philosophy. The essays collected here hopefully inspire activists, students, and researchers everywhere to build their own movement and create solidarity across borders to fight against imperialism in its new guises.

---

110. J. Mazumdar, "A Story of a Neglected Freedom Fighter of India," *The Indian Libertarian*, February 15, 1958, 13.

111. Vasant Paranjape, "M. P. T. Acharya." *The Word*, October 1954, 143.

112. Meltzer, *The Anarchists in London, 1935–1955* (Sanday, Orkney: Cienfuegos Press, 1976), 29–30.

A note on the collection

The essays collected in this volume have been gathered from archives across Britain, France, The Netherlands, and Germany, as well as libraries and archives that have recently digitized magazines. Wherever an original English version essay exists, these have been used, but otherwise texts have been translated for this collection. As Acharya's essays were often reprinted in other magazines, information about simultaneous or reprinted essays is provided after each text. Acharya wrote variously under the names Mr. Bhayankar, M.A., M. Acharya, M.P.T. Acharya, and the pseudonym Marco Polo, and to give the best possible rendition of his personal imprint these names are used for each essay. Without changing the meaning of the original essays, grammar, spelling, and punctuation have been edited where necessary to make them more accessible to the reader. Furthermore, many of the essays contain original footnotes, which are marked as such. I have included additional footnotes to provide historical context and other information. To give a better sense of Acharya's political development and key thoughts, the essays have been arranged chronologically.

1. The "Communist" Program: A Critical Review

Mr. Bhayankar

It will be remembered that last year just before the Indian National Congress session, Messrs Roy and Mukherji issued a joint appeal from Moscow to the Indian National Congress. The appeals were printed and sent from Moscow or London. They were also sold at the rate of two pence in London too.[1]

This year the same is being done from Zurich—but without the signature of Mukherji who has in the meanwhile fallen out with his original co-worker Mr. Roy.[2] The program intended for the hearing of the National Congress calls the Congress a coalition of all the forces oppressed by the foreign domination. But in his report to the "Bolshevist" press in Europe he calls the same organization, "a motley political organization, which for the last 5 years arrogated itself the right to speak for all the dissatisfied in the country, while it really stood for the interests of the petty bourgeoisie." Again in the December issue of his *Advance Guard*, Roy's organ, it is written in a leading article on the coming session of the Congress: "Every Congressman must understand that the so-called 'National Unity' is an illusion and that the National Congress is not a cohesive political party."

1. M. N. Roy (1887–1954) was an Indian revolutionary and Communist, founder of the Mexican Communist Party, cofounder of the CPI, and founder of the Indian Federation of Labour in 1941, after a split from the AITUC; Abani Mukherji (1891–1937) was an Indian revolutionary and Communist, an early ally of M. N. Roy, and cofounder of the CPI. Executed in Russia during Stalin's purge in October 1937.
2. M. N. Roy, "A Program for the Indian National Congress" (1922).

Contradictions

For the first time it also appears that Mr. Roy writes that the domination of foreign imperialism in India has led to economic ruin, industrial stagnation, social degeneration, and intellectual backwardness for the people of India.

For before in the Moscow papers and others, he and his quondam friend Mukherji used to write and sing that the British Government had brought development and civilization in economy, industry, intelligence, and society. Probably the new face is put up and maintained for the program meant to be accepted in India.

In this program, it is also proclaimed contrary to all accepted principles of his Russian Bolshevik party that the first and foremost objective of the national struggle (our movement for national liberation is freely used in this program) is to secure the control of the national Government by the elected representatives of the people. The principle of election is also declared to be the democratic principle of universal suffrage. All these principles are boldly, rather audaciously, and falsely proclaimed—probably to accept his program or at least to draw others into a discussion on them. The same game was played in 1917 by the Bolsheviks to capture political power, i.e. governmental machinery, and now there is no democratic universal suffrage in Russia, not even a free election by the workmen to their own soviets, as everybody knows. Even here there is only election maneuvering and election corruption and terrorism. Probably Roy and his would-be followers think that they are expert enough by this time to wire pull the electioneers and come out at the top.

In spite of these contradictions in the theory and practice of his own principle, supposed to be the principle of "communists" all over the world, the Indian National Congress is made to declare or the declaration is made by the "program" writer several points as program of National liberation and reconstruction such as absolute independence, supreme authority of National Assembly and federal republicanism. It must be remembered that federalism will not be countenanced in any shape by the principle of the Indian Communist Party.

Social and Economical Program

Among the social and economic suggestions in Roy's program are the confiscation of all large landed estates without any compensation and ultimate proprietorship of the land to be vested in the National State. Formerly Roy used to write up the distribution of large properties among the peasants, which was done by the peasants in Russia, but which the present Government did not want. Probably the Communist International now learnt the lesson and has warned its Oriental agitators not to talk such foolishnesses. The would-be Lenins being statesmen as any set of Lloyd Georges, Roy also talks of co-operative banks of the State established for the agriculturalists, of selling agricultural implements on easy terms and taxation upon incomes.[3] When banks, selling, and taxation are established, there can be no end to the work of these revolutionaries as in Russia under the new economic policy. There will also be the new bourgeoisie to which all Russian "comrades" of Roy belong.

Education and Religion

Nationalization of the means of communication including mines "under the control of Workers' Committees for the well-being of the whole nation"—not for the profit of would-be-communists like himself and his underlings—is the fifth point in the program. Minimum wages (wage-slavery being the object of abolition by all socialists) and 8 hours a day, always talked of by the socialists themselves and not enforced even by the communists in Russia except at the cost of further reduction in the necessities or for want of work at all—these form the 7th and 8th points of the social and economic program of the Indian Lenin.

Employers will also exist in the Soviet Republic of Roy's communist party. "Laws" will be passed to provide for the well-being of workmen. And labor organizations will be given a legal status

---

3. Lloyd George (1863–1945) was British Prime Minister of the Wartime Coalition Government.

and workers will have the right to strike—two things which exist in name or not all in Russia. Workers' Councils will be formed by the Roy State in all big industries as they are formed in Russia—and these will defend the rights of workers in the Bolshevik sabotage. Profit sharing will be introduced where there shall be no profits but everything will be distributed for "the use and benefit of the nation."

The next point is about free and compulsory education. This will be legislated for and carried out with State aid—if, of course, the State has any "money" left after the swindling done by the commissars, otherwise full ministers.

Freedom of belief and worship will be guaranteed. But when believers and worshippers quarrel and recruit partisans, will the Roy statesman sit idle and allow them to fight against everybody?

Army

The last point is about an army. There shall be no standing army, says Mr. Roy. The entire people will be armed to defend national freedom and every citizen will be obliged to undergo military training. Who the people and citizens are, what the national freedom is, and when Mr. Roy will be in a position to arm them, before or after his resolution, cannot be imagined from the whole ideal program.

The Program

"The aims and aspirations of the great majority of the Indian people are embodied in the program," says Roy confidently, "Swaraj is no longer a vague attraction nor is it a mental state. The object before us is now clear." Further boosting of his own plan is done in the following rhetorical manner: The program will raise India to the state of any free and civilized nation. The Liberals are appealed to, saying "the program does not injure them." But "we know what to expect from both quarters; British Imperialism will not change its heart and our upper classes will never risk a comfortable present and promising future for real freedom to the nation. Our immediate task is therefore to involve in the struggle all those elements whose welfare demands the realization of our program." Further on, "their understanding is still limited and their vision not far reaching but we will convince them in actual struggle how their everyday life is bound up with the destiny of the entire nation."

The immediate program consists of (1) organizing militant peasant unions, (2) abolition of traditional feudal rights and dues and repeal of permanent and talukdary settlements,[4] (3) confiscation of large estates to be managed by councils of cultivators, (4) reduction of land, irrigation and road taxes (by the existing government!), (5) fixed tenures, no ejection, abolition of indirect taxes, low prices and finally abolition of all mortgages, (6) then come demonstrations with mottoes—as if these will bring the means mentioned, (7) then agitation for the freedom of the press, platform, and assembly—three things which don't exist even in Russia and even for revolutionaries in sympathy with the Bolsheviks, except when the organizers belong to the clique of the most corrupt among them, (8) to enter the councils of the government (ostensibly with the object of wrecking them from within them). In this Mr. Roy is decidedly with the semi-moderator.

The object of all this is clearly to create a third party, as he writes in his *Advance Guard* of December 1st. This he hopes to do by sitting in Moscow or Berlin and appealing to that reactionary body, the Congress in India. "Gaya must see the abdication of the orthodox non-co-operators from the Congress leadership" is another sentence from his leading article.

But who is going to take the place there vacated? Roy himself asks and answers: "In the period immediately following the Gaya sessions, the leadership of the Congress will pass to the control of liberal intellectuals."

He condemns the non-co-operators as unprogressive. Theirs was a short but spectacular career—his usual phrase about everything not his own.

---

4. An aristocratic, land-owning ruling class in India during the Mughal Empire and British Raj.

Finally Roy bluffs: "We must go to Gaya in order to declare our intention to initiate this new stage of the movement, viz., to bring forward a program of action—our program—and to invite the progressive intellectuals to subscribe to such a program. It is clear what we shall do at Gaya."

May he go there and may he succeed! Especially as he says next and as he pretends in spite of his abuse to be interested in saving and keeping the Congress "as the traditional organ of our national struggle. Left to the mercy or orthodox non-co-operators the Congress will receive nothing but a solemn burial at Gaya." We know Mr. Roy can go to India. He has been several times in and out of India, in spite of his being condemned to death and hanged a hundred or at least a score of times, both according to his own statements to his former dupes and according to the Rowlatt Report.[5] Even so late as March 1921, he told the people in Kremlin that he would go to India to work further and he would manage to do it. Even now his agents are going and coming through Kabul and Baghdad between India and Moscow. Why sit in Berlin comfortably or uselessly when he must go to India. He, like his Bolshevik Indian agents, will surely be connived at by the British Government so long as he is attempting to break up the Anti-British front in India. Was not his wife last year in England and, after having been recognized and arrested, and simply deported to Mexico, did she not escape with a false passport and return safely to Moscow? If his wife can do all that, he can do a thousand other feats, as he is more experienced.

"The sincerity of the various factions participating in the Congress will be tested by their readiness to subscribe to a program calculated to intensify the struggle—his program made not to advance the interests of certain small sections, but to open the way to progress and prosperity to the majority of the people." By the way, there is another Indian program maker who calls himself the

---

5. The Rowlatt Committee was formed in 1917 to evaluate the impact of terrorism in India, the influence of the German Government during the war, and Bolshevist influences.

servant of mankind and the latest incarnation and prophet of God but who is also a pro-Russian (Bolshevik) and pro-Afghan—though not of Bolshevism. His name is Mahendra Pratap and he is also a friend of Roy.

Roy is convinced that "Gaya should mark the Renaissance of the Congress" after all, since he has published a program and it will be accepted by the secretary of Congress. "We must go there," so ends his article at least, to "herald this new phase of our movement and begin to fight to base the national struggle on a really revolutionary foundation by making it a vital problem to the masses."

The Hindu (February 14, 1923), 30–31.

2. Communism in Its True Form

Berlin W. 62,
Landgrafenstr. 3A II.
18. V 26[1]

To the Editor of *The Mahratta*, Poona.

Sir,—In the 2nd article of one Dr. from Lahore on Communism, which I happened to see produced in your journal, the author threw a fling at supposed Indian communists in Germany as wasting their lives instead of trying to do something by being at home in India. I do not know if the gentleman so advising is trying to propagate communist views of "sympathizers" with Communism, but from the "exposition of Communism" in several papers, I think that he is only propagating a false understanding of Communism altogether. If and so long as one propagates wrong ideas about anything, one need not be afraid of remaining in India or returning there to do so. Proof: Moscow propaganda trickling down into India even through the columns of the *Times* of London and the foundation of communist or similar so-called labor parties with connivance of the all-eyes and all-ears authorities. If communism is anything so-called by that name, I may point to our learned book-doctor that, still, communists are not themselves quite agreed as to what Communism *should*

---

1. Acharya's name is not given as author of this essay, but he was known to live at this address in Berlin at the time.

be like, let alone whatever number of people might call themselves and agree they are members of *this* and *that* "communist" party. It is evident to any child, not quite wholly depraved and deprived of intelligence, that Communism and socialism are not party and government affairs or methods but social and communal "government" of all affairs (i.e. social self-government) but without any *uppermost government*. To say that any party or government represents Communism is an absurdity, being evidently contradictory to this social, communist (common) idea.

In this letter I would simply refer to the words and understanding of Eugene Dietzgen, the proletarian materialist gnosologist who, with Marx and Bakunin, was the greatest figure of their times.[2] He wrote:

On April 20, 1886: For my part, I lay little stress on the distinction whether a man is anarchist or socialist, because it seems to me that too much weight is attributed to this difference. While the anarchists may have mad and "brainless" individuals in their ranks, the *socialists have an abundance of cowards*.

On May 17, 1886: I was of opinion that the difference between socialists and anarchists should not be exaggerated.

On June 9, 1886: I call myself anarchist and explain what I mean by anarchism. I define it in a more congenial sense than is usually done. According to me—I am at one with all better and best comrades—we shall not arrive at the new SOCIETY without serious troubles. I even think that we shall not get along without wild disorders, without "Anarchy." I believe that *Anarchy will be the stage of transition* (from non-government to Communism). Dyed-in-Wool, "Anarchists" pretend that Anarchism is the final stage (Lenin), to that extent they are rattle brains; but we are the real radicals who *work for the communist order above and beyond Anarchist disorder*. The final aim is socialist order.

---

2. Eugene Dietzgen (1862–1929), son of Joseph Dietzgen (1828–1888), was a German-born manufacturer and socialist. Acharya seems to confuse Eugene with Joseph here, as he quotes from Eugene's introduction to his father's *Some of the Philosophical Essays on Socialism and Science, Religion, Ethics, Critique-of-Reason and the World-at-Large* (Chicago: Charles H. Kerr & Co., 1917, 1st edition.), 27.

Further, language serves not only the purpose of distinction but also of uniting things, for it is dialectic. The word and the intellect cannot do anything else but give us a mental picture of things. Hence man may use them freely, so long as he accomplishes his purpose.

On April 9, 1888, i.e. a few days before his death, Dietzgen wrote: "I am still satisfied with my *approach to the anarchists* and am convinced that I have accomplished some good by it."

From this dialectic of a materialist monist and above all proletarian and gnosologist (without digesting whose writings, no man can speak correctly of Communism) it is evident: Communism is the last stage of society, beyond Anarchism even. What about the cowards who pretend to be communists without being at all Anarchists? They are counter-revolutionist traitors to *the idea of social unity*. Anarchists may be individualists but communists are opportunists *and legalized reformists*. So when the Dr. from Lahore pretends that what is called today Communism "becomes" Communism really, then he is preaching and propagating *false Communism as it was tried, failed, and is being practiced by Bolshevik rule in Russia. Communism can come only through and beyond Anarchism* not before and behind it, as Lenin predicted and died broken-hearted and mad. And the British Government knows and tolerates false Communism preventing the true.

The Mahratta (June 13, 1926), 306–307.

3. "Anarchist Manifesto"

M. Acharya

OUR COMRADE M. ACHARYA (deported from the United States during the era of Mitchell Palmer), publishes in *The People*, Lahore, India, an anarchist manifesto as follows:[1]

I have been following your paper and other Indian papers' suggestion for eradicating communal and other quarrels. Most of these are serious and of a constitutional nature. But how any constitution will solve the problem of unity, I do not understand. The very persons drawing up the constitution as national (although the nation has no voice in it except to vote if wanted), even if they continue to agree till it is drawn up on paper, are sure to quarrel about the interpretation and application of the constitution.

Secondly, all constitutions say: "Thus far and no further"—as such they are the beginning of conservatism. A change is impossible within the constitutional limits and every fraud practiced to change in spite of it leads only to further corruption.

Thirdly, constitutions allow decisions only by the *wish* of the majority against minorities, whether such decision is good or bad, just or unjust, or expedient or not. A majority is not always right, just and all that—nor a minority always the opposite. As a matter of fact, a minority is often more revolutionary than the majority. A minority has a clear solution, but a majority makes a muddle of all ideas, solutions, and applications.

---

1. Acharya was not deported from the United States in the so-called Palmer Raids (1919–1920), but sentenced in absentia in the Ghadar trial (1917–1918).

I object to dividing a whole into any categories—even majorities and minorities are divisions. Where such divisions are created, there can be no unity at all.

People now object to communal franchise and still want a franchise. What does it matter whether the cleavage takes place on religious, property, or political lines? It will continue to exist, and its existence in any form is not unity.

The parties carry on their divisions through the whole mass of people under a national universal electoral system, instead of localizing or abolishing divisions in any region or small hamlet. Why should any division at any point create divisions throughout every village and hamlet?

All quarrels and squabbles are political, i.e., made in the interests of a few who can afford to see people quarreling. How?

Let us take communal representation. Who wants it? A few religious fanatics on *all* sides, and a few "Zemindars" and "Jagirdars" in every community, who can gain the reputation of being communal and religious, and a few office hunters, present or would-be, who pretend to serve the interests of all these.[2] The mass of the people has nothing to gain under the present quarrels or by their future agreements, but have only to lose more.

I am convinced that no unity can come out of constitution mongering either for the present government or for any future government. Constitutional schemes can only regroup the quarrels, but not avoid them.

Do you want real unity? Or do you want only this political "ideal" or illusion called by that name? Politics is neither ideal nor practical in the sense of being good for the vast majority—who do not constitute the small minority of egoists and parasites called politicians.

If you want unity, peace, and harmony:

---

2. "Zemindar": official or landowner and tax collector during British colonialism in India; "Jagirdar": official or landowner and tax collector, particularly in South India.

1. Give up looking for political or economic central government, of any kind whatever.

2. Give up looking for any kind of constitution, legislature, even village legislature.

3. Give up *all* religious, political, party groupings.

4. Mind your immediate living affairs from birth to death—such as food, clothing, housing, work, instruction, recreation. Assure these for yourself in common with others.

In order to assure all your necessities and comforts—and of others:

a. Don't look for superior or inferior positions as of right or of charity; don't look for salaries and representation, don't take them.

b. Give up ownership rights and join together—to make others give up theirs.

c. Don't look to arranging the whole country's affairs nor begin with the country *first* in anything—work in your local surroundings wherever you are. Try to bring out economic contentment there by bringing out order in production and supply for all. That is the beginning to reach the country.

d. Abolish money and wage and salary and profit system and introduce common ownership and common production for the use not only of your immediate neighbors, but for the whole country later on. There should be no question of not only buying and selling and profiteering for anybody, but also no question of bartering and exchange even *in kind*. We produce as much as we can of what is necessary for all in the village, town, or quarter. Let there be no employers and owners, no salaries and wages, *differential or equal*. Let all the bodies of persons be treated as *one and indivisible*. Let everyone go to work voluntarily wherever he wants and is accepted—making work easy and pleasant for all, like play, and making it short. Money produces nothing—nay, *production is kept down by money and by private ownership, profit, and the supply and demand of buying and selling.*

e. Provide equally for the necessities and comforts of every individual—working, as necessary, for any incapable member of your village, town, hamlet, or quarter. You are nobody's servant but *your own employer in society, not even society's servant.* Do not keep people doing unnecessary work, for that is encouraging parasitism.

f. Let there not be twenty newspapers telling all confusing things in every spot. One is enough for all and may be had as an organ *for all* who wish to write. Let no editor act as bureaucrat censoring other people's views. That is government and tyranny by individuals.

If all these are done at every place in the country, then a uniform flow of wealth can be arranged for all regions simply by occasional conferences of different regions, simply *consulting* with each other. No government of fatly paid, idle, parasitic "specialists" is needed to improve society, which they never do.

It is no doubt difficult to make vested interests to give up their privileges. But to make them give up, to fight them down to join all, is the first condition not only for this scheme but also for any unity in the country. It is not practicality to give up first fighting for it, in the name of being practical.

Not only vested interests but the vast majority in every community will probably be against such an abolition of privilege, helped by the corruption all around. But if people think they can abolish privileges which create divisions by not fighting first to abolish them, if they think that is *"being practical"* not to fight privileges—well, they can go on with their unity-creating game forever without profit to some individuals, till disunion becomes intolerable and impossible.

What is noted above is the only practical thing to do, everything else is postponing *practicality and work* for trying to prove a theory of "practicality."

We have no international matters to care for till we come by our own in this way. Make yourselves an example for the world and that is the best internationalism. Otherwise, the world will not come by to help you nor can you help it.

The Road to Freedom, 3.1 (September 1, 1926), 5–6.

1.   The Mystery Behind
the Chinese Trouble

M. Acharya[1]

THE CAPITALISTS ARE PROPAGANDIZING FOR the Bolsheviki by using the Chinese trouble as Bolshevik intrigue. Nothing serves the Bolsheviks better in their propaganda against revolution. And the Bolsheviks scratch the back of the capitalists abusing it in their turn as only capitalist intrigue. But the real fact is the Bolsheviks and capitalists are together playing their different parts in their capitalist aggression on China—the so-called state, and the purely private—individual, capitalist parts. For while the Bolshevik parties are well with the capitalists in diplomacy and capitalist enterprises against workers in the name of post-war rehabilitation, the spies of the capitalists and the propagandists of the Bolsheviks very nicely collaborate to do provocation and putsch in revolutionary ranks the world over. In fact it has been a puzzle to the man of the rank and file in labor movements, why the results of Bolshevik propaganda and tactics have only helped to strengthen capitalism by dividing the workers in their trouble and trial for existence, to fight against one another on this and that "form" of state and communism.

The trouble in China is only another form of Bolshevik disruption in a far off country. The Chinese nationalists are nationalists as in any other country, although extremely democratic as led by the late Dr. Sun Yat-sen.[2] They are not for any social revolution in

---

1. Original footnote: M. Acharya, a Hindu revolutionist, deported during the reign of Mitchell Palmer from the United States, became well acquainted with the macchiavellistic politics of the Bolsheviks during his sojourn in Russia. M. Acharya is a keen student of international affairs and an eminent linguist—having the command of English, Chinese, Russian, French, German, Italian, and the Scandinavian languages.
2. Sun Yat-sen (1866–1925) was a Chinese revolutionary and first provisional

the western radical sense. They have been very progressive, for they knew that in progress was success. And the Chinese as masses are not at all bigoted in their political or social views, accustomed as they have been through centuries of experimental communism. We know for example that in China the businessman and landowner, doing nothing beyond amassing profits for private, individual, self-enrichment, were considered, till recently at least, as parasites of the society and therefore held in contempt. (Anyone who wishes to know about the history of the social system in China would do well to read *La Cite Chinoise* by Simon, published in the middle of the last century, and the chapters of Edward Carpenter in his "Towards Industrial Freedom," besides the parts referring to China in Lebournaux "Evolution du Commerce.")[3]

Under the capitalist disruption of Chinese society during the latter part of the last century, the culmination of which was the revolution of China under Sun Yat-sen, there is no doubt a capitalist class is coming up even among the Chinese. But the mass of the people is yet indifferent to politics and state-making revolution, knowing and wishing to know nothing of these essences of modern science. But capitalism, especially of the foreign imperialist variety, not leaving them in peace, they have to react in China as elsewhere to one set of foreign and native capitalists or another. Naturally they make sympathetic cause with the Kuomintang democratic party of Dr. Sun.

The communists go where there are a large number of people calling themselves a revolutionary party. So they went in China, in their Moscow statements, interests, as only sympathizers of the Chinese national capitalist democrats. They even became advisers of the democratic governmentalists in Canton, while the communist state diplomats made treaties with the so-called national goat in

---

President of the Republic of China (1912) and later Premier of the Kuomintang.

3. Acharya refers here to G. Eugène Simon's *La cité chinoise* (1885), Edward Carpenter's *Towards Industrial Freedom* (1917), and Charles Letourneau's *L'Évolution du commerce dans les diverses races humaines* (1897).

Peking and then barbered it with the reactionary goat that succeeded it in foreign capitalist interests. It is curious therefore that while Karakhan was doing that kind of diplomatic trade in Peking, Borodin (Gruzenberg the arch Menshevik and Kerenskite of Chicago who "turned over" to the Bolshevik state) became the adviser, sent by Karakhan and the Third International pontiff Zinoviev to Dr. Sun—who was making war against all the changing Peking authorities.[4] How is that possible for a "revolutionary person and government" to deal honestly and in a friendly way with both the warring sides of "counter-revolutionary" governments? That no labor leader seems to have questioned, let alone found an answer for. If analyzed and answered, the conclusion must lead naturally and logically to the fact that both the official and un-official representations as well as their fetish in Moscow were only doing counter-revolutionary treachery in the name of revolutionary duty in Peking and Canton alike. No wonder then, China bled and warred within itself and fell prey to all the capitalists, old and new would-be ones. I have read an article in a Chinese national democratic magazine where the Bolsheviks are denounced as imperialist aggressors much as the British, Japanese, and Americans. With Karakhan and Borodin and their "guns" behind in Moscow, nothing better could be expected either in result or in the Chinese opinion based upon the actions of the Sovietic and communist tacticians and "non-officials."

Not only was it treachery but deliberate treachery to any revolutionary cause, nationalist, democratic, or labor—what these high-class, decent representatives of Bolshevism practiced in China. Nor can it be anything else. For though they are representatives of Leninism, they actually, whether secretly in the communist or

---

4. Lev Karakhan (1889–1937), a Menshevik turned Bolshevik, was the Deputy People's Commissar for Foreign Affairs (1918–1920 and 1927–1934), issued the Karakhan Manifesto (1919) on Soviet policy toward China, and later ambassador to China (1923–1926); Mikhail Borodin (1884–1951), alias of Mikhail Gruzenberg, Comintern agent in China (1923–1927), who restructured Sun Yat-sen's Kuomintang into a centralized Communist system; Grigory Zinoviev (1883–1936), close ally of Lenin and chairman of the Comintern.

anti-communist camps, belong to the international provocative organizations, as their known history must lead us to conclude. At the time of the Bolshevik agitation against the Kerensky regime, Borodin was conspicuous in the U.S.A. in denouncing open meetings that anti-Kerenskyites were all German agents—this same hero of Bolshevism today! And Karakhan is hand in glove with such a man. It is known to anyone in the United States that Borodin was Kerensky's trade representative sent to Bakhmatieff via Norway.

Not only are Borodin and Karakhan great friends, but they are altogether equally hand in glove with Nuorteva who, as representative of the Lenin cabinet, was denounced in the United States as an Anglo-Saxon agent.[5] Of course, he went to England and Canada at that time to negotiate unofficially the friendship of England but was ostensibly arrested, exchanged, and released to Russia on a British man-of-war. This raised him to the position of the chief of the Anglo-Saxon department under Chicherin.[6] But in 1921, the Cheka itself arrested him as an Anglo-Saxon agent and his secretary, an English deserter from Archangelsk, accomplice with Nuorteva in sabotage, provocation, and espionage and therefore shot. But still, thanks to the intervention of Chicherin and Karakhan, Nuorteva was released, although real or false documents and means of escape were found in his possession when arrested. Not content with releasing, Nuorteva was offered the ambassador's post in England!—As if to prove he was maliciously arrested!

But as Karakhan was leaving, whether forced or voluntarily, to go to China, who else could represent him under Chicherin than Nuorteva? The latter refused to proceed to England pretending he would be accused this time as surely a British agent and was therefore given and accepted the old chiefship of Chicherin's Anglo-Saxon section. The Anglo-Saxon section, due to the Soviet government's

---

5. Santeri Nuorteva (born Alexander Nyberg, 1881–1929) was a Finnish-born Soviet journalist, involved in Finnish affairs in the United States, deported to Russia in 1920.

6. Georgy Chicherin (1872–1936) served as the People's Commissar for Foreign Affairs in the Soviet government (1918–1930).

attempts to obtain credit from the United States and England, being the most important section of foreign affairs, the chief of that section becomes automatically the chief advisor of Chicherin, whoever be officially so or not.

After this description of the intricacy of Soviet diplomacy, the mystery behind the Chinese troubles may be considered illumined. The troubles there were entirely an Anglo-Saxon financial affair, arranged via Moscow.

Chicherin was informed of the certainly of *conspiracy of the Entente (Anglo-America) through the triple set Karakhan-Nuorteva-Borodin*, already in 1921, and he was challenged to institute (by the present writer) an inquiry by Cheka or any other interested party. But Chicherin, who promised to think over and reply, only took the side of the conspirators "out of pity" for their honest work and difficult situation. After all, the Bolshevik offices are personal affairs of the chiefs, helped or hoodwinked by their secretaries.

Under such a system called Sovietic, the Chinese troubles, even if made in the name of or by the Soviet diplomats and agents concerned, are only an Entente concoction in which the Chinese are the victims on both sides. So long as Dr. Sun was alive, there is evidence to show that he went cautiously and with restraint as to the advises of the Bolshevik agents and diplomats, but the recent events show that his successors completely fell into their snare and treachery of their advisers, whether these be called directly Bolshevik (or Entente) agents. The last Canton episode, although due to very real and deep causes of exploitation and tyrannization, as the Bolsheviki and the democrats as well as non-partisans of both say, will have exposed the Bolshevik role to the Chinese democrats and both to the Chinese masses—and although the capitalists of all shades might have temporarily profited by the premature, provoked, and misled rebellion will surely lead the workers of China to organize themselves against British—Bolshevik—Chinese treachery. That will be the greatest thing for the Chinese masses.

The Road to Freedom, 3:4 (November 1, 1926), 2–3.

WE ARE ANARCHISTS

5.   In India

M. Acharya

Development of Industry

According to official reports, in 1925 there were more than 6,000 factories employing 1,500,000 workers (men, women, and children). Out of these, 68,725 are children. The number of work accidents this year was 12,600.

It cannot be denied that class struggle is becoming more and more crucial in India. In recent years there have been trade unions in the country's most important industries and among civil servants. But these unions have not yet been recognized by employers or by the government.

Since the communists tried to infiltrate the country, other organizations were set up to counteract the communist conspiracy. The communists themselves were divided into two distinct fractions, one prepared to follow all orders from Moscow, the other preferring a sympathetic attitude towards Moscow's Marxism. But neither the authority of Saklatvala, an Indian member of the British Parliament, or the Pontiff of Indian Communism, Roy, had been able to unite the small handful of Indian communists on the basis of Bolshevik communism.[1]

At the same time, efforts have been made to render impossible any attempt to establish a revolutionary class struggle movement in

---

1. Shapurji Saklatvala (1874–1936), Indian-born MP for the Communist Party in Britain.

India. To do this, a Fabian Society, a social democratic organization, and a Workers' Party based on the British model were set up.

All these parties and leagues have nothing in common with the class struggle in India. Their aim is to stifle this spirit of class struggle or, at the very least, to channel it into a legal path. The influence and support of these political parties in India is very weak.

The workers' interests are mainly oriented toward the trade unions. But unfortunately these are in the hands of unstable leaders. Due to the great number of illiterates, the cultural level of the Indian working class is very low. But they have, on the other hand, a robust instinct, and although they are ready to follow anyone that makes promises, they turn away from them if these promises are not kept and will even stop paying dues. The leaders of the trade unions are, for the most part, leather workers and politicians, who are pleased not to work anymore. They often receive pecuniary assistance from the employers, provided they do not lose the sinecure. But the workers movement cannot be created this way, because the Indian workers are used to seeing everything practically and only consider positive results.

There is yet another class of parasites within the Indian labor movement. It is the British pious who, in the guise of well-paid inspectors or liberal elements, come to compromise everything and end up playing the role of martyrs. One of them, C. Andrews, a former missionary, is now president of the Metalworkers Trade Union of India.[2] He has traveled around the world paid for by the bourgeois Indian National Congress and posed as a friend of the Indian worker in the British colonies.

A European workers' delegation recently came to India to be celebrated by the bourgeoisie and the capitalists. The delegation was led by Tom Shaw from Britain (Minister of Labor during MacDonald's ministry), and Furtwängler and Schrader from Germany.[3] This del-

---

2. Charles Freer Andrews (1871–1940) was a Christian missionary in India, where he became a close friend of Gandhi and supported the independence movement.

3. Tom Shaw (1872–1938) was a British Labour Party politician and trade unionist.

WE ARE ANARCHISTS

egation will have absolutely no influence on Indian workers, who cannot understand how these workers' delegates can be celebrated by the enemies of the working class.

The situation of the Indian worker is that of every exploited worker. They must fight simultaneously against brutal capitalism and against politicians, because capitalists, government, and reformist leaders collude in their activities against the interests of the working class. What is needed for the Indian proletariat is new workers' organizations, of a revolutionary syndicalist character, which alone can tear it out of the misery in which it grows. Only federalist organizations, given their complete independence, can create a solid foundation for class struggle in India.

"Dans l'Inde," *La Voix du Travail*, 2:9 (April, 1927), 16.

Franz Josef Furtwängler (1894–1965) was a German trade unionist, Foreign Secretary of the Allgemeiner Deutsche Gewerkschaftsbund (a confederation of German trade unions), and took great interest in Indian labor and independence. He and Karl Schrader, head of the German Textile Workers Association, described their trip in *Das Werktätige Indien* (1928).

6. Disruption of Marxism[1]

M. Acharya

SO MUCH IS MADE IN THIS CENTURY, especially after the establishment of the Bolshevik State, about Marx and Marxism that to say
that their theories of Society and Production are far from perfect
is considered either heresy or madness—or at least nothing better
can be offered by their opponents and critics. It is therefore very
daring, nay—perhaps foolhardy of Mr. Eastman to come out with
a book at a decent socialist publishers' trying to prove that Marxism
is metaphysics and simply inverted Hegelianism, the acme of
Metaphysics.[2] Mr. Eastman himself has been all his life a Marxist,
although a critical Marxist, unlike the blind and senseless worshippers and defenders of the Marxist "science" miscalled Socialism.
Mr. Eastman himself considers Marxism far from being a Science,
although most admirers of Science are themselves being mystified
by those "in authority of them" into abstruse metaphysics covered
by terminological jargon.

Long before the War, a work appeared in German to the bulk
of 750 pages criticizing the unscientific Marxism as taught by the
political Marxists, even of Marxist "intelligentsia" themselves. It was
called *Die logischen Mängel des engeren Marxismus* by Ernst Untermann,
the American translator of *Das Kapital* and other works of Marx—and

---

1. Original footnote: *Marx, Lenin and the Science of Revolution* by Max Eastman (Allen
& Unwin).

2. Max Eastman (1883–1969) was an American socialist writer and political activist, who
spent almost two years in Russia (1922–1924), and became critical of Stalin's regime.

one well versed in Logic and Dialectics (materialist and monist) and believing thoroughly in Marxism.[3] This book appeared already in 1910 as an attack showing all the inconsistencies in the writings of Marxians—from Plechanow to Mehring—and it appears that Lenin made use of this gentleman's arguments without supporting himself on the source, when he began to thunder against all his political Marxian opponents. But Mr. Untermann writes to me that this chief contribution of his to the study of Marxism was never taken notice of by the very persons he polemicized against, nor even by their anti-Marxian "counter-revolutionary" opponents. It is quite natural that the politicians of one kind or the other thought it best to keep quiet about this deep going volume, because firstly neither found themselves capable of attacking his anti-bourgeois standpoint nor thought, secondly, it would help their misleading common causes to support or attack Mr. Untermann's arguments.

Now, this book of Mr. Eastman is on the same line as Mr. Untermann's criticism of Marxian writers, speakers, and actors—but even a little more daring in some respects, even more heretic—because he is also pro-Marxian yet. Both writers criticize wisely not merely Marxians so-called or self-styled but even Marx's own writings and show clearly how Marx himself was not free from the metaphysics of Hegel, but carried metaphysics into the economic understanding of Society by mere inversion of Hegelian Dialectics. Marx and Engels did not free their methods from metaphysics at all, but kept it up all through. Hence no originality can be attributed to their works, unless it is original to invert Hegelianism and apply it to analyze Society. Metaphysics is a product of dualism, want in a unified, synthetic standpoint by which alone all contradictions can be avoided and the opposites can be shown in their proper places and proportions. But neither Marx and Engels nor their most devoted metaphysicians have left us a heritage of that synthetic

---

3. Ernst Untermann, *Die Logischen Mängel des Engeren Marxismus: Georg Plechanow et alii gegen Josef Dietzgen* (1910); Gerhard Ernst Untermann, Sr., (1864–1956) was a German-American socialist author and translator.

understanding. We must confess that not even our best critics of Marxism, Untermann and Eastman the scientific as opposed to political Marxian writers, have given us that understanding—because they are also Marxians avowedly. But they have done their best, as analysts, in the two books named and it is the duty of every admirer and denouncer of Marxism alike to study these books seriously like an unprejudiced, unsophisticated thinker and scientist. So far, they are the best contributions of the age in the field of social thinking as attempted by Marx.

These books are an attempt to correct and better Marxian thinking and therein lies the heresy of the writers, according to the stupid politicians calling themselves "also Marxians," and "socialists of this or that type of Marxian variety."

In the first part of Mr. Eastman's book—which is by far the cogent part in comparison with second styled the Science of Social Engineering—the author exposes thoroughly the claim of the Marxians and of Marx himself to be the only thoroughly "objective thinkers." Objective thinkers they are only so far as their object of establishing on paper their theories are concerned, but no more—as far as the object of their investigation is concerned. That is Metaphysics in excelsis. All that does not suit their one-sided theories either does not exist or is perverted to fit into them—hence metaphysics has to be resorted to. It is time that the Marxians recognize that Marx himself was metaphysician, at least partly so, if they want to work for Socialism—not mere capitalism of and by the State machinists and manipulators.

To Mr. Eastman, however, the establishment of the Bolshevist State by Lenin's group of Sophists—who he considers to be heretics to Marxism—is itself a distinct advantage on the road to Socialism, because according to the author it enables the proletariat to dictate. So Mr. Eastman is at one with Lenin that the proletariat can dictate to itself only through the state established in its name by a party called "proletarian and communist." Here Mr. Eastman contributes consciously to the illusion—illusion is Metaphysics— kept up by the Bolshevik Marxists. Mr. Eastman claims to admire

Bakunin, who heroically fought against the State metaphysics of Marx, and even claims that Bakunist Anarchists have been the only ones who completely abolished—naturally thereby—the entry of metaphysics into the ideas of Socialism. Eastman also doubts very much, nay distrusts and denies the Marxist and Leninist assurance of "withering and dying out of the proletarian State" and knows well how these Bolshevik theorists of the "proletarian State" are doing everything, for example—by teaching wrong Socialist theories of even Marxism and by suppressing every freedom of thinking even of the Communists in their State-Soviets, besides of course restoring capitalism, native and foreign, to prevent proletarian socialism from raising its head. And this, Mr. Eastman calls a step forward in the direction of Socialism—because, forsooth proletarian dictatorship as understood by Lenin and himself. If that is a step forward, well, Capitalist concentration and trustification can also be called a step in advance because thereby capitalism will bankrupt itself even when it thereby becomes all-powerful against the working class. Similarly, the Bolshevik capitalist trustification called State management is only an advance upon private capitalist non-state trustification. Yet, Mr. Eastman thinks that there is some metaphysical virtue of proletarian dictatorship in the Soviet State, a state managed by one party exclusively for its own "ideology," i.e. interests covered by ideals. When the Anarchists denounce this kind of "proletarian" dictatorship of the Communist Central Committee State over the working class as inhuman and anti-socialist, Mr. Eastman calls them visionary about the Socialist idea, because they have not pointed out "a better way" than the Bolsheviks—as if the Bolsheviks have gone on any good way to any good object even while doing evil as Mr. Eastman himself sees. Is it proletarian class dictatorship when the workers have to elect only communist party members to dictate to them in the name of the proletariat, and they are dictated in the capitalist interests of the elected in office and paid fat salaries and obeyed for not doing anything good but all evil to the working class? What difference is there then between this "proletarian" dictatorship and that obtaining in the so-called democracy like U. S. of unproletarian system? Both say: You have only to elect us but not check us in our actions so long as we keep the power to act! That is the dictatorship of the proletariat and workers in both advanced and backward regions of capitalism.

In the second part of the book pompously called the Science of Revolutionary Engineering, Mr. Eastman is not so clear about that Synthetic Science as he has been in the first which is the Analysis of Bolshevist and Marxist metaphysics. Hence, it must be concluded that he has not contributed anything substantial to that Science: He has simply further analyzed the other movements and that also badly. The trouble is Mr. Eastman is too erudite and intellectual and that he calls Scientific: It is perhaps analytical science of a kind but does not contribute to the synthesis of the subject, Socialist as it should or would be when realized. What does a science help if it cannot or does not show a way to construct, or even show what that constructed thing should be? It is pseudo-science, which can only analyze and pretend to have destroyed. But the Anarchist Socialists—even when they have not established "an anarchist rule"—which is probably what can convince the anti-anarchists—have told a definite, positive thing, have given a synthesis when they said that socialism can only be without rulerships of any kind by a part of mankind—however vast a part that be—over the rest, and therefore the abolition and prevention of every rule by man over man is the first condition of realizing Socialism, equality, democracy, brotherhood, and oneness. If this is not clear, then—the mind of him who says so is evidently incapable yet of grasping because it is accustomed to metaphysical suppositions and theories based thereon: It is not emancipated enough—however Socialist it may be called—to understand practical, synthetic socialism but must wait till the rolling of events will force it to abandon illusions. However, let us try to put the contents of the Socialist Idea, the free, human social idea—in a different way from the usually accepted:

Since the "withering away of all superior human force over man" is the beginning of Socialism in practice, that Society can only be one, indivisible, organic socialism—or social organism. Since that is and can only be one indivisible whole (whatever be the "parts")—no parts of Society can represent the whole and still be identical with the whole. So long as the parts, together or by turns, undertake to represent the whole by some trick of drawn up constitutions, be it called revolutionary, proletarian, and Sovietic of workers—there can be no organic society, Socialism. Therefore, only when rising states are kept suppressed by human beings, can Socialism begin. But the Marxist metaphysical politics is to keep up a new state after abolishing or allowing to die an older one. That is not contribution to Socialism but preventing Socialism, postponing it, working against it—fighting against Socialists for capitalism even in the name of being Socialist and working for socialism. It is creating newer illusions or keeping up the fundamental older ones to preach that a state of some kind yet untried is a necessary step as transition to the organic society, Socialism. To demand a dictatorship of a party or all parties together through the State is to demand of the proletariat to help the rising capitalists—perpetuators of falling capitalism—to help them to keep up the dictatorship of capitalism over the workers, though in a coming form, a newer form. Mr. Eastman only helps to keep up the metaphysics of Marxism when he preaches that the Anarchists have not shown any way although they have dismissed completely all forms of metaphysics. Instead of doing so, he and all who desire socialism should incessantly point out that Marxians are metaphysicians, that Anarchists alone have once for all thrown metaphysics to the lumber rooms, they are therefore *the only practical people* to join if one wants socialist success and then preach only how Socialism is impractical with State (manlike)—thinking. Then Mr. Eastman and we will have something to contribute to Socialism—which we cannot do to any extent because we have all the time to dispel the arguments adduced by each other, at least to neutralize them. For one anarchist paper, which can be established with great difficulty, there are hundreds of so-called socialist and really capitalist publications written against Anarchism.

No, Mr. Eastman has not tried to bring out the Socialist idea. Since we analyze only with the capitalist historical learning, we try to understand, like Marx, Socialism only with the Capitalist thought process—which makes Socialism more, rather than less, difficult to grasp. We can only understand Socialists anarchistically as follows: In the far deep recesses of human history no man owned anything: Nothing was owned by anybody. Later on one by one or group by group began to get possession of this and that, finally everything. Now the Socialist problem is to get this everything for the Society, for the needs of all, as social capital or wealth. But the Marxists are trying to postpone this Socialism by trying to make all this Social property and wealth into State property, capital, in order to prevent it all from coming to the good of everybody—taking advantage of the capitalist idea ruling in the minds of all that some group of men must specially exist in order to decide for all others how the social wealth should be applied. Hence private capitalism "necessarily" leads to combined capitalism of the few, whether of the State, party, or managers. Well, to call this Socialism is to misunderstand and prevent Socialist thinking. It is of course called by the Marxist transition dictatorship of the proletariat—which Mr. Eastman knows is not and cannot be.

We who want or pretend to be socialists must therefore not postpone Socialist thinking of the people by metaphysical arguments advanced to show how the Anarchists are idealists but visionaries and do not understand the problem or the subject, and therefore the Bolshevists or Marxians are right, but assert that Marxism and Bolshevism lead only to the concentration or centralization of Capitalism in the hands of the State, but does not bring the people any nearer to Socialism, and even tries to postpone the realization and materialization of Social-Society. If anarchism is wanting, we must supply the want—instead of confusing it with Marxian metaphysics as statesmen do. But learned Socialists seem only intent to prove, at the most, how Marxians and Bakunists are both wrong and still Bakunism is the correct ideal but cannot be realized and therefore is not worth considering. This attitude does not contradict and controvert Bakunism and cannot prove that Marxism and Bakunism are finally the same although as poles asunder.

The postponement of Socialist anarchism is entirely due to the faults of Marxian and anti-Bakunist writers. It is due to the want of their seriousness about the Socialist object. If they will become workers in the socialist cause, they must give up this anti-Anarchist and therefore pro-Marxian or pro-Bourgeois attitude, and think without inhibitory influences, which are the only hindrances to the realization and establishment of Truth and Well-being for all. They must become emancipated from the bourgeois historical prejudices. If that is not done, all talk of Socialism is and remains "talk" without meaning but good for the bourgeois, anti-social rulerships of every variety, of which the latest is the so-called Socialist rulership.

If Mr. Eastman and others of his type who show a healthy sign of critical attitude would only go a little ahead, Socialism will not be waiting far away from the present and succeeding generations— waiting for any dictatorship to be established, but will be at our feet today. It is fatalism to say that the Marxians are fatalists and the Bakunists Socialists who are against Marxism are visionaries. Either Marxism or Bakunism is going to win private capitalism: if the former, we will have Marxist capitalism to get rid of; if the latter we will have made a beginning towards Socialist Internationalism and equals and brothers in Solid Unity.

The Road to Freedom, 3:12 (July, 1927), 6–7.

7.   From a Bolshevik

M. Acharya

Erinnerungen und Erlebnisse von Angelica Balabanoff, Berlin: 1927 (*Memories and Experiences by Angelica Balabanoff*)[1]

The author, a Ph.D. of German, Swiss, and Italian Universities, a Russian lady by nationality—has been an almost religious Marxist ever since her youth and is a well known figure in the Italian and Russian political labor movement for nearly three decades, and is therefore known internationally. She was a student of Antonio Labriola, a professor in the University of Rome, and a Marxian, well known as the author of *Essays on the Materialist Conception of History*, where he shows how wrong all history writing must be for want of a monistic understanding of historical developments.[2] She was one of a handful of Socialists who stood against the capitalist war of 1914–18, according to the resolution of the Stuttgart Congress in 1908—which all the so-called socialists violated by joining their national Governments.[3] For all practical purposes, the authoress may be considered as the founder of the so-called Zimmerwald-Kienthal movement against the last war, which with Lenin was instrumental in establishing the Bolshevist Government in Russia. She was

---

1. Angelica Balabanoff (1878–1965) was a Russian-Jewish-Italian communist, secretary of the Comintern and later influential on Italian socialist politics.

2. Antonio Labriola, *Essays on the Materialist Conception of History* (1896).

3. Acharya's associates in Paris, Madame Bhikaiji Cama and S. R. Rana, attended the International Socialist Congress in Stuttgart held in 1907 (not 1908).

secretary of the movement from its very inception at the beginning of the War, later on the first Secretary of the Third International. She describes in this book the treacheries of all "revolutionaries" from Mussolini to Lenin, Zinoview, Radek, and others whom she came in intimate contact with in the cause of her Marxian career. She has bitter disappointment with them all but is rather sporting to Lenin, Trotsky, and Bucharin—although she does not consider them much worth as characters, or wise and solid, dependable men. When Lenin became sick, it was her turn to be excluded from the Communist party for so-called "unworthy behavior"—i.e. criticism of the Bolshevik demi-gods in private. It has done her good, for she can come out openly against them, which she would not have done out of "party loyalty" if she kept within the sheep's, black sheep's, folds. Those who knew Balabanoff (as the writer knew), know how religiously scrupulous, and unselfish she is, even to the point of martyrdom.[4] She looks at the proletariat like an ascetic with pity, but that did not prevent her from co-operating with and justifying the actions of a newer state for a couple of years—because of the danger to the Russian proletariat from *other* states. The result was that she was responsible for the betraying of the proletariat to a new set of oppressors and exploiters instead of liberating them. That is the sad end of all Marxian "science." She is still very naïve, for she hopes another state will be required to emancipate the proletarians; the Marxist prejudice inculcated by herself and maintained through more than a quarter of century gives her a kind of respectability, which she dare not shake off, for fear of being an apostate or called so. So she will die in the Marxian dogmatic schism.

In the whole book, she delivers a kick whenever she mentions a Syndicalist or an Anarchist—true to the tradition left by Marx. If we have to believe what she mentions of some syndicalists she met for we cannot negate what is attributed to them both owing to her truthfulness and want of other information to contradict her—even

---

4. Acharya met Balabanoff at the third Zimmerwald conference held in Stockholm in September 1917; see Introduction and Chapter 48.

then there is no reason why Syndicalism and Anarchism should be wrong and unscientific while Marxism (or State Trustification) must be the only Socialism, or the necessary step toward socialism. Our contention is that if some Syndicalists and Anarchists are wrong, all Marxians are thoroughly wrong. Syndicalism and anarchist thought may be improved, are possible of improvement, but even the "reddest" Marxian thought will remain incorrigibly petty bourgeois, if not grand-bourgeois. She could not produce any Marxian example of such thorough selflessness and practical, unprejudiced, useful heroism, as that of the immortal Anarchist Tema, whose worth she recognizes by devoting a couple of pages because he died for the revolution, even if it turned out to be a Bolshevik *coup d'état* in the Tzarist palace! Otherwise Balabanoff would also have sneered at him because he was an Anarchist. There seems to be to the Marxists, one good revolutionary among Anarchists—that being a dead Anarchist. The same as what the English used to write during the war: There is only one good German and that is a dead German! There is probably reason for this attitude of the Marxists—in their authoritarian instinct, Balabanoff supports authoritarianism outside the Bolshevik party but not of the leaders over the party—an attitude which cannot be justified in theory or as practical. Authoritarianism outside the party must necessarily lead to the same thing inside the party—as there is no gap between outside and inside in practical life. We are Anarchists, because we do not want authoritarianism outside or inside, because to us anti-Marxists, life and society must be, imminently, one indivisible whole impossible of mechanical separation, as the Marxists inorganically think and believe.

The book is well worth reading, not only because she is a well known figure in both the successful and fallen Bolshevik camp, but because it describes the inner life of a movement, part antibellicose and part-militarist, which has not been described hitherto. Balabanoff is no doubt the best fitted person to write about the origin and storm of state power in Russia by the Bolsheviki.

The Road to Freedom, 4:6 (January, 1928), 3.

8. Mother India

M. Acharya

IT IS NOT GENERALLY KNOWN HOW the Indian troops were brought to Europe at the very beginning of the World War, how they were treated, and how they fared in internment camps, and therefore it may be worthwhile to begin this essay with a little description of these events.

When the War was declared, the British Imperial Government sent the soldiers in India simply on board of troop ships promising to pay their families a couple of months' wages in advance, but did not tell why this generosity! On board, they were disarmed and placed under guard of English soldiers. They did not know where they were going to, but thought they were being transferred to another station. The ships came to Egypt, but still this voyage was not at an end. Thus they landed in Europe—for the first time in the history of the Indian troops. Being on foreign soil, where everything was bristling with arms, they had been marched to the front and had to fight under compulsion. Naturally, throwing of flowers and such shows to put enthusiasm into them were arranged when they marched through the French towns and villages—not forgetting the chances to please their sexual instincts with sickly French women.

The soldiers were paid practically nothing when on the fighting line. This fact can be proved by statements of prisoners taken by Germans, because when they were captured they had no money while English soldiers still had some. Thus they were made to fight for nothing, but whatever was advanced to their families. Thus the

British Government saved the cash, while making the faithful soldiers of the Empire, their much advertised heroes, bleed and die for good words enforced by bayonets and laws.

While these ignorant, imprisoned soldiers were removed from India, raw territorials from England replaced them in India. Thus the Empire in India was made safe for British rule and profits, while the loyal empire sent its sons to die in the nick of time for nothing when England was quite unprepared to send picked British troops to Belgium and Northern France.

The troops in India are divided into regiments forming members of one caste, race, or tribe. But in France, besides setting the Indian officers against the possible treachery of soldiers and similarly setting English soldiers against both in the first lines, these being told to shoot from behind them on the least suspicion, similar trouble was created among the fighters by putting soldiers and officers of different castes and races together and encouraged to watch and report against one another. The Indian officers are all of the lowest rank, and even then they are only moral leaders of the respective caste and tribesmen, having a superior position in the different castes and races. Even the highest officers, called captains and majors, have only the title without training authority to supervise and cow down the morals of the soldiers and under-officers.

Thus, out of nearly 200,000 Indian troops, nearly two-thirds of the total Indian soldiers in existence, only 50% are reported to have returned home, and only 600 or so were reported captured by the Germans. The rest perished in the battle fields or from serious wounds, not only because they were placed between two fires, but also in the most impossible, undefendable sectors of the battle front without being properly equipped or trained for a European warfare against the modern armies of European imperialist powers. No doubt, they fought bravely, according to the tradition of their caste or race, and would rather perish then give in or retreat. This also contributed to their decimation. It is in fact owing to the traditional profession of soldiery practiced by certain castes and tribes in India that they are taken into the army, a tradition which carries with it high bravery and chivalry of the olden days. Even of the 600 Indian prisoners of war captured by the Germans, about 200 died of sickness contracted during long years of sitting in internment camps in the most inhospitable climate for the hardy races.

The one result of this senseless, merciless use of Indian soldiers was that when they went home invalided and uncared for, and their castes and tribes came to know of their innocent sufferings, the whole races became turbulent and rebellious. These tribes and castes began to fight militarism, and thus a strong anti-militarist movement came into being. Therefore, the British authorities disbanded many cavalry regiments, which refused to do any more military services. Realizing the ultimate danger of this new born Anti-Militarist spirit among the illiterate common soldiers, the British imperialist Government made concessions to the Indian bourgeoisie, whom they want to fight this spirit.

The invalided soldiers were no doubt partly given "employment," i.e., badly paid long hours of work in flour mills and such hard works or provided with insufficient plots of land for cultivation, but these keep them more prisoners than free men for the thankfulness expected of them. They can neither work nor make use of the charity shown more in words than in conditions. Some months ago, a few score of ex-soldiers in the Punjab went in a body and occupied the lands by force (more shown than employed) of a betitled man who was given a present of the lands they wanted to have. When the minions of authority went there to the help of the already rich bourgeois and inquired why they did so, they replied that they were more in need of the land than the Gentleman-Landlord to whom the lands were presented by the Government, while they themselves went starving after fighting and bleeding for the rulers. You have here an example of feeling and intelligence obtaining among the simple soldiers not yet perverted by capitalist ideas of being well off.

But the Government called "of India" is preparing for worse times to come—worse for itself both inside India, for it has to face the consequences of pauperization of the population practiced for many generations, and outside India, in coming war of Imperialists for the world markets. It wants now to give up its old policy of keeping Indians aloof of military profession but to draw the Indian possessing and would-be bourgeois class as recruits for its purposes of capitalism at home and abroad—as concessions for the Indian bourgeoisie to fight against Indian workers and peasants and for a part of the foreign export market. The long cherished dream of the Indian nationalists to enter the army to fight anybody who may be coming along and happen to be helpless is being realized subservient to British imperial interests—against the interests of the Indian working, producing class as a whole. The British Government has promised to train Indians as officers of the army—provided they would be "good boys" ready to fight loyally for its imperial purposes in India and abroad. Nothing pleases the stupid nationalist bourgeoisie—nationalist only in name and bourgeois internationally in the capitalist sense, friends of its own oppressors. Just, now, a few loyal Indians of the aristocracy or powerful vested interest class are being sent to England to have a questionable underling military training. Military training is promised to the "higher class" college boys of unquestioning loyalty. If things go on at this rate, we may not be surprised to see a civil war of pro- and anti-British bourgeoisie as is now passing before our eyes in China—for international capitalist interests of exporters. It is the greatest danger to the peaceful well being of the teeming millions of India coming in the form of a doubtful "boon." It is therefore all the more necessary to struggle against the militarization of India—called the "indianisation of the army."

⌒

Mr. Gandhi is known throughout the world as a great and consistent pacifist and anti-militarist. But unfortunately, it must be said that he is never consistent and never was. Hence his pacifism, because it is half pacifism, now in this interest and again in another interest, avails nothing. While he is violently opposed to violence in general, he is more opposed to the mass liberation from violence than to the violence of Governments. He does not believe that the violence established by Governments at their expense creates and necessitates the violence of the people at times. While he wishes to abolish the violence of individuals and groups, he believes that violence of governments is impersonal, necessary—nay perhaps in the end good. This psychology is opposed to the very idea of non-violence and peaceful, brotherly society. If any group of people is entitled to establish or having established—to maintain their violence in he name of Society, nation, and order—what prevents others morally to overcome their violence with other violence in order to impose a new violence of their own? Thus we have party after party coming up, all agreeing together that some violence or other has to be imposed and kept up over the people in the name of constituents and States. And Gandhi is not different in this respect—not better—than the usual run of man poisoned by habitual submission to violence of one kind or another. He talks of bandits and robbers—without trying to distinguish whether those who have already got possession of Social Wealth or others who want to get possession of them from these are the actual and virtual robbers. In that case, the legalized sanctity of robbed social wealth by some—whether these are private bourgeoisie or state managing bourgeoisie—has to remain forever, according to Gandhi. They are not then those who want to abolish violence and robbery, but want to maintain their own violence and robbery to benefit by social wealth and ill being. So long as the psychology of Socialists, pacifists, and humanitarians exist, we need not expect any betterment and any improvement of individual and society by non-violent means. But we are here to better and improve people, to struggle for it, by non-violent means: That means is to din and drive the Social truth home by untiring repetition.

I do not mean to say that Gandhi is himself directly concerned in this or any other Governmental violence against people, but still—so long as he does not denounce all governments, i.e., parts of Society over the whole and at the same time countenances some government against others, he is indirectly with that violence. I personally think that Gandhi would not take ministerial part in any Government, but that he would support the election of some Government rather than denounce all constitutions making governmental violence against people possible is enough to prove my statement.

Fortunately for India, not all people are fit nor willing to enter into the army, even if any Government will ever be in possession of sufficient money and authority to introduce universal conscription. The danger to India and the world is nevertheless less—if at any time any Government is capable of recruiting one million fighting men out of the 320 millions of India's population. During the last war, India's forced contributions were more in money and materials than in men. Out of the 1½ (one and a half million) or even 2 million men recruited there during the last war, I do not think more than half a million carried arms nor even a quarter million were on the firing line. Yet their capacity to keep tens of millions in awe— and under contribution for the destruction of materials—cannot be minimized or condoned.

As India consists of one fifth of the globe's population, the field for anti-military agitation and action there is not only great but it is all the more necessary on account of its magnitude, if the next War prepared by our capitalist and "anti-capitalist" state rulers have to be foiled in their recruiting—although foredoomed—attempts. But anti-militarist and paternal socialist words alone are not enough. It is necessary to preach and agitate for a Socialism, the only real socialism, where every organization of violence will become inevitably impossible. And that can only be when the would-be socialists see that the rule of a part of the population over the whole of their electors, by however vast and complicated a constitution, be it called workers' or proletarians, is not accepted as even the transition form of Socialist Commonwealth and bitterly fought against establishing itself. All constitutions must necessarily serve as a damn against life and movement—for conservative reaction coming under so many forms. We cannot cry against war and violence—international or civil—and at the same time accept even the reddest of constitutions. Constitutions suppose the violence and the organization of violence of some over others—finally leading to civil and foreign wars.

Since the final object of Society and Humanity is to become organic in order to avoid violence within itself and of any part of it against another, the keeping of violent divisions must necessarily lead to another rearrangement of violence—of a new violence against the old and against a still newer one.

Remember that no part or even all separate parts "together" can ever represent the whole and still be identical with the whole— an illusion pervading even after so many centuries of civilization. The only constitution we can therefore recognize is the constitution innate in an organic, undivided Society whereby the wealth of every individual increases the wealth of the whole Society—instead of depleting and concentrating it in the hands of a few or in the State (which cannot be different for the people at large)—for their separate benefit.

If we establish, accept, or do not struggle against the split up basis of Unity, by which one part reduces all the rest to so much dead material, be that part composed of the representatives of so many divided and dead parts, we can never cope against militarism, however sincere we be, but will simply go on raving against it, leaving it peacefully to rule.

In order to arrive and achieve that organic unity of Society called Socialism, we must struggle for that idea from this very moment, instead of deviating from it on party, constitutional, and so-called transitional lines—as all our "also Socialist" friends are doing. We know they are doing it—i.e., deviating from Socialism and class-unity, in the name, if not under the plausible excuse, of being practical. Practical we must all be no doubt, so long as we live—we can only be practical; otherwise we will be living theoretically and ideally, i.e., away from this society and humanity rises above capitalist, imperialist, and militarist conditions, and succumbs to it with metaphysical inventions called arguments, instead of overcoming it all for conscious living as social, united, organically thinking beings. Unfortunately, our many socialist party friends do not see the nature of their party actions but, therefore, invent newer arguments and parties on unreal suppositions for good.

Only when we can hinder violence of every kind, from individual to governmental, even of socialist Governments of whatever name and accident, we shall be nearer to Socialism, classless Society. The illusion that the State will do what the Society cannot or will not do must be destroyed root and branch if we are to be Socialist in the good sense. It is being destroyed slowly, because we do not attempt to destroy it in all consciousness, and with all our intelligence.

Naturally, in a Socialist society that we attempt to preach, there can be no question of wages and salaries: It is Social insurance of every member by the Society as a whole that we want. Who shall pay and accept wages and salaries, however great or equal? It is work alone with that object that can give us that Social insurance, the work that is now taken away for war, wage competition, and reduced production. Wages and salaries are inevitable in a society—if it can be so-called at all—where the means of production and the products belong not to the whole Society but to a group of private owners or political representatives. Therein, exchange and balance of power is a necessity. But for Socialists who want Society as an organism, conscious, undivided (class and party-less), and whole— where is room for Exchange and Balance of Power Systems and their manipulations? The Society, nation, and humanity works to produce all that it requires and can produce out of materials, which now belong exclusively to a few owners and governments for their own aggrandizement. So long as this is allowed to exist, all practical work to abolish organized and unorganized violence is an illusion and eternal talk. If we would work as we want—to abolish both state and private violence—we must work for the ultimate goal of the future Society.

The Road to Freedom, 4:9 (April, 1928), 6–7; reprinted as "Der Anti-Militarismus in Indien," *Die Internationale* (May, 1928), 14–17.

9. Principles of Non-Violent Economics

M. P. T. Acharya

ANY SYSTEM OF ECONOMY, WHICH IS run neither in the interests of the consumers nor is administered by them must necessarily impoverish them and then disappear. For it is only the consumers who can work and maintain the system—by their work and by their intelligence. But in order to function, this system must then be free from all domination or strict regulation—or even control—on the part of those who from outside want to make it serve other ends than the consumers' interest. Now all state systems, whether Bolshevist or purely capitalist, can only be run from outside, since they are part of society that feeds on the majority, namely the producers and consumers. This system of parasitism must be abolished and not tolerated or reinforced by a metaphysical, mental, or spiritual method of support. The Bolshevists suggest as solutions nothing but a cerebral metaphysics exactly as the capitalist suggest that the present economic system is designed by God for his profit.

Practical Economy System

An economic system, which is practical, must at the same time be scientific and social: It must be able to dispense with money, with exchange, and with one part controlling the vast masses. It must be essentially of exemplary simplicity, even if it were to be described as "primitive." This primitive economic system that was a social system was abolished not only by the industrial revolution, modern capitalism, and social wars; its destruction goes back to an even more remote period, viz. that of the establishment of individualism with its laissez faire economy whereby the state would allow unrestricted exploitation, which enabled the accumulation of wealth in fewer and fewer hands.

Even if this theory of primitive society and its aim were erroneous, the consequent result cannot be doubted. The peoples are not born to objects of exploitation and domination in the interests of a few individuals and groups. Yet, rightly or wrongly, the people suffered, tolerated, and allowed the dominations and exploitations, but that is no reason why the moderns should believe that they had acted wisely and therefore imitate them, leaving the march of evolution to its fate.

Autonomous Communes

Monopolies—state, private, or combined—can function only at the expense of the majority of members of the society. In order to lessen distress of humanity, both in peace and war, the sole remedy lies in abolishing these three systems and not in experimenting with them and tolerating them. The only system, which can replace them and the other equally erroneous economic methods, is the administration of production by the consumers for the purpose of establishing equality of consumption. It is, however, impossible of attainment without the abolition of the privileges of property (state, private, and combined), and the dissolution of ownership of these organizations peaceably, violently, or otherwise, and the establishment of locally independent society within which each member will be equal to another member and will represent himself instead of being represented by somebody else and ordered from above. It is only in "autonomous communes" of this kind that social solidarity and social work is possible and that universal "democracy" can be ensured and maintained to an equal degree. It is only thus that the energy of all members of the whole society can be liberated and directed into social and international channels—bringing pleasure and prosperity to each and all. All control and government authority of any kind will thus become superfluous—as each individual will make his nearest neighbor and his most remote fellow-creature feel his responsibility. Anti-social persons—who are at present the products of the anti-social organization of economics—will be rendered innocuous far more effectively by the individuals who surround them than by the state, which is distant with its organs or surveillance and punishment.

Decentralized Society

In these small communities, it would be impossible for anyone to remain as idle at the expense of his neighbors—the more so as work will have replaced money as the world standard of value. In places where the possession of money is necessary and sufficient to procure utilities for consumption, people work as little as possible and this is quite natural—since money represents the right to acquire utilities available and a chance to acquire still more money.

All these factors must be taken into consideration if one wishes to create a system that will function securely—for all these factors are human and the men called upon to implement an economic system, whatever it may be, are "human" too. Otherwise, a system, which appears on paper as marvelous to a limited and dry intelligence, will prove impracticable as soon as an attempt is made to put it into practice. In a society, a nation, an international humanity divided into communist-social groups without authority, these groups can be easily led to coordinate their economic efforts VOLUNTARILY, needless to say, in view of their common and equally profitable aims. No impediment will be placed in the way of co-operation by any central authority and no autonomous commune will be materially self-sufficient, be it in a question of necessaries or comforts, not to speak of luxuries. It cannot be, it would not possibly be, by exchange that such co-operation will be realized, but by a common participation in production and by a proportionate acquisition of products by the different communes.

A registration office created by the various communes in co-operation, and the use of modern technical means of communication for broadcasting wireless messages—day and night—indicating the total utilities available for the total population of a union of federated communes, would suffice to enable each federation to know how many utilities can be consumed in the communes considered separately. Telegraphic and telephonic messages will suffice to direct the utilities where they are needed.

Similarly, the needs of the communes can be totaled up by the registration office, and communicated by wireless to the producing regions and communes, which, hand in hand, will look to the ways and means of satisfying those needs as rapidly as possible, having recourse of the best technicians and workmen working voluntarily in order to make constant improvements in science and technology.

Local Autonomy

Apart from the question of determining what necessities are to be satisfied as indispensable to all communes, the communes should be left entirely free to distribute the utilities "democratically" as they think fit. They should be left entirely to themselves as regards all that concerns their productive and consuming functions and their internal affairs. There should be a variety in life—advantages and disadvantages, liberty of movement and change, liberty of choice in responsibilities too—for each man or each woman who wants to stay in or leave a commune—and a similar right for each commune to receive and keep or eject any man or any woman. If the question of food and other needs of every man, woman, and child is thus solved; if there is certainty of work for every capable adult and education secured for every child, all conceivable varieties of marriage and separation, and the protection of every child are problems easily solved with the help of the collective community. In these communes, the child cannot be a burden; he will, indeed, be welcome as a member, for he contributes to the improved welfare of the whole society.

Diffused Democracy

It is the communes enjoying an economy of this nature that can constitute a "real democracy." The democracy of the Bolshevists and the anti-Bolshevist constitutionalists is but a snare; it is of no consequence that the law gives them right to vote several times. If nobody can observe or control the actions of those elected who can justify what they want without any possibility of contradiction that is the only thing possible, the electoral rights become only a farce.

No written constitution, whether uniform or uncertain, is necessary for these communes, each member of which represents himself on each and every question to be solved. All party quarrels are avoided. No discussion is dragged all over the country to split humanity and awaiting the decisions of a handful of men in session somewhere.

These communes cannot possibly recognize the permanent institutions of barbarous justice administered by judges, police, and executioners, who receive salaries and are compelled on pain of losing their jobs to inflict the most cruel inhumanity on certain of their fellow beings. The severest of punishment that can be inflicted on anti-social persons would be to drive them out of one commune after another until they correct their behavior and become useful members of society. There would be no need for the communes to lodge hostile troops or to maintain forces at their expense in order to see that the vile decrees of distant authorities are respected. If an armed force becomes necessary, it would be levied at the call of the communes, right on the spot.

This federation of independent communes has within itself no need whatever for a foreign office. If commerce or exchange with the outside is necessary, a common commission can be constituted to sell the surplus products outside and with the money thus obtained procure necessary utilities—the operations passing outside at the prices current on outside markets. With the federation itself, there could not possibly be any question of prices, exchange, or monetary complications. Hence, no money and wages. If a region outside the federation inquires for products—so long as business continues outside, the objects for which there is a demand can be assembled or produced in the same way as if it were for internal consumption— the money thus obtained being spent to purchase from outside such utilities as the federation lacks.

We may rest assured that a short time after the creation of a federation of communes of this nature, be it anywhere, the life and liberty of each individual being ensured without formalities, the various countries in the world would, one after another, rally to such a system. There would then be no necessity for any "foreign policy"!

Economic Bulletin, no. 1 (International University of
Non-Violence: University of Calcutta [1930] 1947);
reprinted from *Kaiser-i-Hind*. This article originally
appeared as the second part of a longer article in
L'en dehors, *La Protesta*, *Die Internationale*, and *L'Adunata dei
Refrattari* in 1928 and 1930; see Chapter 13.

10. Unity—What For!

M. Acharya

FROM ALL COUNTRIES COMES FORTH THE CRY—unity, freedom, happiness, peace, good will, and material well being, ever the cry, organize for socialism, communism, and a better world in which to live—workers and peasants, arise and throw off your chains!

What is all this for? How shall we bring about all or any of these things? Many talk glibly of things they plan to do but few stop to reason out the way.

It has often been asked how to bring unity in the midst of a divided society. But society suggests an already existing unity among its members. Any attempt to force unity upon those who live upon a normally divided and mutually warring basis only results in great confusion. Zeal without sense and words without meaning were worse than no movement nor effort at all.

Those whose empty plea for unity, freedom, happiness, and peace is intended only for themselves, actually seek division, slavery, misery, and war for all the rest of mankind.

Human selfishness is always with us in the individual, but now we have the spectacle of a huge concentrated effort to crystallize this evil into a mass movement by organizing the workers and peasants for an undefined and indefinable Socialist Communism!

What is the meaning of all this? More division without reason—more confusion without solution! The socialists and communists know what they want but they do not want anybody else to know. They want new division of ownership based upon capitalistic premises and supported by state ownership and mastery of human lives. They combat the private ownership of wealth and the sweating of the workers not because they oppose the dictatorship of life and material needs per se, rather because they oppose those who maintain the dictatorship. One of the great lessons we may take from Russia is that social ownership is no part of the socialist-communist program—but a scheme of nationalizing all human life and effort for the benefit of the few at the expense of the many.

These usurpers of ideas have no conception of social justice and because they are totally bankrupt of all social feeling, their cry for justice is false and their plea for unity is a fraud.

The socialists of all parties are quite in agreement as to what they oppose in individual capitalism to the end that they may introduce state capitalism for themselves. Regardless of their internal bitterness and internecine quarrels they stand united against all those who hope for a socialism wherein there shall be no state, no party, and no division. They cry out against the capitalist state to induce the exploited victims of private ownership to come over into their camp that they might be crushed and robbed more fiercely still.

They take advantage of capitalism through just or unjust abuse of its functions as a camouflage. They sabotage every real revolutionary effort with their bourgeois morality—they say that socialism can only be achieved through gradual processes and by legal means, that the uncompromising socialists are mad and impractical idealists and traitors. What better could suit the supporters of capitalism?

In this way do the well-known socialist politicians in the capitalist states sustain their positions and make them pay handsome profits as pseudo leaders.

But have these betrayers of the masses ever attempted to call a conference to discuss the merits of the socialism of the masses, and what means are necessary to bring it into operation, and make it practical and realizable now, within our own time?

No, never have they made any such attempt, they have no time for purposeful work. They do not want a socialism wherein self-rule prevails; they conceive only a state-ridden, divided social life without harmony, unity, or agreement. Their program calls for a continuation of tyranny and exploitation of the workers even after the disintegration of the present capitalist state through the ravages of competition and international war. Their plans are to capitalize upon the bankruptcy of bourgeois morality so that the position of the leaders shall be secure, whatever else may happen.

This betrayal of the worker's interests for the benefit of the leaders is willful and deliberate, and their persistence and continued defense of their policies under the subterfuge of evolutionary necessity is provocative of defeat for every revolutionary attempt to bring about better conditions for the masses.

Whether the sabotage of all sincere socialist propaganda is sponsored by ignorance or dishonesty makes little difference, for in the last analysis the result is the same—defeat for the workers!

So long as leaders who profit by their positions are permitted to remain where they may use their influence for their own private gain, just so long will the toilers of the human race remain victims of their own stupidity in recognizing the authority of any ruling group.

But it must not be forgotten that these State-socialist politicians are not blind to the ends they seek. When they oppose the anti-state Syndicalists and Anarchists, they know that they are facing a social group that knows their schemes and foresees their ends, therefore their unrelenting warfare against all anti-authoritarian idealists is based upon their understanding that they represent the only living force that is able to drive them from office and make them seek some honorable means of earning their bread.

The Anarchists represent the real social ideal because they expose the humbuggery of the state socialists with their proletarian armies, their spies and ignorant, ruthless dictators as evidence of which it is only necessary to turn to Russia where alleged communists have set up a military bureaucracy and system of slave economics, which surpass anything the world has yet witnessed.

Only by repudiating these false leaders and setting out to achieve our own ends through the conscious efforts of a united mass movement, knowing what it wants and knowing how to get it, can the capitalist and socialist politicians be rendered harmless by being shorn of their power. And when their right to mislead is no longer recognized, the fiat of mandates can no longer impress, and the workers can at last come into their own—a free society based upon love and understanding, unity, and harmony where no man can force his will upon another.

The Road to Freedom (September, 1928), 8.

11.   Why This Judicial Murder?

M. Acharya

IN THE FACE OF THE FACTS establishing the innocence of the world's two greatest men, and I say this because they were heroes of the first water, and in spite of the protests of millions of men and women of diverse nationalities and diametrically opposed views, our comrades have been reduced to ashes.[1] Why so? Evidently for the prestige of official justice.

Sacco and Vanzetti expressed the truth of time through the most advanced thoughts and incarnations of humanity. Yet they were murdered, burned at the stake, as it were, on the altar of modern official hypocrisy and deceit called the law.

What is this law, this justice, and the state? They are the creations of the great financial interests, the banks, the stock gaming markets, and gamblers of human life and destiny.

The courts, parliament, and government are but the watchdogs of the banks and monopolist in money—against which these two men struggled in life and thought. Feeling the truth of their ideas so vividly and realistically, they condemned these institutions as lies and shams, conceived in cruelty and nurtured in corruption. They were willing to die to defend their ideas.

They worked to create an order in which every man, woman, and child should have an equal chance at life and well being.

---

1. "First water" meaning "of the highest quality."

That is exactly what the banks and the state institutions do not want to broadcast.

But the ideas of Sacco and Vanzetti are the expressions of time in the womb of the future and they will come into being just as inevitably as the changing of the tides.

Hence, the bankers and statesmen shiver in their shoes, steeped as they are in crimes against humanity and glory with the blood of innocent men.

By such token do the spokesmen of these criminal institutions falsify the truth and drag culture in the mire by burning the precursors of time in the electric chair because their activities threaten their tottering institutions.

The Road to Freedom (August, 1929), 8.

12. On Jealousy

M. Acharya

Dedicated to my partner

THE BARBARITY OF JEALOUSY DATES from the time when man began to buy cows (that is to say, to exchange objects for other objects, as we do today with money) and considered that his money would be lost if he did not protect said objects against loss or use by others. Later, by exchange, abduction, or otherwise, he acquired the *possession* of women (as he acquired cattle or other objects for everyday use, of luxury gold ornaments whose use or abuse by others could bring him loss), and he had to worry about monopolizing their contact with him. Their acquisition cost him as much money, effort, and utilities as any slaves, draft animals, or laborers, objects of consumption, or pleasure. He meant being their owner and their only usufructuary. Women, being objects of acquisition, did not possess more soul or intelligence than cattle or material things. They were at his disposal to be used or misused, as he pleased, to be unused, sold, or killed like sheep. Women had to be content with their fate. This system has prevailed so far, because the laws continue to guarantee the man the possession of his wife (of his love!), and to prevent the alienation and the transfer of his affections to someone else.

Women have become so accustomed to the slavery of their bodies that their minds are never tired (like slaves) of asserting and believing that it is legitimate—permanently or momentarily—to belong to only one man and to love him. To think otherwise is shameful, even for the woman who thinks.

Monogamous love is transformed into an axiom, at least in women. They claim that they cannot "share" their love and affection between many men. Their duty as slaves to a single master is so painful that they cannot want—and naturally—to please all masters or even only two.

Why would they "share" their love since it is on *the order of the men* they love? It took a slave mentality to conceive of ideas such as "giving love," or being complacent and helpful to male love. Do women not have enough sense, intelligence, and organs to serve and please themselves first—as men do, even when they "love"?

Thus, *language itself* betrays the slavery and contradictions of the feminine mentality, despite its "love" polish. All natural physiological necessities are sacrificed to this slave mentality, inherited from the traditions of the past. Feminine bodies have no other value than that conferred by the wearing of useless ornaments, intended to make them "pleasant" while remaining "modest."

An Irish lady has written somewhere that the roles are reversed and that women have learned to lead men. They have sharpened their intelligence and make use of various devices, including make-up, clothing, coquetry, "love." This development of their cunning has been achieved at the expense of the carnal desires of their bodies, by calculation and by "culture"—the culture of coldness.

It is true that the new demands of the female owner are used now to keep men on a leash. Women today demand the "love" of men in the same way that men have demanded their bodies and their bodily fidelity. Although the roles have been reversed, there is no equality between the two sexes. Women are still forced to meet the sexual needs (or not meet them) of their husbands. Voluntarily or not, they are attributed or delivered to a single man. It is only the women who are described as non-respectable or the hypocrites who arrive, from time to time, to satisfy themselves with someone to their liking. But what are the risks? Many of these "satisfaction" cases are not directly aimed at meeting the physical and physiological demands of the female nature. The sex of the woman is a shame to him unless owned by someone. It is only with a legal husband or, at the very least, an owner with whom the woman allows herself to satisfy her sexual demands. To change partner, for a woman, is a shame even more than a loss. This is what we call "love," in and out of marriage. Even "the freed woman" cannot invite anyone to satisfy her sexual impulses. It's the man who has to start talking about love. The woman will not confess her love if we do not make love to her. The jealous woman is certain of the love of her companion—husband or lover—only if he is also jealous. What is present love but the expression of jealousy?

But what is jealousy in love?

It is a feeling similar to the owner's love for his dog, his seat, his garden, which he has bought or conquered for his exclusive use. Whether he uses it or not. Whether or not he finds pleasure in using it. He *acquired* it. It is for this reason that these objects cannot be used by anyone else. The woman of today says: "I have acquired this or that man for myself, for myself alone, thanks to my knowledge of the art of loving, in other words, by being careful against the sharing of his love, and no one can rob me of this property." Jealousy reduces beings to the order of things—it makes them objects of possession. It ignores "the soul"—the autonomy of organs, feelings, mind, physical affinities. Jealousy leads to the loss of agreement, harmony, and love in the so-called beloved person.

"Whether we love or not, jealousy is still the best"—this is the motto of our barbaric humanity.

"De la Jalousie," *L'en dehors* (November, 1929), 6; reprinted as "Shittoshin no mondai ni tsuite," *Fujin sensen*, 2:2 (February, 1931), 14–17.

13. Trusts and Democracy

M. Acharya

IN A SERIES OF ARTICLES FROM *Foreign Affairs*, London, Francis Delaisi discussed this problem.[1] Delaisi at the time predicted the war, long before it broke out. He is already talking about another war today: that for petroleum, which will be much more horrible than the last one, that concerned colonial markets. Delaisi was persecuted in France, his birthplace, because of his anti-war attitude.

In the first of his articles, Delaisi described: Trusts. Pools or similar conventions are horizontal groupings: they unite all manufacturers, and when they are international trusts, they also refer to foreign competition. Then they are masters of the market, and at the same time determine production quantities and prices. They take advantage of their position to drive prices higher and higher. But there is a limit here. If prices are too high, consumption will go down and production costs will grow. To counter this difficulty, one reduces the wages and extends the working day (and develops a whole "science" in order to reduce the production costs). Thus, the limits of a productive production can be adjusted up and down. Presented with a fait accompli, consumers can do nothing more than either rebel or be content. Likewise for the workers: under the threat of dismissal, they must either subjugate or revolt; strikes, however, are undesirable and annoying, and sometimes people cannot resort to these measures. (Throughout his entire article, Delaisi tries

---

1. Francis Delaisi (1873–1947) was a French, pan-European economist, journalist, and syndicalist.

to convince the reader of the need for an agreement between the trusts and the workers.)

Now the author turns to the model government, which was set up to remove the damage of private capitalism by state monopolism, and said:

Capitalism, which emanated from individualism, has come to industrial unification. But he went only half way. Let us therefore drive the process to its end, and put all industries under one and the same control, through "socializing" them. At a stroke, all opposing interests will disappear if all the tools of production and exchange belong to the state, which represents the totality of the consumers. This is how the problem will be solved, the Marxists say.

This, however, is how it will only be solved on the surface, says Delaisi. The Russian experiment has shown that the management of all factories was neither entrusted to the workers, nor to a state bureaucracy. It was deemed necessary to organize all factories into trusts constituted as closed capitalist societies with their own risk and financial profit and loss account. Certainly these trusts do not distribute dividends to shareholders, but they nevertheless regulate prices and set their own production costs, leaving a margin for profit and repayment on borrowed capital, reserves, percentages to the administration, and workers' shares.

In this way, such a body tends to increase prices and lower wages. It is in conflict with the resistance of trade unions, which sometimes leads to strikes, as everywhere; it continues to be in conflict with the trusts that obtain their products. Undoubtedly, the state, the sole or principal shareholder of all these trusts, is their sovereign master. It regulates all its activity. The State Planning Committee (Gosplan) determines the mode of production and the prices each year for each industry, each sector, and for each local trust. But the only way to determine the manufacturing plans is to have discussions between the complementary and interrelated trusts and the workers' trade unions (recognized by the state as entrepreneurs). These tripartite agreements take place from time to time everywhere to establish the figures to be provided. They are then often modified later by similar periodical consultations. In short, the digits of the Gosplan serve more as guide numbers and "means of control." The "dictatorship of the proletariat" passively surrender to the game of these economic plans and forces.

With one word, the author of our article says, whether we choose a bourgeois or a "socialist" state, the solution to the problem is the same.

In the sections of his article so far described, Delaisi unmasked the Marxist or Bolshevik myth that their state was anticapitalist and social, and this proof is a meritorious work. His work should open the eyes of all those who still believe that official monopolism and state trustification of all means and materials of production could either lead to socialization, or at least have a different and better effect than the private monopolization of social life by a few hundred thousand, with or without trusts. Neither one way nor the other can be pursued in the long run, since private monopolism necessarily leads to statehood, and vice versa, as Russia shows today. But where is the solution to social gain and national welfare? Here Delaisi does not appear to be any better or wiser in the search for a solution than the Marxists—be they Bolsheviks or anti-Bolsheviks. He also proposes a three-way co-operation, which is not very different from the Bolsheviks: cooperation between the trusts, the government, and the organized workers, although he himself believes that such an experiment, as the Bolsheviks have done, is not the best for productive trusts, the state, and the workers. Delaisi merely calls for a minor modification of the Bolshevik system, in the interests of the private capitalists, which in his opinion will also only be beneficial to the interests of the state, workers, and consumers.

But he anticipates the objections to his own scheme, when he himself remarks: as this, one might say, is very complicated; would it not be much easier to get rid of the conflict of interest rather than to settle it through such a complicated mechanism? It is precisely here that he makes his proposals, but he leaves the correct and real solution out of consideration.

Delaisi's arguments for his proposal are the same as those of the Bolsheviks: if only a one-sided interest is advocated, such as, for example, in today's trusts, this will lead to tyranny and exploitation.

When two spheres of interest oppose one another, there will be a struggle. However, if three different spheres of interest are opposed to each other, a better adaptation between them is possible.

On the basis of this argument, therefore, it could be argued that the more diverse interests that are involved, the more possibilities of adaptation possible in the free play of the forces between them. But Delaisi limits the various interests only to three.

On the other hand, we must ask: how can we eliminate the conflict of interests, as such, rather than try to settle it through such a complicated mechanism? We see that Delaisi's own fears are correct and do actually materialize.

Why should humanity recognize three different spheres of interest to the detriment of their own and all common consumer interests? Is mankind only born to fulfill the function of the interplay of the "different" interests of the state, the employers, and the workers, the latter being connected with the former by the trade unions mentioned—against all consumers? Can people only live as long as one can sell and others can buy? Do people have no right to exist simply because they are born? And Delaisi—just as the Bolsheviks, and exactly like the anti-Bolshevik capitalists—in his entire system does not appear to be too keen on the consumers, who comprise the whole of mankind, whether they are tied to work, or incapable of work, or cannot find work (as today).

In every system of the national economy, the interests of the consumers should be the basis for the organization of production— not the advantage of the manufacturers, the state, or even a limited number of workers in limited trade unions. For these three parts can only be an infinitely small fraction of every nation that neglects the interests and welfare of all the rest. Especially the systems proposed by Delaisi and the Bolsheviks subordinate the interests and prosperity of the great majority to the "business" measures of manufacturers interested in profit, further to the politicians who raise taxes and some hundred thousand or millions more qualified workers, who depend on their masters for their wages. Such a system, in which the interests of a minority dominate the broad masses, cannot be called either national or democratic.

Even from the point of view of entrepreneurs (whether these are capitalist or state trusts), such a threefold system cannot exist, as such, precisely because of the nature of such an economic order, which takes more than it gives, while a large number of people ready to work cannot even transform their work into goods and profits for the masters.

The main obstacle to maintaining such systems comes from the fact that, for their preservation, more must be fed into the system than can be given by it. Otherwise the maintenance of such a system would soon become impossible. This is the case, too, of how many things may be produced, whether by the improvement of technology, or by the unrestrained exploitation of the physical force of millions, who seem to be born only to serve the production process and the producers, states, and capitalists, for more or less the same amount of money, or even during limited circulation, and decreasing and declining circulation; the means of consumption are very small for the great majority of the population compared to the high prices demanded by state or private capitalists, and even for those who can lead a "decent life" (it is only the few) it is impossible to buy up all goods. The problem thus faced by modern businessmen is how to get people to buy, and this problem cannot be solved by a state, private, or tripartite trust, because it is an antisocial system that takes more from the people than it gives and wants to give. However, this is theoretically possible, but not practical in an economy with a ruling class, which aims to buy and sell the people. As long as the majority of people remain mere commodities for the entertainment of the banks, the state, and the capitalist businessmen and manufacturers, they must suffer the whole existing order with them, and finally they must go bankrupt or be eliminated by force. Unfortunately, the bourgeoisie is told by professors and men of the state that the system is capable of improvement, despite the fact that it is becoming more and more alive, and the workers are united by various parties in the belief that time is not far off when the system will bring them prosperity: by the state, private trusts, or arrangements between both. The most recent history of mankind, above all the industrial revolution, has sufficiently proven that modern industry in connection with the state and capital has only proletarianized and impoverished mankind, rather than rendering it richer and safer. And this despite the tremendous treasures from all corners of the world that have been accumulated through the labor of people and in the hands of a few men. All the systems promulgated by Bolsheviks or anti-Bolsheviks can only restrain the decay of this hopeless state, which can only be sustained with loud false propaganda and the silencing of the masses.

"Trusts und Demokratie," *Die Internationale*
(March & April, 1930), 110–113, 134–135;
the rest of this article was reprinted simultaneously as
"Principles of Non-Violent Economics" (Chapter 9).

11. Project: Intended to Wrest Small Industries from the Clutches of Capitalism

M. Acharya

THERE IS NO DOUBT AN INFINITE number of small producers who suffer not only from the need for capital (government money)—and this unfulfilled need prevents them from running their businesses properly—but are unable to find buyers. Money, in fact, is monopolized and controlled by the bankers who use it for their own interests. The current result is that its small producers cannot continue to live or keep their products and their goods: they are forced to discard them (or mortgage them, which amounts to the same) at any price, thus abandoning their last means of existence. It is to save them, as well as those who are destitute and unemployed, that I have imagined the following project.

If small producers (farmers and craftsmen) agreed to unite and combine their bargaining skills, they would do very well, thanks to their production power. Even small capitalists who do not know or place their economies elsewhere than in the banks or in the shares of capitalist enterprises—even if it means losing them one day— could, by investing them in profitable enterprises, make a living for life through the use of tools belonging to them. Unfortunately, these small capitalists persist in wanting to speculate, and they lose all their money in the hope of getting big interests. They are stripped by financial companies, which are controlled and handled by the international monetary powers. However, they can only face bad days by turning to self-employment, rather than avoiding speculation. Speculating to get by does not pay; we must give it up, for they end up making themselves bankrupt even if they make others bankrupt.

It is not government money that provides well-being, it is productive work; even to a few, it can provide this money. All that the government's money can do is to make everyone work for a pittance—and this for the benefit of the state and some banks—driving the unemployed to their deaths (and their number is increasing).

It is important to understand the character of the government-protected currency (wrongly called gold).

If this currency is accepted universally, as has been the case so far, it is sufficient for some of its holders to withdraw a certain amount from circulation, either as profits or because they do not want to part with it, so that the cogs of the economic mechanism stop; millions are ruined, condemned to starve, exploited, or killed, whether they revolt or not. In these times of crisis, one does not sell or buy, no matter the amount of utilities offered. Sometimes there is plenty of money, but it does not circulate; sometimes there are plenty of goods, but they are expensively priced and the worker is not paid enough to buy them. This is the cause of unemployment and labor troubles, which are going from bad to worse.

State-protected banks have many other tricks in store to ruin the poor world, and the monopoly they enjoy allows them to operate safely. For one sterling gold, banks are allowed to issue 7 pounds of banknotes. Assuming that the bankruptcy of their creditors causes them to lose 1, 2, even 5 of these, they still make a profit. There are banks that issue 20 times the gold guarantee they have in reserve: what an epidemic of bankruptcies in prospect!

Whether the evils caused by the monetary system (gold or paper), and whether unemployment or pauperism can be abolished without the intervention of the banks or the state, is a question that must be left to Messrs. bankers and statesmen! But those who want to save themselves from their clutches must do so before it is too late to use their money and tools. This can be done right away without waiting for the political and international changes promised by the statist theorists or the handlers of capital. This can be done in any village, in any neighborhood, without a central organization. The system I propose eliminates the fierce competition that leads to the ruin of large numbers of people for the benefit of some in the name of the so-called theory of the "survival of the fittest," that is: the right of the strong against millions and millions of isolated producers.

If, in every village, every city district, the farmers and craftsmen (including home workers) UNITE on *the basis of mutual production and service rendition*, they would meet the needs of the workers, and they could increase their production, as well as the needs of the homeless and the unemployed. The more they produce, the more they will be able to sell for money after satisfying their consumption. Money acquired through the sale of surplus products can be used to purchase equipment, merchandise, and new tools. It is, moreover, only in relations with merchants or traders who produce nothing by themselves that it is necessary to use government money, or still to procure products or instruments that are not on the premises. Current shopkeepers can be used to sell to workers in the locality or neighborhood, but if they invest funds to buy objects from outside or sell to passing customers, this can only be under the control or direction of the producers of the locality or the district, after consideration of their needs and their requirements.

If it is deemed necessary or preferable, special stores can be created, supplied only by the associated producers.

How can all this be administered without resorting to the statist currency? A nominal value shall be fixed for the goods produced and credit vouchers representing the value of the work done or the services rendered shall be given to the workers or employees. These credit notes can be converted at any time into merchandise, in stores, at the prices indicated. The producers, who would hand them over to their workers or to all others with whom they would be dealing, would issue these credit notes. Those who run the stores would also be paid in credit vouchers for the services they will render: store administration, distribution of goods, etc. We would also pay the rent with these vouchers. Similarly for taxes or taxes of one kind or another: should the tax collectors not accept this method of payment, we would pay them with the statist money received from customers outside. This would not be advantageous, since it involves a premium on the sale, but it cannot be avoided at first. Be that as it may, the principle would be not to sell, except to obtain the official money necessary for transactions with the outside world. Profit and competition would therefore be repeated day by day, while solidarity and the fight against monetary power would be strengthened more and more.

This system would not avoid the need for official money, but it would minimize its use and the disadvantage of selling and buying statist money, the use of which, we know, leads to losses and bankruptcy, especially for the poorest producers.

These credit vouchers can be used across many villages or neighborhoods as well. It is sufficient either to issue them for this purpose or to issue transferable credit vouchers valid for a department, a province, or an entire country. One can consider the creation of a credit voucher office to transport goods or make payments across a given territory.

Those who work, produce, or render services of one kind or another—those who rent out land, rooms, objects of any kind—those who teach, do accounting or have a useful occupation, would have the right to receive these credit notes issued by the producers affiliated to the Union, or otherwise *known*, or the persons authorized to use them. The only exceptions are those unable to work or hosts received by affiliates.

Any producer who supplies goods to the stores may be authorized to issue these credit notes up to a certain amount. Better still, the producers' union can reach an agreement and authorize the issuance of a certain amount of credit vouchers by a central office—for a sum based on the real value of the utilities produced. No loss, no waste, since credit vouchers do not exceed the nominal value of the goods to be distributed to the holders of the vouchers. If there is surplus production, it is reserved for sale to outside customers and the official money thus acquired is used for the purchase of new equipment, such as improved machines and tools, and for transactions with those that you cannot pay in credit vouchers. That's the whole system in a few lines.

The advantage of this system is that it is not affected by crises, fluctuations in the commercial, industrial, or monetary market. All the unemployed, manual or intellectual, qualified or unqualified, can be employed and live, certain that tomorrow will come. They do not have to worry about "buying" statist money; they will work less than if they had to work for official money, which requires a lot and pays little, at least in most cases. They will do their job with more pleasure, the supervision of foremen and pointers becoming useless. The official monetary system and the enmity it creates between men will prove to be obsolete. It will be good for everyone.

"Projet: destine a arracher les petites industries aux griffes du capitalisme," *L'en dehors* (April, 1930), 5–6.

15. Gandhi and Non-Violence

M. Acharya

WITHOUT BEING A FOLLOWER OF GANDHI, I am an admirer of Gandhism as practiced today in India. Therefore, I think I am correctly interpreting the attitude of Gandhi to violence, although I have no authority from him. In his letter to the viceroy, which he wrote just after his arrest, he says:

"I have said that every violent act, word, and even thought interferes in the progress of non-violent action. If in spite of such repeated warnings, people will resort to violence, I must disown responsibility, save such as inevitably attaches to a human being for the acts of every other human being. But the question of responsibility apart, I dare not postpone action on any cause, whatsoever."[1]

I understand this as applying not only to the people's but also to the government's violence. Finally he says:

"If you say that civil disobedience must end in violence, history will pronounce the verdict that the British Government, not bearing, because not understanding, non-violence, goaded human nature to violence which it could understand and deal with."

That is: Pacifically.

I ask: Is this climbing down to the Government or condemning only the people's sporadic (because provoked) violence? The bourgeois press says the former, and the Stalinist press the latter.

---

1. Gandhi's letter to the Viceroy, Lord Irwin, May 4, 1930. Edward Frederick Lindley Wood (1881–1959), also known as Lord Irwin, was Viceroy of India from 1925 to 1931.

It is another matter what Gandhi *would* say later on, when the Government will deal with him. No doubt, Gandhi puts non-violence *as principle*.

In this connection I would point out that Gandhi had often said before he was arrested: "*Violence or non-violence, there is no going back from the program of civil disobedience and non-payment of taxes.*" He preferred violence to cowardly sitting with folded hands at the policy of the Government. That is why the Government could not answer his letters with anything but repressive violence.

Even in his most pacifist days, he had written: "Rivers of blood are more to be welcomed than sitting in slavery."

Now, he started his revolutionary pacifism irrevocably and makes the Government responsible for *the provocations of violence*.

A further example will illustrate his attitude better: In 1922, when the Sikhs were prevented by the Government from carrying any steel instruments, which might be used as arms and they felt it as an insult to their war-like religious customs, they asked him whether they should or not resist the order of the Government, even at the cost of their authorities' lives.

Gandhi said: If they feel bound to resist it, they must not put up with the order, even if it should cost their lives. They must have the courage of their convictions and must take *risks and responsibility*. As regards himself, he didn't want any arms nor considered it *his* necessity or religious duty to carry arms and therefore did not want to go into a struggle for insisting upon the right to carry arms. Those who believe it is necessary *must go* into the struggle and carry it to a successful end whatever the consequence may be and he, Gandhi, is morally for them in the struggle. Surely, he advised them to carry arms (which was their right, as not to carry arms is *his* right), but use the arms *responsibly*, so that nobody, however powerful, need be killed *unnecessarily*. It, of course, depends upon the interpretation of what one considers necessary or not—Gandhi thinks on principle the *use* of all arms is unnecessary.

He cannot be brought to agree with us: he believes only in social force of solidarity (he calls it soul force) to bring any

Government to its knees and he insists on suffering even to the point of getting killed.

That means of course giving the rights of killing only to the government, to expose its "peaceable cloak."

The result of Gandhi's advice was the Akahi peasant movement, which wanted to expropriate the temple lands. They marched daily in batches of hundreds to take possession of the lands most peacefully in spite of the provocation of the Government in placing machine-guns and ordering not to march beyond a certain line on pain of firing upon them. That did not prevent them from crossing to their object and they had the whole town in their favor, soon the Government withdrew their threat. I do not exactly know if they achieved their object of getting possession of temple lands or they and the Government entered into a compromise with the temple trustees whom the Government wanted to protect against the Akahis. I suppose that some compromise was arrived at. If that did not satisfy the Akahis, they would start the struggle again. They are mostly ex-service men and enjoy great reputation for bravery. Although they are accustomed to violence—in killing for the Government or getting killed by the Government—Gandhi twined their bravery into channels of non-violence, where they showed deathless bravery. Morally at least they defeated the State.

Without going into abstract ethics of non-violence, it is good to point out to all subject people that non-violence is the only principle that prevents resisters from *falling victims to governmental provocations and provocators*. It is most practical to colonial countries in finding out who leads the unwary into provocative channels by subtle hypocrisy coming as the "necessity for violence." Gandhi has made in India hypocrisy in politics impossible. By clearing hypocrisy out of public life, Gandhi has cleared the field of open hypocrites. If it were not for that, millions of people would not have the courage and immunity to break the laws purposely. It is more easy under oppression to break laws than to break the concentrated apparatus of war, therefore millions of people go into the movement and it becomes the force of social opinion.

I do not regret Gandhi's preachments of non-violence. He has demonstrated that laws can be negated and made into a dead letter the moment people want to do so. Not only that, *he has led millions of people to do so.*

The Road to Freedom, 7:1 (September, 1930), 1.

16. The Problem of Exploitation and Its Elimination

M. Acharya

COMRADE DETTMER LOOKS IN MORE detail at the question of "reasons for exploitation,"[1] and notes that exploitation is a consequence of unfair distribution, and a change can only occur when the workers take over production and distribute it among themselves according to the principle "from each according to his ability, to each according to his need."

The capitalists or even the state can and will exploit as long as the workers agree to receive wages for the delivery of their products, while the products are distributed by non-producers. For the private capitalist or the state, there would be no incentive to possess production and material if the workers refuse to surrender their products and deal with their distribution themselves. Exploitation is made possible and conditioned by the right and entitlement to the products, and only secondarily by the possession of the means of production itself. Today even the owners of the means of production are in servitude of the pure money-capitalist; the mere possession of money allows him to continually seize the profits of production. If money were to be abolished altogether, and the workers would take over the products themselves, the possession and exploitation would come to an end, and the owners of money and means of production would have to work themselves. The trade unions and the socialists, however, are so much dependent on money, on private property, and on the beautiful motto:

---

1. Fritz Dettmer (1898–1962) was a German anarcho-syndicalist.

"Entitlement to higher wages" they deny their class interests and thus become standard-bearers for private and state property. Money economy is always a capitalist economy, and those who demand money thus exemplify capitalist thinking and capitalist economy. But money is nothing more than robbed work. This socialism is consequently nothing more than a new form of bankrupt capitalism.

Comrade Dettmer further notes that a free disposal of products, et cetera., as is possible for the privileged members of the capitalist economy, would be impossible in a socialist economy. If the capitalists were to be given free choice, nothing would be improved, for some would always be wasting and needing more than they are entitled to according to their achievements, while others therefore would have to go hungry. This is capitalism with or without money. If you let a selection happen between different objects, most will likely choose the superficially beautiful, but fewer will choose the really good and will mostly get it too. It is roughly similar with our money system; it looks like freedom but is still slavery. If, as Comrade Dettmer proposes, one were to issue good or impersonal credit vouchers for the procurement of particularly desired goods, some might be able to fulfill their desires, but a large part would certainly not receive anything and would have to exchange the vouchers for inferior goods. This is freedom in injustice and selfishness, as today.

A solution is possible here simply by the local authorities distributing the desired goods fairly in relation to the total number of members. This distribution would, of course, take place under public control. If a person foregoes the acceptance of the goods, he still does not acquire the right to exchange it with another category of commodity, since others who may have a right to their share would have to receive less or go without any. Above all, this would lead to confusion in the distribution and create difficulties and dissatisfaction. If circumstances allow, it will always be possible to exchange, but there is no claim to it. In addition, of course, the claims of all have to be compensated, but no one can be harmed in any way. It is also important to ensure that everyone regularly receives what they need or use, without having to make an exchange first. I have observed in

Moscow how some German delegates, who had no use for chocolate, cigarettes, and similar luxuries, took what they were entitled to and exchanged it for other items from other people. Some even sold these exchanged items openly on the market. It was an incentive for doing business. Immediately after, the market was full with all kinds of goods that had just been distributed. Compare this with the customs of the inhabitants of Samoa, who always take from the common stock what they are entitled to, with the necessary consideration for others, without anyone checking. They have learned for generations to adapt their needs to the same needs of all. This is the true communist spirit, the development of which should be the goal, but this cannot be achieved under the slogan "individuality before general right."

The only possible (and necessary) socialist distribution apparatus of goods is formed from the number of persons it concerns. This may require certain instructions (goods instructions), but no money. Money is a one-sidedly limited instruction without regard for the people, for whom it should serve to facilitate the supply after all. These are the commands that humans control by their limitations. The socialist order will be a distribution order based on the number of people, and they do not restrict the people's freedom of disposition of the goods. The non-socialist order requires a centralist administration and the socialist (anarchist) a local administration of production and its distribution. The latter requires and brings about the summing up of all in the common task: the provisioning of each individual.

There is no transitional stage between non-socialist and socialist order, even during a revolution. Every peaceful transition would be a combination of the two principles, which are opposed in their essence, in other words, a contradiction. Such a transition can only be Marxist: first the revolution, then the transitional stage and only then ideology and reaching the goal.

This ideology of all capitalists and "socialists," which says that exchange of means is necessary, is an obstacle to the spread and development of the socialist idea, which finally ends in Bolshevism.

Exchange is a capitalistic form of economic life. In order to facilitate the exchange, at least two types or classes of proprietors are possible; for example, proprietors of labor and proprietors of products. After all, the strongest always rules the other, and the proprietor of the finished goods and also the raw materials, whether a private capitalist, trust, or state, will rule the workers, if exchange is recognized as indispensable and "there is no other way," as the socialists say. In a socialist ideology, exchange and exchange theories cannot and should not be talked about? Work, products, and society are inseparable. It is not even a question of an exchange of commune to commune, since all communes are nothing but parts of a large common commune, all members of a commune are simultaneously members of the common whole. They are all under one roof, like a family. Is it a family if they work according to the exchange principle, when the father issues money as a reward and receives products from his children and his wife? Do family members work in return for food, clothing, and shelter? No, they work so that everyone is adequately supplied with the necessary resources without separate property, without disputes about how much the individual gets. Only when products are under the same roof will they be distributed among the family members as required and by agreement. If there are not enough products for everyone, they are distributed among the most worthy and needy. Everyone simply contributes their best, in their own interest, so that they are taken into account for the distribution.

When the Native American tribes went buffalo hunting, the chieftain did not condition them; they had simply agreed to distribute the buffalo meat amongst themselves. They knew no wages, no profit-politics, and no disputes. They had no capitalists or rulers, but only technical leaders, whose word was not law. To conceive of this communism differently would mean capitalist thinking. The exchange idea leads to individualism, and finally ends with the necessity of a judge or dictator with all the harassment.

The book *White Waters and Black* (G. Maccreagh) describes the democracy of Indians in Central Brazil. There, the leader is simply the executer of the will of the tribes and their advisers. The members do not always have to agree with him and they do not. If one does not wish to acknowledge the leader anymore, he is set aside, and if he exceeds his powers, another is appointed for him. If he becomes hostile, he is killed. The author of the book recommends this system to the inhabitants of the United States.

The indigenous people of Typee (in the book of the same name of H. Melville, the German [translation has been published] by Scheffauer Knauer Verlag) did something worthy of imitation by building houses, dancing, and jumping, without knowing who would occupy them later. If a house was ready, and one of them had a desire to live in it, they would leave it to them for this purpose, without saying a single word about it. It is claimed that the children never argued there—until exchange and modern civilization were introduced. Another device is the "taboo;" it is a principle, which is not violated by anyone, because everyone has agreed: "there are no punishments, but no awards either, they are superfluous!"

In Taipei or Central Brazil, terms such as my (or not my) father, brother, sister, my wife, etc., do not exist, because everything is mine. Everyone there lives like a single organism. Can I say this finger, this hand is mine and the other is not?

Especially in the areas of social organization can we learn from primitive peoples, but not from those who live in exchange civilization. Exchange is the beginning of capitalism. Unfortunately, such primitive peoples no longer exist. But civilized and technologized people can also form a society without exchange, and this will be scientific, free, and anarchist socialism.

It is interesting to read about the culture of such societies in an unpublished book, *Die Romanze des Saragossa-Sees*, by Blencowe. If someone enjoys painting, they ask permission to paint the walls of some house. When they have finished their "work," they go to another house. For the painter, their labor thus becomes pleasure, they do not think of accepting any payment for their work or even of wanting to exclude the public from it. He creates joyfully for himself and others. This would not be possible in an exchange civilization, in which money is always the decision for quality, for possession, indeed for the mere consideration of a work. If socialists cannot separate themselves from their theory of exchange, they will never be productive as socialists; they will only ever be a safe support for capitalism.

Whoever exchanges is not a socialist, but a brute, an eternal bearer of political enmity, never a socialist or a pacifist, who acts according to the "give and take" principle.

In America, there has been a colony of 300 people for the past seventeen years, who live as socialists without exchange, money, wages, without religious, political, and ideological disputes, without police, prison, thieves, murderers, and without crises caused by unemployment. If desired, I would like to write a special article about their cohabitation. These 300 people work together in industry and agriculture and do not abide by any laws. Their only principle is: joint ownership and co-operation, distribution of labor and products according to the need of all. Everyone is sure of the social and comradely attitude of their neighbor, everyone can, without a disadvantage, exchange their jobs; physical and mental work are valued equally. They live according to Kropotkin's principles. The most peculiar is the fact that they were all gold diggers, who have often won and have lost even more regularly, and who renounce the benefits of civilization in favor of life. There are personal checks for food and items. No matter whether someone is married or not, they have to work and serve the public. We could learn a lot from this.

I have shown in another article how all the villages can be converted into such colonies without money, how socialization without exchange is possible on a local or world basis if the people, or at least the workers, would agree or at least apprehend it. I showed this article to a Chinese student who was convinced by the idea and who wants to try to propagate it against bolshevism and capitalism in China. I am always ready for a discussion and, in every respect, can satisfactorily answer the questions raised in the article. Without clarity about socialism, this is impossible. The question must be clarified before the revolution breaks out.

"Das Problem der Ausbeutung und ihrer Beseitigung,"
Die Internationale, 4:6 (April, 1931), 131–134.

17. Some Confusions Among Workers

M. Acharya

WHEN TRADE UNIONISTS ORGANIZE WORKERS—and speak in the name of workers—are all workers meant and included? The unemployed, according to the trade unionists are only such of their own members who are out of employment. Are all unemployed and badly-paid workers not workers? Are those office and intellectual workers who are not in Unions not workers? According to them, those who don't and can't pay into the unions are not workers or only second-rate workers, adjuncts to those who pay. Are all who are employed in parasitic branches of industry, such as those employed in non-manufacturing or luxury producing for a few, workers? They are only workers in the sense that they work to produce profits for those who are intent on money, without any use to society or the useful, producing, starving class.

Is any party or union a working class organization, in the sense they work for the benefit of the workers as a class? Every union and party claims to be a class organization of workers, the vanguard of workers, but based as it is on group formations and bound as it feels to the capitalist conditions of money, it is bound to serve the interests of its own limited membership—even if thereby it may be contravening the interests of all other groups, and the whole class.

Is a socialist, communist, or democratic political or economic party going into the struggle for the spoils of office and rulership that which its label should stand for? It is like every other openly anti-socialistic, anti-communist, anti-democratic, anti-economic party.

The only difference between the openly anti-worker parties and the self-styled "workers" parties is, if at all there is any difference, one of openness and slyness for the same objects, of telling things honestly and hypocritically for the same object. Thus a party that pretends to be socialist, communist, democratic, and serves its own membership by excluding all others refuses the very things it pretends to serve, and finally even serves against its own party members who stand for these.

Can a unity be brought about by "joining together on a divided basis"—as when different workers organizations confer to agree on anything? Such a unity is not possible and even when pretended as achieved can only continue so long as they are not compelled to act. The moment the circumstances for acting comes, the unity can only break up. Hence every unity and federation must be based on the breaking up of group interests, and therefore of groups. The same thing applies to workers economic organizations such as unions by trade, politics, or country. All the leaders sitting together in conference and passing obligatory resolutions upon members can only lead to rulership of the members by the rulers ("leaders") in clique. There can be then no union between the members of the various groups.

Can class struggle be conducted on a wage struggle basis? Since wage struggles are conducted for getting higher wages from economic owners and rulers, every wage struggle necessarily leads to concessions and compromises with the wage givers, whether state or private, and thus is a compromise and acceptance of the rulership of a class or group, a recognition of its right to give wages and be in possession of the means and materials of production. It can only be a class struggle if the struggle is carried on to abolish wages (which is rulership by group possession). Otherwise, it is only a struggle to get higher wages *for a few*, not for the whole class, but leaving the abolition of the wage-paying state or private class in the rights to possess the means of living.

What is a monopoly? If some or most have what all have not, it is monopoly of those who have against those who have not. It matters not whether the majority or minority possesses a thing. It is both anti-socialist, where socialism must mean social ownership, undivided and absolute. That a state is owned by a group or administered by a group does not make it the property of all, even if all, or only those who elect, are supposed to own it. Thus there can be no proletarian, workers', communist, social, or democratic state in the sense in which these words are supposed to be understood. Every state being a ruler over all, the state negates the power of the voters so long as its administrators, the owners' (party) or inside men's interests are supreme (the supremacy of the state interests.) Hence it cannot represent the interests of the people who have voted or accepted them. Thus every state turns out to be an illusion after voting. A state can only regulate in its own interests—even if these interests are against the society, in a "workers," socialist, or communist state—against the workers', socialist, and communist interests. Thus socialism, communism, "workers' interests," and even democracy become illusory under a state. That is because of the monopoly of rights (laws) given over to the state. Having become established in any name whatever, the state becomes of the enemy of that *thing*. It is inevitable so long as a state is different from and superior to the people. No state can be identical with the people who elect it or accept it "in their interests." A people's state can only be one where each individual is self-acting at all times in his own and, out of identity with his neighbors', in all neighbors' interests. That will be the only social state, with self-determination for all at all times in all matters. All other states are the negation of self-determination even if power of voting to the state is given, the reality of voting being the right to deceive oneself, by voting to one or other of the deceivers and their groups.

Is class and civil war a step to socialism? If it was a step we must already have socialism, since there was always class struggle in capitalist society, the struggle between owners and employers, rulers and the ruled, the exploiters and the starving. The theory that class war leads to socialism, directly or step by step, is disproved by history through all these thousands of years. Socialism means that the class war must be stopped—by abolishing classes of every kind, by undivided solidarity. The class war is forced upon mankind by capitalist and other classes—not by socialist "necessity" in a non-capitalist ideology. The socialist necessity is the abolition of the class war (civil war) enforced by the capitalist society and ideology. Thus when a social-democrat hypocritically pretends to stand by the working class in its struggles against capitalism or the communist of the same variety pretends that class and civil war is almost a religious duty of workers, and therefore the establishment of a class-state to suppress the capitalists, a class-state wherein the communist dictators' party becomes the ruling class, is inevitable and imperative till the present capitalist class is extinguished, both are wrong as socialists but taking advantage of the present socialist ideology, come down from capitalism through Marx, they want to prolong their own period of might, and their right to exploit workers in the name of socialism and communism. The capitalist society makes it appear that one of the two is right, while both are as wrong as this society. The class war and this state is forced "as transition" to another class war and another state as "transition" by the capitalist nature of society—the future state is the continuation of the capitalism that now rules and a new form of capitalism, not the period of transition for the abolition of capitalism but for the prolongation of capitalism in other forms. There will also be a class war against the new state and society of "state socialist" order, against the new, proletarian rulers forming a clique, forming a party to dictate to the proletariat itself. It is by the conscious suppression of the states that class war and capitalism can be abolished, since all states must live by the same methods of exploitation, of one class clique over others, viz., by manipulating money, wages, laws, police, and army in its own interests, which means perpetuating capitalism as far and long as possible. What difference can there be between a socialist or "communist" state and a private exploiting limited company? If the socialist state is co-operative, the private limited company can also be called socialist—but socialist only among exploiters of workers as in a socialist state. Every socialism that excludes from work and management even only one willing man is a misnomer and is capitalist exploitation. Socialism does not require and cannot conduct affairs by employing money, wages, laws, police, prisons, and arms to be used by a few to enforce others. If it is pretended that these are necessary to establish socialism or communism, it is a sly argument for the rehabilitation of capitalist tyranny and exploitation, not to speak of misery for workers, so that a few non-capitalists may rule like capitalists in their own interests, to perpetuate their individualism against the interests of the majority. No socialism can be attempted with capitalist means and therefore just the opposite of capitalist means and arguments can alone establish capitalism without the transition period to be utilized by rulers of labor. If the capitalist state and society is centralist—decentralism must be the means of socialism: if conditional autonomy is the capitalist principle, absolute autonomy not only for all parts but also for each individual should be the rule for socialism. If territorial centralization is the rule for capitalism, local independence should be the socialist principle and method. If prevention of initiative and responsibility for all is capitalist, freedom of initiative and responsibility for oneself should prepare the way for socialism. If property by a group as a monopoly is the capitalist-socialist principle, no property for any group should be socialist. There can be nothing in common between socialism and capitalism whether in methods or objects. Every period of transition is a trick to make socialism adapt itself to capitalism—whether legal transition or dictatorial transition. It may be good for a few socialists and communists to do nothing for socialism or communism, but to those who really want socialism and communism, there can be no such period of dictatorial or democratic transition to be fixed by the rulers. The period of transition can be shortened only by working for the abolition of money wages, laws, prisons, police, military, and gallows—and not establishing a class-clique for dictatorship for a period of transition. Nature alone combined by the will and intelligence of socialists can make the transition shortest, provided they act with a clear and honest purpose.

The Road to Freedom: A Monthly Journal of Anarchist Thought and Interpretation, 8:3 (November, 1931), 1; originally published as "De quelques confusions parmi les ouvriers," *L'en dehors* (September 15, 1931), 6–7.

18. Who Are Workers?

M. Acharya

IN THE CAPITALIST SOCIETY, ALL WHO earn money are workers. So are the soldiers, the munitions workers, the speculators in bonds on the exchange, the tax collectors, and the writers of nonsense and their adjuncts, so-called artists, literarymen, art critics, and a countless number of useless and even harmful persons. All the shop and booze owners and tingle-tangle men are workers. Like statesmen and the army of officials who write papers and get money out of it. So are the fellows who buy cheap and sell dear by establishing offices that produce nothing. The legion of scribes who make black look like white and write black in the name of public opinion and welfare, and the hordes of lawyers who live on the quarrels of others and earn money just by the tongue, whether or not justice is done. The judges and law-givers (parliamentarians) who know nothing about anything except hearsay on which to rail justice, i.e., to get themselves paid. Surely all these are workers in the capitalist society and the more they earn, the more important workers they are. All commission agents and pimps who earn money by seeking buyers for anything and anybody are also workers, and are necessary for capitalist waste called "economics." The bankers and bank palaces and their employees and directors are the innermost sanctum sanctorum of the whole business, and they do nothing but count papers and add interest and keep signed contracts. Every firm has such departments and all employed therein are also workers. The actual producers of all things—which, by consumption alone, all the locust swarms mentioned exist and fatten upon—are the worst paid and the least part of workers. The actual producers of wealth are the poorest paid, because they give only labor that is essential, and the consumers of wealth produced by them are the greatest number and often the richest. Only a few thousand or hundred thousands of trade unionists, engaged in producing export, munitions, and poison gas goods have some benefit thanks to their serving the interests of their masters.

How can one expect that things will grow and must grow better for all when a few who produce tons of goods get the least and those who consume everything get the most as reward "for organizing and taking all risk of economy?" The day is near for the end of this organizing and taking risk *for wasting*. Economy as understood today and till now is waste for the money in it. Mankind must congratulate itself that this parasitism of locusts is coming to an end. It has lasted all too long and was all the time worse than a nightmare because it consumed the blood and bones of millions through ages. Not all the Bolsheviks and Marxians can save the system, which is universal in decay and therefore is rapidly decaying. (In two years 45% of world trade is gone forever.) Yet they talk of simplifying the system of parasitism by managing through the state as owner. It simply won't work, even then, hereafter. And in any socialism, all these cannot be "workers" again, they will have no place.

If and when a new system has to replace this, the term "workers" must be clarified. Who are workers? First the producers of food and raw materials, then transformers of the latter into houses and clothing, then those who contribute service in the form of health and sanitary arrangements and give instruction in various things. Those who keep houses and streets and means of communication in good repair are also equally essential workers as those who construct these. The transport men are equally useful but they will have less to do than in the wasteful and speculative society. All the amusers of society, whether of pen or of mimicry, may be considered useful but art production, which is enormous in quantity and meaningless in quality now will be greatly diminished, especially as art is a form of expressing the curiosities of inhibitions and commonplaces and complexes that will cease to exist. Whether art should be paid for as now, because people have now to earn by any means and make a profession of anything for money such as the dictators and the managers of art, or whether those who have art to express should do so for their own pleasure of creation or to get a name, cannot be decided at present, one way or another.

In any case, most of the parasites, their names and number are legion, who live and fatten well upon the most essential producers must be put out of the business and profession of consumption (including professional wordy political artists) and will be laid off to find food by useful contribution of essential labor. Because much can be produced by a few hands under rationalization and Ford and large-scale system, there is no reason why a few should work hard and long and bleed and starve for a pittance. The productive and useful work, as well as consuming powers, should be generalized and distributed to make life bearable for all, not only for the most wealthy.

But most unproductive and consuming "workers" and "works" are maintained and are meant to be upheld—if possible, at the misery of a few and an army of unemployed miserables. This won't go because it cannot be kept up.

Any planned economics must fulfill the conditions sketched above or it works not in practice.

The Road to Freedom: A Monthly Journal of Anarchist Thought and Interpretation, 8:9 (May, 1932), 1–2.

19. Is the Exchange Between the City and the Countryside Economical?

M. Acharya

SYNDICALISM, LIKE OTHER MOVEMENTS, proposes the theory of exchange between the products of the city and those of the countryside, for the time when workers take possession of all current property. Will it work?

The city's products contain additional work on agricultural production. In addition, they use a great quantity of materials from the field to transform them into a myriad of products. In the case of the countryside, forces of nature contribute to the production, and this does not happen as much with products from the city. As a result, many materials have to be used, and much more is required to produce those materials, before the city's industrial products can be finished.

To pay the price of the city's products, people from the countryside have to produce a great quantity of materials and have to provide tremendous labor so that the city and the industrial workers can produce a limited amount of finished goods. In addition, food, shelter, clothing, and clothing materials must be provided to enable the city's workers to live in the countryside.

Under these circumstances, the countryside workers acquire the city products at a higher price, precisely because of the exchange; in practical terms, this cannot last for long. That is also the reason why there is nowhere where industrial products, or even agricultural products, can be sold. In Bolshevik Russia, peasants have to buy industrial products that are more expensive than the fruits of agriculture, which they provide, and they have to sell large quantities of agricultural products to buy small quantities of industrial products. Even the State itself, which produces industrial and agricultural goods, will have to pay much less for the latter and ask for a much higher price for the former, if you make the exchange between the two departments based on wages, and wages and prices disbursed, this could not work otherwise in any exchange system. In the abovementioned system it is futile to sell large quantities of agricultural products, and even to produce them is difficult, since the profit of agricultural producers is not for their own benefit, and as a result they cannot be sold or exchanged, soon leading to overproduction. How can trade unionists or anarchists do this work, technically impossible in practice? Hoping to achieve it will always be guesswork until it is tested.

The only way to avoid this impossibility is to put agricultural products and industrial goods together as a whole, for general consumption, and then simply distribute them in equal proportions among rural and city workers; this will be a social and equitable balance for both rural and urban workers, with the same advantages and disadvantages for both groups. No exchange system can be fair for everybody at the same time. And exchange is antisocialist, since property is divided between the workers of the countryside and those in the city, instead of being owned together by the workers' society, without distinctions. Property being split in groups is no more socialism than the association of private companies.

> "¿Es económico el intercambio entre la ciudad y el campo?," *Orto*, 1:5 (July, 1932), 321.

20. A Response to All "Economists"

M. Acharya

I HAVE CAREFULLY READ AN ARTICLE by Comrade B. Lachmann, after having studied similar plans, the trial and partial practice of which have taken place in Germany and Austria (*Argennot*, that is, Work against Distress) and in the United States (*Industrial Exchange Association* of E. Z. Ernst, Los Angeles, California).[1]

While these plans work as palliatives, they cannot satisfy their members, neither from an ethical nor from an economic point of view. Only for a technical reason of arithmetic. But people exhaust themselves by trying to swim against the current to look for the impossible. Whether everyone possesses anything, or whether we are only exchanging work—with or without the intermediary of money—it is necessary for any exchange to calculate a certain price. Mr. E. Brokaw, of Del Rosa, California, asks to fix the price per hour (the so-called Equitism system).[2] It is certain that all that is necessary for the production of each utility cannot be produced individually, and if it were tried, people could not succeed in producing all that they needed, even through the family system. Even those who possess many things or something in particular cannot produce on equal terms, because of their different mental, temperamental, physical, and natural circumstances.

---

1. Benedict Lachmann (1878–1941) was a German author, bookseller, and editor of *Der Individualistische Anarchist* (1919–1920). E. Z. Ernst, co-founder of the Freedom colony in Kansas in 1897 and later leader of the Industrial Exchange Association, was an early proponent of the equitism system.

2. Warren Edwin Brokaw (1860–1943) was an American proponent of the equitism system.

In any exchange, price and competition affect its conditions.

I know that trade unionists and anarchists-communists also preach the necessity of exchange: utilities versus utilities, utilities for labor, and labor for labor. Furthermore, they even assume that some kind of money is needed (see A. Berkman in his *ABC of Anarchist Communism*).

There is no more communism when some groups have more compared to other groups—it is property and group traffic.

My objection to group ownership and individual property, as well as to control and ownership of the state, is rather of a technical nature (from an economic and ethical point of view) than an ideological or a philosophical one. This is practice. I think that the technique of exchange—contrary to ethics—will lead to oppression, exploitation, and ultimately economic upheaval as it is now. Finally, this is impracticable and *impossible*; moreover, we cannot try to experiment right now. For the simple reason that if a man possesses and makes use of something, or has only his body and his abilities to use, it costs him something to maintain it. He must add this cost to the cost of the raw materials that he has to get from others (including the raw materials necessary for his existence), in the calculation of the total prices, since all work under different circumstances and with different capacities—the total prices will differ according to different producers—as well as the total quantities produced at the same price. In the exchange system, some will offer less and others more for the same price and of course buyers will go to the best market and lower the prices of those who should be paid more for working with different abilities and in different circumstances. This fact will suffice to make this system unethical, and can only be justified by relying on the vile Darwinism that the "less capable" must disappear. Later, the same problems will reoccur with the most capable survivors. If there are men who live only by sale or exchange of labor, they will surely suffer from this process, as they are paid for work alone, not the many ways of keeping one's body alive.

From an economic point of view, any exchange system requires: raw materials + labor + the subsistence cost of the production organizer. These last two can be gathered together in the same individual. Current production and demand potential will determine the prices. Thus, the selling price must combine these three elements, which is more than the current price in the current system of production, which is only raw materials + labor. But the person who administers things must also subsist, he must, therefore, be paid by the buyer, the exchanger. Thus, individual property as well as property or group management requires that each organizer be paid extra, which does not take into account any plan: capitalist, labor, or anarchist.

We must not approach the question from the point of view of whether we like communism or not. The point is whether communists are right, even from the point of view of their achievements and their theory. Communist exchange theory will lead to the same dislocation as capitalist theory, or other individualistic theories, not to mention ethics. The ethics of equality cannot be practiced in conditions of inequality—in the society of exchange that anarchist-communists want.

From a technical point of view, only a society *without exchange, even anarchist*, is possible. It does not matter if it is called communist. I am for individualism as a force of dynamism and even of social economy. But this individualism can only find its expression under conditions equal for all—not in the inequalities that any system of exchange will entail. If people do not want equal living conditions, they suffer under exploitation first, under oppression, and then tyranny.

In addition, I consider that technically any exchange is materially impossible in the future. Therefore, there is no other way than to be ready to accept an anarchist Associationism without exchange, based on "competition" of individualistic capacities.

The future society will be anarchist, it will be decentralized, founded, and federated on localism. I have described, several years ago, how such a society can be organized, and will be organized (in the article "Trusts and Democracy" published elsewhere, No. 133–134, May 1928).[3]

I think that the time of the Proudhonist experience has passed, whether we like it or not.

"Réponse a tout les 'économistes,'" *L'en dehors*
(February, 1933), 52–53.

---

3. See Chapters 9 and 13.

21. The End of the Money System

M. Acharya

THE GRANDIOSE PROGRAM OF Prof. Rexford Tugwell, which is fa-thered upon President Roosevelt, speaks of, and is spoken of, as, drastic measures.[1] But it is not even for Capitalism, which is based fundamentally on export trade facilities and surplus. It is the export trade alone that can pay the tributes of interest, rent, taxes, profits, and commissions. Prof. Tugwell, like so many other Marxian and capitalist theoreticians, supposes that money with or without gold has life innate by right of issue. Money is any dirt which people have been accustomed by habit to use, no doubt, but has no such life to impart. For it is not money that is contained in objects but labor and material (including means of production) that sustains life and keeps it going. Money comes in only as taker of interest, rent, taxes, profits, and com-mission—to those who are privileged to charge these. Most of every single dollar contains only these charges. Whether one or the other components are increased makes no difference. For example, whether as Prof. Rexford Tugwell and Roosevelt want the turnover tax screw is not applied but only income and inheritance taxes are increased makes no difference to the final consumer or if interest is reduced and unnecessary expenses are made (including doles to needy workers) or other measures as increased police and military or simple administra-tive expenses. Whether one or more of the items contained in money are increased for these additional charges, it comes to the same thing.

---

1. Rexford Tugwell (1891–1979) was an economist, who became one of U.S. President Franklin D. Roosevelt's economic policy advisers.

After all, the men in possession of all things will put all these charges over every article sold and lent. In spite of some losing by reduced prices or charges, others will gain, but not that final mass of consumers. For money is there to be earned and collected by every operation, be it by as few persons as possible. Interest, rent, taxes, profits, and commission are different names and forms of tribute, i.e.—the right to fleece consumers in return for the privilege allowed to consume or use. The robbed labor (from exchange of labor with the money paid as wages) is sold to others inland and abroad in order to extract or exact more money. Money alone is the final object of business, not consumption—under Bolshevism and Capitalism. Every mill is finally turning out more money even when producing goods, otherwise it has no use for producing same. Consumption is only an opportunity to get more money—if possible.

What is the balance between wholesale and retail prices? The retail prices will always be, will have to be, higher than wholesale prices. But if turnover is less as now, the wholesale prices have to go up and the retail prices too, under Capitalist or Bolshevist business. There can be no balance, for there is no law or norm to be enforced upon all doing business. Even under State capitalism in Russia, the prices wholesale and retail will vary according to not only the margin of profit and expenses desired by those in management and possession but also according to the different natural and distance conditions, and according to the total quantity of products available and resulting. There can be no thumb measure for determining the difference between wholesale and retail prices in every case, for the margins of profit must ensure recovery of expenses according to circumstances. Capitalism, whether state or private, is not anarchy but chaos. If rent or taxes or interest is increased even by a single individual, because something has become less and dearer, then all will gradually increase the prices to be sure of their profit. Otherwise they are likely to fail in business.

Money can no longer pay its interest, except so far as it can be taken away from those who still have it. Without interest, money— the keystone of business and present civilization—will destroy itself and the system. That is exactly what both Bolsheviks and Capitalists do not want to see. But there can be no interest-less system of money. Keeping money alive will mean interest first, its initial force or momentum. Production and consumption come last, for without interest money has no value, profits out of which interest is paid are unlimited interest.

All the useless expenses, interest, taxes, rent, profits, and commission themselves eat up the value of money, out of necessity to earn these. It is by the dwindling or stealing of the value of money that more money is earned. But that is necessary for the money system, even if it ruins those who have earned it or necessitates their holding in their hands the dying money. The exchange transactions serve only—served till now—only to get hold of all the money that there is in the world. Hence it does not go any more, even if money is killed thereby. To the banks, states, owners, and traders, it is immaterial whether all pay the tributes or only some—provided they pay enough. Here is the key to the economic crisis—it is not an economic crisis but the failure of the money and exchange for money system. To increase money or extend its range among more people without incurring losses is a dream even if those who have already all the money will be compelled to part with their money. That cannot prevent the depreciation of money, for the present money has still to earn, even in other hands, if it has to be kept alive and stable. Hence changing hands will not make money more alive and will not produce more purchasing capacity.

Healthy or sane currency simply cannot exist. Currency has always been insane, eating its own tail and being based upon it, all people and business are eating themselves up—for currency. We are in the tertiary stage of this insanity, of currency sickness and mental insanity together. Prof. Tugwell like all private and Marxian Capitalists conveniently forgets, like his colleagues in professorial and university wisdom, that money exists for business and business for money, not for supplying things for consumption and use. As peoples cannot consume, both money and business are at the end of wisdom.

Surely none wants inflation but wishing to keep the gold standard is no more guarantee in the U.S. for keeping it than it was in England, Japan, or Scandinavia.[2] None of these countries wanted to "go off gold" but as they were compelled for want of favorable trade balance, so it will be with the U.S. we may hear one day, soon after the failure of the debt settlement if not earlier—that the U.S. also reluctantly gave up gold as backing of her currency. Then there will be a pandemonium in the world, because INFLATION MONEY CANNOT EXCHANGE AGAINST INFLATION MONEY.

When that time comes as it is inevitable, the Anarchist production for distribution and use, not exchange for money, will be the only possible solution of the crisis, the only inevitable way left open. Those who are not prepared right now for that situation will be drowned in blood. The choice is whether people want to reach Anarchist social economics—without trade, finance, and state—safely and deliberately and systematically, i.e., by prearranged transition and volition, or to wade after blood is shed vainly. There is no third choice even for the U.S. The bridge of safety to the future consists in volition and conscious transition. Otherwise, there is a complete break with the past—whose history cannot work anymore.

Man! A Journal of the Anarchist Ideal and Movement,
1:4 (April, 1933), 1, 8.

---

2. Original footnote: Comrade Acharya wrote this before the bank crisis had taken place here. – Editor.

22. Nationalism in India

M. Acharya

NATIONALISM AS INITIATED BY GANDHI is pacifist. It is national only in the territorial sense—territorial independence. True that Gandhi also dreams of a national state and a constitutional state. But that is due to the reaction even upon Gandhi's mind forced on the part of an imperial, foreign, and unconstitutional government at the present. This statement is true notwithstanding the force of fact that there are many groups within the Gandhian camp who wholly stand for a dictatorial militarist and imperial India—some day.

It is well known that when a constitution was drafted by Indian leaders some years ago and Gandhi was invited to assist it, Gandhi refused to take part in the drafting saying it was after all not so important as passive resistance to authority. And he started the famous Salt tax violation march (direct action) with only 64 adherents saying he would do so and persist in it even if the constitutional leaders considered him quixotic and the national congress refused to support and follow him.[1] Gandhi was more courageous, audacious, and foolhardy than the Indian Congress and leaders and soon his movement became the fashion, custom, and religion. It has come to stay. Today violation of laws has become the hallmark of respectability

---

1. During British rule of India, the production and selling of salt was a monopoly of the British, meaning that Indians had to buy expensive, heavily taxed, and often imported salt. As part of his non-violent campaign against British rule, Gandhi led a march through Gujarat to Dandi to pick up salt from the sea, thereby breaking the law. Along the way, he encouraged Indians to break the law (civil disobedience) and pick up salt.

Gandhi is a lawyer and religious man. But for him law and
religion are only means for social well-being. In this respect the
irreligion and anti-legalism of many a revolutionary is backward
and only the means to another legalism and religious mind. Gandhi
felt the pulse and heart beat of India when he started his march to
Dandi salt deposits of the government. The atmosphere was sur-
charged with violent thought swaging and the government wanted
it to grow looking for an opportunity long sought to crush violence
with super-violence of tanks and gas bombs—in the name of law
and order. But Gandhi, by sanctioning and initiating passive polite
and unarmed violation of salt monopoly law, intervened successfully
between governmental and popular violence and led the violent
energies of the people into channels of inconquerable solidarity
against the government and its laws. He overtook and unnerved the
government and its readiness to use and justify its own violence over
all. As such he acted like an Anarchist tactician of the first magnitude, caring for no laws when he gave his personal ultimatum to the
Viceroy—through an English follower, Mr. R. Reynolds, a former
Labour Party man, and when Gandhi refused to yield an inch of his
ultimatum it was thought that on the day fixed for the Salt march
he would be arrested at his door-step.[3] But the government lost its
nerves at the lightning rapidity with which he maneuvered—according to his ultimatum. Since that day pacifism has come to stay and
grow in India, going from success to success—not halting in spite of
his repeated incarcerations Gandhi made the movement go without
and against leadership—it is a great autonomous education to the
people. In one stroke he killed off both Marxism and its opposite,

---

2. Vithalbhai J. Patel (1873–1933) was a prominent member of the Swaraj Party,
which opposed Gandhi's civil disobedience movement.

3. Edward Frederick Lindley Wood (1881–1959), also known as Lord Irwin, was
Viceroy of India from 1925 to 1931. Reginald Reynolds (1905–1958), a British
Quaker, socialist, and critic of British rule in India, wrote extensively on Gandhi's
non-violence campaigns.

authoritarianism. That day we must reckon as the birth of popular Anarchy in the world—not only in India. He planted the seed of Anarchism—even if he did not want or know it, because he wanted nothing should intervene and cross pacific education. Gandhi had openly proclaimed that schools as they are, are slave manufacturies and the people go to prison as to places of pilgrimage, calling it Gandhi's College. They have thus liberated the prisons by flooding them in. Is it not in Anarchism with a vengeance?

Asked if he would take position as Minister in India, Gandhi replied he may not, probably will not. Nay certainly, he cannot, for he cannot accustom himself to the cribbed routine and cramped spirit of ministerial formalism (bureaucratism), which keeps ministers buried in the grave as it were of formalities. He wants to be a free man, moving freely among people.

Gandhist volunteers not only resist government passively and without arms but also prevent violence against Englishmen themselves or of Indian provocateurs of England against Indians themselves. When driving a great demonstration in Bombay the son of an English general got mixed up among the crowd and these wanted to manhandle him, Gandhists at once jumped to his rescue and relieved him of dangers. They teach chivalry and sportsmanship to Englishmen without boxing or shooting them, as they want to do. That tells effectually upon soldiers, civilians, and policemen. It is sport and feast, which Indians want to call fight against bayonets. An arrested civil resister is not an object of pity but worthy of congratulations at public meetings—a lucky and honored person. Can anything be nobler in fight without arms to defend oneself? When the most cowardly and craven feels a spirit of emulation at Gandhist action. Naturally, the brave in bayonet charging feel like cowards unless they are the froth of humanity.

The Gandhi volunteers prevent provocation by the police. At a great storehouse when crowds were looking at boycott posters in a most orderly manner, the police could not find an excuse to charge upon their admirers. A civil clothes policeman slyly took a stone to throw into the shop window. Alert as the crowd was they held his hand and pulled him to the Congress office. To their surprise, they found him in possession of a civil clothes police badge and the Commissioner of the police had to ask for the release of the man.

Again the Congress volunteers take away from the police the duty to keep order and traffic regulation. When a great demonstration of millionaires and workmen, numbering half a million or more of Bombay's population was moving against police prohibition, it was very rough in the eyes of the onlookers to shoot into them. The police made a cordon and the procession sat on the streets a whole day and a whole night refusing to disperse. At last there was nothing but to parley and agree with the leaders of the demonstration who were pressed from behind to march on and who could not push the crowd back. The compromise was arrived at thus: the police agreed to withdraw and the leaders agreed to care for order. The triumph was great for the crowd. The police were robbed of their office and authority at least for one day without a blow.

Nowadays such skirmishes are not done en masse at one place. Such battles are given at twos and threes—at hundreds of places at the same time to separate and weaken the force of the authorities. The people have become wiser and surer since the arrest of thousands of leaders. The leaders are the first to set the example and go to prison—instead of directing and sending others to prisons as in the West. Bourgeois they are in India. More honor to them than to the proletarian leaders of the West.

The Indian national movement has all the essence of war without hurting the minions of authority. It split the brains of the opponent without breaking the skull. (Read: R. B. Gregg's *The Psychology and Strategy of Gandhi's Nonviolent Resistance*, 2 vols.) Have you ever heard of this type of nationalism, without leadership except among the leaders themselves?

Nationalism in India is self-determination of one and all at all times and places. The only program of nationalism in India is to choose a point among the prohibitions of ordinances as target. Each one may choose and act against it as one wills. Surely it is not Bolshevism to break laws and decrees. Is it nationalism as we know it? It is anarchistic direct action by individuals and groups that goes territorially as nationalism in India because it has not become general throughout the world. Will such a discipline and self-determination, and self-education leave traces of any government? Impossible. If it is not nationalism, it is nationalism without fixed purpose and program, a kind of Makhnovism. Like Makhnovism— Gandhist nationalism fights without arms between two fires and fronts: inner and outer violence. The men participating in this fight cannot be expected to submit to or tolerate a native violence, be these Bolshevik or constitutional dictatorial. Gandhi has given an education and foretold—nay prepared them to meet successfully every violence with non-violent unarmed resistance, simply by mass refusal to obey and submit.

It may be nationalism against imperialism but still it is international in spirit and purpose, because it is pacifist and simple. All nationalities are welcome in this struggle. In India or outside. It believes each nation and individual knows its or his affairs better than anyone can tell. Leave us in peace and live in peace. That is Indian nationalism.

It is more international than Bolshevik state bureaucracy in Russian territory. It depends least upon business and money and arms—because it depends upon and is born of the people instead of being superimposed. It is educating people not to depend upon leaders and armed forces and state paraphernalia. It is a self-moving tye, organically naturally, spontaneous. Uniting all its parts and including engulfing all into one mutually interested whole. It is a rock in formation against which all armies of the world will fail—for armies are automatons having only wheels within wheels—unthinking and tyeless. The party and state movement depend upon the principle of exclusion, while the Indian movement is all-embracing. Hindus, Mussulmans, Jews, Christians of all classes and races. Men, women, and boys and girls taking an equal part as independent beings in the movement. If it is nationalism, it is greater than Socialism, which try to include only a class, no, only actual workmen organized in unions or party politicians in the name of the workers "as a class."

It is abolition of classes and class war, which is going on in India peacefully in the name of nationalism.

The movement gives anarchist training, which is exactly what the Bolshevik and anti-Marxian world is afraid of, and even anarchists are mistakenly skeptical about. But India is teaching in practice the anarchist principles—to the whole world. Be it national because territorial at present. Nonetheless it is anarchic, anti-bourgeois, and anti-Marxian. It is stealing a march over coming anarchy in the West and in the world. Hail Gandhism because it is anarchic—it is new to a fossil world of ideas.[4]

Man! A Journal of the Anarchist Ideal and Movement
(July, 1933), 2.

---

4. Original footnote: I rather think that the anarchic claims for Gandhism by comrade M. Acharya are more of an inspired wish than a triumphant reality as yet. – Editor.

23. On the Question of Race

M. Acharya

In Germany, they are discussing the purity of the race and trying to rid the Germans of all traces of foreign blood. They were ordered to produce certificates establishing that no drop of Semitic blood flowed in the veins of their forefathers. Germans and even today's Hindus cannot show that they do not have any non-Aryan blood in their veins—because the system of birth certificates does not extend beyond a few decades, and nobody cannot guarantee that the Semitic blood is lurking somewhere in their ancestry. Even in India, where purity of blood was the basis of the caste so that no one could eat or marry out of the caste, especially among Brahmins, children were taught for thousands of years to remember the names of the authors of the Vedas, whose blood runs in their veins, it is not possible that the blood be purely Aryan, so that there is no certainty of purity of race.

Naturally, the Brahmins are taught to believe and to proclaim that they are pure Aryans, because they descend from Vedic writers and therefore possess a few drops of Aryan blood. Despite the rigidity of the rules of the caste, even with regard to food, rules observed until recently, each village and each family has a variety of types that range from Mongolian to Semitic and mixed-race European and even Negroid. In India, if it is therefore difficult for races to be pure, because out-of-caste marriage was strictly forbidden, what about "pure" Germans, "pure" Latins, "pure" Slavs? In Europe, where marriage has long been a private, individual affair, and where female sexual chastity has not been rigorously followed? Even in India itself it was not observed. How many children in a marriage are not the results of adultery?

Even in northern India, however, where Aryan blood is most prevalent, it is impossible to find pure Aryan even among Brahmins. For Aryan immigrants or invaders mixed with the primitive Indian population. The Hindus of the North were never as strict as those in the South with respect to food and marriage into another caste. In spite of this, despite the fact that my caste, which kept its blood Brahmin and pure Aryan, even safe from contact with other Brahmins, what percentage of Aryan blood actually flows in my veins?

It is certain that the first ancestor of my caste, in one way or another, married with the natives of southern India (when it was only among their priests), and yet called his children "Aryan," because they had Aryan blood, while others did not. But that does not make a Brahmin a pure Aryan, despite any amount of Aryan blood he has. Was there ever a law imposed on Europeans so that mixed blood ceases to continue to mix? No. Yet they speak of the purity of Latin blood, of Germanic blood, of Slav blood—because they imagine that it must be—and that it is. It can only be less pure in Europe than in India, because no law was applied on marriage to keep offspring pure. To discern purity is now an impossible task after thousands of years of mixing. This applies just as well to the Semites of Europe, who have tried to keep their blood pure—for how many of their children must be born out of wedlock or come from adultery with Europeans. So there cannot be any pureblood Semitic children in Europe either.

Some anthropologists have claimed that Europeans mixed somewhere with the Hottentots. Because many European shows traces of what is called *Hottentotenschürze*—the apron of Hottentots, either totally or in a reduced form. The esteem in which female posteriors were held—both by men and women (and this appreciation is characteristic in painting—especially German)—could be attributed to the innate Hottentot psychology in the blood introduced into the European race. It is claimed that the Hottentots once possessed a high culture accompanied by an adventurous and conquering spirit, and that they invaded Europe. Millennia and millennia ago, South African kefirs had a high culture, and traces have even been found that some African tribes knew how to turn iron into steel long before it was thought of in Europe. From all this, it follows that it is not unlikely to claim that the Hottentots "defiled" European blood before it was aryanized by the conquerors of the North or by Caucasians.

Moreover, the purity of the race lies in endogamy, incest, in a sense. If incest really leads to degeneration, exogamy must be considered healthy and therefore encouraged. William II knew what he was doing by encouraging Germany's degenerate aristocrats to enter into marriage with Semitic women, not only to revive their coat of arms, but also to regenerate their impoverished blood by cross-breeding.

Once, when an Indian preacher celebrated the glory of our ancient Aryan blood, my female friend rightly pointed out that it was better to have monkey blood and be free than to be human and enslaved. And the worst of all chains are those of the mind.

"Sur la question de race," *L'en dehors*
(September, 1933), 174–175.

21. Is the Present System Doomed?

M. Acharya

THE WORLD IS WATCHING THE capitalist dictatorship experiment of adjusting prices and wages to suit each other. It is a dictatorship like any other dictatorship, bound to fail and destroy everyone.

But it is not necessary to see and wait for the effects. Anyone with open eyes can see in advance it is bound to fail—much earlier than the most pessimistic can think. Prices and wages can never be adjusted to SUIT each other, both are inimical to each other. One may as well go on mixing oil and water into one compact mass.

The total amount of money paid as wages—to some or all—can never be enough to rebuy all the goods produced; it can only buy a part of the goods because it is only a part of the money put into producing the goods. Hence the wage payers, be they state or private persons, must sell a part of the goods at the total cost incurred to produce all the goods. That will make the prices unattainable to the wages paid to the workers. This holds true as much under the capitalist order as under the bolshevist one.

It is easy for anyone to understand that the higher the wages paid, the higher the prices must be, will be. To suit the wages to prices, wages and prices must be increased with every production. To increase wages and prices is tantamount to reducing the purchasing power of money. Every reduced purchasing power of money will necessitate further increase of prices—or reduced consumption and sale, and therefore less employing chances. The only way capitalists or State can recover costs without increasing prices and reducing employment is by reducing wages AND selling abroad a large part. And selling abroad means there must be money and no restrictions should be placed upon import of goods and export of money into other countries. That is exactly what is not possible now or hereafter even with inflation money. If only other planets can buy and pay, it is possible to work the price and wage system. Let them wait for this—meanwhile dwindling down trade. That is what is going to happen due to this impossible experiment.

It requires no experiment, for it can be calculated on paper to find it is impossible. Why make such experiments or let others make it unless all mankind is idiotic. Today only what is hundred percent certain can work and will work. If that is not understood, the collapse will come with a crash upon the heads of all—manufacturers, traders, peasants, and workers alike. And it will come as inevitably as dawn after night.

Such a hundred percent experiment is only one without prices and wages—just production for direct consumption. That can only be done by decentralist, non-dictatorship, democratic arrangement—through control by all equally. It is the only arrangement that is possible and therefore bound to come after the crash.

Under such an arrangement, all will have a say as to what shall be produced, what not, and under what conditions. Under such a system or anarchy, food, clothing, housing, and comforts for all will form the preliminary basis for all other activities, not luxury first as now for a few.

It is nonsense to say that ANY MONEY system with its inevitable prices and wages can be controlled by any form of state or by all. Money will control all by the laws and impossibilities (contradictions), which ruin all first and itself afterwards. There can be no elastic money with or without gold, which can include the lives of all. That is why money fails and business becomes impossible. Every money system is defective. Yet they try what is obviously impossible to maintain.

Either mankind lives without money, prices, wages, and state— and trade, or will learn to do so after going through all sorts of hells.

Man! A Journal of the Anarchist Ideal and Movement
(October, 1933), 5.

25. A Belated Forecast for the Year 1934

M. Acharya

"MERRY X'MAS" IS OVER and a "happy New Year" has come. What kind of a happy new year? The last of the old kind. 1934 will show that; that no more of this classic, traditional, unthinking, automatic kind will come; no more of this brainless repetition is possible. Happy are those who could celebrate it in 1933, but their happiness in the new year of grace will be short lived.

And the journalistic canaille, oh! To put X'mas enthusiasm in the public, they show by curves in diagrams and by statistics, that the lowest point in the depression is over—even when none is sure of his livelihood for the next day. Every country is described as the only one on the right road and all other countries must copy its example—will copy it. The question is only: "Higher armaments or present level of armaments"! "Business as usual"—if not better than before. How can mankind live otherwise! Just what present man is accustomed to is told to delight the ear. It is a consolation in these depression times to hear so—to be told by those "in the know" of the future trend of affairs. Surely what is 9 months in the "thousands of millenniums" they are just preparing the ground for? History is safe in their hands. Those who say or even think otherwise will be sent to hell. This is A.D. 1934.

And their opponent political parties, leaders, and wiseacres gloat over the fact that the present regimes will crumble down in 1934 and they will come to power and conduct the state of affairs—affairs of the state. They know how to get over the depression better. They alone know it, and the people will help them to get on top of the saddle and put the yoke over their (people's) necks. There is no harm in wishing them "good luck!" For they will never come to power if even they are helped. Not even some of the Anarchists are prepared for the coming anarchist situation. They are also dreaming in the old parrot terms.

As to where the depression leads to—nolens volens. Service, exchange, production, and labor are intrinsically bound up and tangled with something of "permanent" or "stable value" called money—not merely printed numbers—but by acquiring, which we could convert and amass the permanent and concentrated force of stuff. Economics is not simply production, labor, and exchange of goods and using services—least of all consuming goods and using services. The object of present economics—so long as it can be maintained by fraud and force—is to acquire and amass that final force or stuff. Whether you are bound to serve, to produce, or exchange, you must help—just in order to live—in collecting this final object for someone or all. Not even the Bolshevik government can abolish this object, subject as it is to the old means. If you consume goods or use services it is a chance, because you obtain—whilst many others don't obtain—the means. You may be satisfied with whatever you get or have—so long as you can get or keep. What about others, outside these "economics" of service, production, and change—who cannot get any part of the chance or rope? You may, nay, will, be pushed out of the chain as others are kept out. "History repeats itself" has only this meaning. All will be thrown out of this revolving table exactly as in the Coney Island crazy town. (By the way, the Luna Park of Berlin is now called National Park Ltd.)

Whatever is termed that final force or stuff—till now called gold—is now being collected into the vaults of a few banks issuing money, and they in turn are unable to collect gold from each other by issuing so-called credits; credits upon which others are born and die debtors. That is why there is no more chance even for a few for serving, producing, or exchanging. The banks themselves, even with a Bolshevik Government at their back, cannot manage business any more.

Hence my conclusion: Banks—even money issue banks—and with them all business will stop overnight as it were—yet in 1934—as soon as France goes off the gold, for being unable to get more gold. People talk of coming war! Where will be any country able to make war when all countries are in the midst of not only "economic" depression but ready for destruction of currency—most of them having already let down their "currencies"? A war can be made only by letting down currency. We shall have finished this war when France has given up gold.

People again talk of the possibility of "creating a new currency" by putting into circulation one without gold basis. Such a currency has never existed and can never exist: for when and how shall people know what value is concealed behind such a currency note?

They go on further—talking about inflation with the help of silver as a way out. Silver currency is no doubt inflation, for it has a relation to gold and the value of silver in exchange with gold determines the value of notes issued with silver backing: one may as well print more "green backs" with gold definition of values. But when all countries have given up gold—on account of France giving up gold—what shall be the relation of paper or silver currency to each other? None can define it with the daily fluctuation of silver and its corresponding relations to goods and services.

Inflation is possible so long as one country at least is ready to part with gold upon presentation of its promissory notes. But when all countries say goodbye to gold—all banks and currencies become impossible. This I contend—notwithstanding all talk of war and preparations for war. Present civilization will close down shutters.

Happy New Year to all statesmen who have captured State and power! They are like monkeys in a burning forest who have climbed up trees: They can neither get down nor stay there.

As if they instinctively know the danger to themselves, they talk of coming thousands of years of their rule and the coming improvement of business under their rod. If they get down, they will be killed for getting on the backs of others only to get down when the danger is near. If they fall when the tree burns, they are sure to lose their lives. To prevent the suspicion of coming danger, they talk with empty heads of wonderful things to come with more brag than before—as if everything is safer than ever in their hands: "Business will go as usual!"

If banks and business closed down, the state closes automatically down with them—for the State of any kind is only a commission agent of banks and business.

In this year of 1934, we shall see the closing down of all business and states, the carriers of all past civilizations. Of that I am sure. When—not if—that comes all statesmen of the world will hang in bunches and in row all the world over with their banks—not in one of two countries alone—for having promised what they never could hope to do. The new would-be rulers will be unable to realize their dreams of founding new states, and will be hanged with the old, as they are now chased out everywhere.

The banks will eat up business and business will have to eat up banks. The state and the army being the right and left hand of banks, these will fall and crumble together with business and banks. Happy New Year and last year to them!

They may prevent pointing out the danger to themselves and the inscribable only solution to it is anarchy—whether consciously prepared application of the principles of anarchism or coming out of chaos arranged and ushered by them.

Just as in 1917, Bolshevism unexpectedly sat on the saddle in Russia—17 years later Anarchism, to the surprise of anarchists themselves will rush in and settle down on mankind for ever. The time is on when it will be impossible to think, except within Anarchism.

Preventing the teaching of anarchism cannot prevent the coming of anarchy. They who "prevent" only create chaos, even when losing their own lives in so doing.

Man! A Journal of the Anarchist Ideal and Movement
(March, 1934), 99.

26. Anarchy or Chaos?

M. Acharya

THE GOVERNMENTS DON'T WANT revolutions—but by making conditions for living impossible they are inevitably bringing revolutions about—against themselves. By conspiring to keep people blind about their own dangers and dangers to their lives, they are calling forth a revolution which will be social, which will put all wars and Bolshevist bloodshed into shade. They are creating experimentally economic conditions which make people psychopathic and more blood thirsty than ever. And yet they cry in horror against revolutions and condemn anarchy—as if anarchy if consciously arranged would be worse than the chaos into which they are precipitating mankind in order to prolong their systems if it were possible.

The anarchists don't want killing—whether by order from above or spontaneously from below. As consistent and logical to the extreme pacifists, they try to prevent every bloodshed. They are trying to help in arranging an elastic system in which all can live without killing or even imprisoning anyone. Provide the minimum necessaries for all and give freedom—all will then go the way of least resistance—but not kill them. Bloodshed? The economic vivisection which all governments practice against all peoples—because the systems maintained and attempted are becoming impossible, that makes bloodshed inevitable, since the people tortured economically to death cannot see in their desperation who is friend and who is foe.

But the gentlemen above and their opponent disciples below, the masters and disciples of violence and bloodshed, are in conspiracy with each other to keep and perpetuate violence—against anarchic peace in society. They are afraid that their lives will be lost if they told they cannot govern them any more, after having promised they could arrange peoples' lives if these only kept quiet and obeyed, "behaved." Not only they are afraid of losing their jobs or profession of "leading" people but they are afraid of losing their lives by confessing they cannot do what they promised. It is a conspiracy of silence to keep people ignorant about their path—till they come to the brink of their graves. High treason? It is always on high. Not far from now, they will come—both the misled people and the misguided rulers to the end of their reign, then there will be bloodshed to make order out of the chaos, where every man's hand will be every other. Will chaos then save the rulers who have blinked all the time the real issues?

Anarchy? Only man has lived till now outside of anarchy and peace. As a consequence, man has shed man's blood murder is a "human" feature. In anarchy alone all can live in peace—for it is as elastic as nature. In anarchy birds and bees have lived through thousands of millenniums with less—far less—bloodshed, and no bloodshed at all among each species, in spite of man's hunting and trying to destroy whole species.

Every man, like every animal and plant, is a boon anarchist—harmonious. But the first bloodshed has made him a man of this "order." There is no return to bloodshed—even for Man. The moment social revolutions start, man will have, will be compelled, to give up arms in favor of the plow. It is possible that killing will interest none but the depraved of this civilization and order.

The anarchists are trying to prepare man for that moment dawning. All others are chaotic boules—not mere boules.

Man! A Journal of the Anarchist Ideal and Movement
(September–October, 1934), 4.

27. The Case for Buddhism

M. Acharya

I DO NOT KNOW WHETHER THERE is any use in discussing Buddhism[1] from the point of view of Swami Ignanakanda, also known as the Swedish O. Lind, or some other authority.[2] Mr. O. Lind is much talked about as a scholar, and he has the advantage of knowing the physical and chemical theories of Europeans. However, as a "Buddhist in practice," Mr. O. Lind does not enjoy a great reputation, because he is only interested in rhetoric, in other words, in Buddhist verbiage—at least according to what I know about him.

Buddhism is certainly a phenomenon that must be studied from a universal point of view and not only from a religious perspective. The best book I have read about Buddhism is *Die Religion der Vernunft* (*The Religion of Reason*), by Grimm, which, as it happens for all good and reasonable works, is hardly known, even among Buddhists themselves.[3]

Originally from India, from a bigoted family of Brahman priests, I absolutely agree with our friend Nobushima that Buddhism has disappeared from India proper, beyond the Bay of Bengal.[4] Burma is only a recent political and military addition to the Indian

---

1. Original footnote: See issues of mid-July and mid-October.

2. Acharya refers to Swami Ignanakanda's (alias of Anagarika Lhassekankrakrya), "pour la défense du Boudhisme," *L'en dehors* (mid-July, 1934), 144.

3. Georg Grimm (1868–1945), *Die Lehre des Buddha: Die Religion der Vernunft* (1915).

4. E. K. Nobushima was a Japanese anarchist, active in the 1920s–1930s, and secretary of the Free Federal Council of Trade Unions in Japan.

Empire; the Burmese are, socially and religiously, non-Aryans, although their blood flows from Indian blood, their culture is partially Indian and they observe certain traditions of Indian origin, that is to say of ancient Buddhism; the Sinhalese are racially and culturally much closer to India than to them. To tell the truth, the Burmese are Mongols, their slit eyes and their yellow complexion prove it. In short, Buddhism is mainly prevalent among Mongolian tribes—Sinhalese being an exception.

What interests us in Buddhism—as universalists and "students"—is not what it has become over the course of history, but what it is.

Or whether Ashoka was a great king and Genghis Khan was worse. Or that Hitler has nothing to do with Buddhism *per se*. It is an opportunity to bicker between Buddhism and its opponents, religious or political. Whether Buddhism is accepted by tribes or isolated carnivores is not an argument against Buddha or Buddhism. What did the Buddha want—not the preacher, but the man—that's the question!

If Buddhism was once so widespread in India, it is because the father of Buddha accepted the declaration of principles of his son. This father was a powerful tribal leader. These teachings became hereditary, and what the kings accepted, the subjects admired, willy-nilly, at least initially. If the Ashoka reign was very prosperous and favored the expansion of Buddhism, this does not necessarily imply that Buddhism contributed to this prosperity or that peace and contentment reigned because of Buddhism—but that the soil was then easily cultivable, produced in abundance, that every kind of religion or ideal could be diffused, that finally Buddhism offered to the people something better than Brahmanism to satisfy their brains or desires. The fact that the kings were Buddhists also played a role.

Buddhism was a revolt against the corruption of priests, religious rites, and wording of words in an incomprehensible language. Buddha himself was led to revolt against the misery of those around him, especially from the point of view of the prince he was, with all he could desire. He may have thought that the misery of the world was caused by the absence of a religious ideal and the spread of corruption among priests. Having experienced asceticism, he came to the conclusion that only philosophy and knowledge could make men better, and, hence, society.

The great virtue of the Buddhist religion is its negative attitude toward life beyond the grave. The metaphysical speculations of learned and well-fed Brahmans are taboo among Buddhists. Many Brahmins lived and still live fighting for the life to come, and procured resources by preaching for the use of their followers. Today, Buddhist priests' erudition earns them a living, interpreting Buddhist scriptures, what Buddha or his followers wanted to hear from this or that passage. There is no less corruption among Buddhist orders than among any other.

Nobushima is right in saying—and Mr. Lind will admit this— that Buddha did not change anything about the Karma theory, as we knew it in India. The principle of Karma is the principle of causality, universal in the Cosmos. It is not based on assumptions, but on the fact that "any effect must have a cause." There is nothing arbitrary and accidental, even in the "divine" universe. But when, on the basis of this idea, it is asserted that a man can be reborn a king or beggar, according to his will and his past actions, the theory of Karma is arbitrarily interpreted. First of all, it is necessary that the positions of king and beggar are acquired before a man can have access to it. The theory of Karma does not imply that a single rebirth suffices to gain access to one or another state (or several attempts at rebirth), but that each attempt has a certain effect—and provides some credit for easier attempts. How many rebirths are necessary, no one knows, for there are an infinite number of previous births against the influence of which we must fight. An attempt to gain access to an unjust object that is impossible to attain may have no effect, for conditions may be lacking for the realization of that object: to imagine oneself succeeding would be to delude oneself into an illusion.

Time is a big achievement factor: everything on earth is conditioned by the length of time. A soul who is born too soon or too late cannot realize the desires and objects of their life or their past lives.

And "earthly" objects are not part of religion, are too vulgar for religion, for Hindus and Buddhists. Both strive to struggle to abolish rebirth—to free themselves from birth and death, for one is necessary for the other in a cause-and-effect relationship. Buddhism and Brahmanism do not admit individual souls: on the higher religious level, the soul equals infinity and indivisibility—nothing more, nothing else. It is the lack of this knowledge and this understanding that postulates rebirth stresses every moment on this negative science. (The lack or ignorance of this science, which implies that one considers the soul as "untouched" and pure of the mind and thought, which are temporary and perishable illusions, is called Avidya). The soul is eternal and intact, exists of itself, independent of thought or absence of thought. "The Vedas say, the mind cannot access."

Buddha endeavored to insist on this principle, proclaiming that metaphysical discussions are vain and useless for the person and the soul. The discussions about the soul are the products of vanity and personality. Ambition must consist in impersonalism.

The cosmic and terrestrial life is the game of the soul. Life is an object in itself—there is no other object or purpose or utility—it is subject and object—the observer and observed. Ignoring and not living according to this perspective is the cause of birth and death—and this is so until the soul is recognized as eternally pure and unaffected by change. The soul does not die, like the spirit. In the soul, there is neither time, nor place, nor state, as in the ephemeral spirit. Nirvana is not synonymous with nihilism, but a state of equilibrium that does not affect any change neither on the inside nor on the outside. Nihilism or absolute emptiness cannot be. This is the content of Sankhya's philosophy and logic, which is the basis of Hinduism and Buddhism. They contain nothing "earthly" in the material sense of the term. That is why the changes that take place in the history of man are absolutely foreign to Buddhism—even to all East Asia. The soul "knows" what changes must occur in different times and places—because it seeks balance, or rather keeps itself in balance. This is the principle of equilibrium: man only has to look for it and he finds it. The "four excellent truths"—true science, real action, etc., aim at La Sagusse's search for the idea, because there is nothing definitively stopped as for the times, the places, the states. Buddhism is simple to understand without intervention of the history and study of Buddhist literature, interpretations, and comments to which it gave rise.

Buddhism tries to abolish in man what in psychoanalysis is called complexes and prejudices (predilections). In a sense, Buddhists are the most universalist in their dealings with other races or religions. They ignore fanaticism—even when they are sectarian. Priests and nationalists may know what orthodoxy is, but to a much lesser degree than in European Christianity or "democratic" Islam.

The Tibetan Buddhist hierarchy is hardly better than Hindu ritualism and priesthood. They associate mysticism and magic— even demonology—with Buddhism. But their theory assumes that it is against Buddha's teaching to save oneself and that rebirth is better than individualistic nirvana. They are ready to be reborn and to wait for everyone to be afraid of Nirvana.

All life, all actions of living beings has its purpose in the economy of the universe—they are perfectly equivalent—such is the fundamental principle of Buddhism and Hinduism (according to the logic of Sankhya).

The imbalance comes from the attempts to change the balance, by means of a higher wisdom considered innate to man only. Problems immediately occur if one or all men, in their vanity, consider that nature (and even man) can be perfected, in the name of "the conquest of nature and the discipline of his forces." It is as if it were a matter of gilding gold or painting the lily leaves to make them more perfect—vain effort that makes things worse. Man can understand how objects are and how the equilibrium is arranged, but he cannot create anything or change "to better help nature"—a claim that is pure scientific attitude. To create you have to destroy and make things worse for you. Leave everything as it is, because all things are perfect, that is the lesson of Buddhism. This is what the

Europeans call "fatalism," they who worsen their lives by force of "activity" in order to "make life safe for humanity." I am confused to write that the Asians allow themselves to be swept up in this rage of destruction in the name of activity, "optimism," and struggle, the brutal struggle, for Life.

If the mind is inclined toward this ostentatious activity, sooner or later it breaks all the brakes and runs to its own loss. Buddhism signals the danger of activity, of over-activity, of deceptive activity. The mind is like a body at rest, whose movement depends on the impulse you give it; if you push him onto a precipice, he will blindly rush over it, and you will not be able to bring him back to his point of departure, just like you cannot redirect a stream to its source. The natural balance gives the necessary impulse at the right time. If a stream runs aground in a pond, a rain can occur that will overflow it and allow the stream to continue its course. Such is Karma. If someone waits without tiring for the opportunity to be in balance, without exhausting themselves looking for it, there will be an opportunity to gain balance and become one with the Cosmos. In no case will he reach this state by throwing himself headlong into his search. Time makes all things grow, just as rain causes seeds to sprout. Sow in vain before the due time, and your seeds will perish; you will speak of "conquering nature" in vain, you will not make the rain fall at your pleasure. If you persist, prepare to die or to go crazy. The conquest of nature, as understood by Buddhists and Yogi, is to prepare to be conquered.

An active man usefully accomplishes only the simplest and most necessary movements if he is wise and economizes his energy. A silent man, a peaceful observer, can be extremely active, because he watches and waits for the right moment to act—all the while knowing that the time has not yet come. Another man may grope in the darkness and exhaust himself in vain searching for something he does not even understand. How much more important is it to adjust the mind than it is to fix machines, which will eventually dominate man, as do the machines with their limitations. Buddhism necessarily teaches that man must be well awake to regulate the mind. Yoga does the same thing.

The Brahmins do not recognize Buddha as a prophet—or see him as a harbinger of atheism—because he considers the mystical, metaphysical sky as a subject of useless discussion. They are waiting for a new Avatar, that of the destruction of the very foundations of sin.

I used to be an admirer of European "optimism" and activity. I see today that this "fury" of automobiles has no economic significance, and is the symbol of a civilization and a type of men who run head-long into the abyss. What is it about doing or loafing that allows a few traders and oil traffickers and spare parts manufacturers in the auto industry to earn a few cents? I live in a neighborhood where, on large roads, there are garages, spare parts salesmen, repair shops, and gas merchants one after another—not a grocery store in these streets, one has to go to the hidden side streets. I am told that the automotive industry is the only one that pays dividends today! Instead of taking pride, it should be a cause for alarm that this symbol of the mad race of men and spirits to the edge [sic!]! Such an impulse, such direction!

And finally, is Buddhism wrong when it screams at every step: stop, watch, listen?

"Le cas de Bouddhisme," *L'en dehors*
(February, 1935), 236–238.

28. Max Nettlau as Biographer and Historian: An Appreciation of His Style, Method, and System

M. Acharya

THE BIOGRAPHER OF BAKUNIN does not belong to the common type of biographers, since biographers are not scientists as a rule, because they are partial, and they lead the reader by resorting to their prejudices and predilections. The so-called biographers are often only literary artists who employ a floaty and fluid language. They work more on the feelings of the reader than on their sense or right and understanding. And they use the common "clichés" of the people as instruments and forms of expression or description, so that their books are known and read or, perhaps, just purchased. Thus, biographies of well-known personalities are written according to the prejudices of the times—from one decade to the next. And such biographers use previous writers in an inaccurate and deliberate way that they take stories and information according to the prejudices of the time. They are, consequently, more novelists than biographers in the scientific sense of the word. The biographed person is only a topic to show off his talent and their artistic language to the trivial tastes of readers full of prejudices. Even the "topics" of the biographers are only for them objects to observe or show the dynamism of the person, not from what is probable in their time, environment, circumstances, and situation, but from the attitude and prejudices acquired in more recent days. Thus, a biography of the Buddha can be made to appear as the adventures of a modern politician or a celebrity hunter. Such books can be interesting for the sake of sensation, or for the insatiable and mediocre intellectualists, but they cannot be exact, accurate in the facts, and therefore, permanent, in the sense of not requiring changes to adapt to the times and prejudices. However, non-scientific biographies can be read, advertised, and sold more quickly. Scientific biographies like those of Nettlau are also an art and a permanent monument that should not be counted among ephemeral biographies. Everyone who reads Ricarda Huch and Max Nettlau can see that they cannot be put together as biographers, since they are very different from each other.[1] For Ricarda Huch it is an opportunity to exhibit her literary talent and for Nettlau it is a scientific investigation, exact and detailed. Is biography a science or a one-sided art? Nettlau's is art and science at the same time. Usually, biographers "chew the pittance," or worse, serve a previously digested meal. The scientific biography was founded by Dr. Max Nettlau, and nobody has surpassed him in that art. That is one reason why, for nearly fifty years, his monumental work on Bakunin remains unpublished and unknown to publishing houses, and only found as a curiosity in the handwritten section of libraries, which is shameful. Publishers say that it is "too strong for general consumption," and that it is unlike the biographies favored by novel readers, who crave frivolous, capricious, and picturesque literature bought in train stations and thrown away by the rail cars. If Dr. Nettlau could not see his work published—his masterpiece— this is completely in the logic of commercial publishing, as it cannot produce profits of 100 percent or more to the publisher-dealer who needs to use the printer in order to make money. This disease of civilization, oh, ghosts of Gutenberg!, is the one that made vile literature multiply, gave way to "great" writers, and is now engulfing all those whose business is related to the disease or ailment of the times. Precisely, the blackening of good paper does not pay more. Biographers and scientific biographies, dispassionate and conscientious, are not necessary in this sick and moribund civilization and, therefore, it is left to a later generation, scientific and healthy, to take charge of the voluminous manuscript and take it to the printer for

---

1. Ricarda Huch (1864–1947) was a German historian and biographer.

the general reading public. In the meantime, I hear that Dr. Nettlau will be able to publish a popular biography of Bakunin, a more manageable scientific biography.

Dr. Max Nettlau's biographical study centers on Bakunin, the unknown, but very denigrated Russian anarchist. Nettlau knows in detail Bakunin's every step and activities. Having personally been in contact with the formulator of anarchism, Nettlau knows all the failures of his ideas and his feelings, his weaknesses and strengths, along with Bakunin's correct and erroneous judgments, at the very tips of his fingers. Bakunin himself could probably not explain why he was acting like he did at the time, because he was *acting*; however, Nettlau is an observer and can, therefore, be objective, as biographers should be.

A few years ago, Nettlau went to Spain to look for traces of Bakunin, because the most insignificant of Bakunin's papers could be missing—almost exactly as a policeman would do in the case of a criminal—but for different reasons. And it is not the first time he went to Spain for such an investigation, which shows that at his advanced age he is indefatigably trying to improve and broaden his biography.

The style of Nettlau's writings is considered "too serious" for the public, because it is very *intensive*. Almost every cell in his brain is working in harmony to give a proper place to a huge amount, to true mountains of detailed facts and to how they relate to each other. Is it not an *art* to order them, place them appropriately, and indicate their relations with previous and subsequent events in a harmonious way? *Each* word is weighed and employed accurately, instead of being used as a worm to produce an effect or "impression" on ignorant and puerile readers. This is where his "excessive" seriousness and "heaviness" lie. Accuracy must be sacrificed in favor of "art," the art of using words in a vague and pompous way. If art is harmony, Nettlau has it to the highest degree and employs it to the highest effect. Compared from this point of view, biographies generally suffer from a lack of balance, even when they are written by the best biographical *artists*, who practice biography precisely because of artistic devotion. I have heard some readers of biographies written by a *literary* artist who found the book "interesting," that is, interesting in its vagueness and one-sidedness, but could not discover the true character, not even the *essential* nature of the person described. It's like music performed in a room with echo and resonance: the confusion of noise or rumors can be interesting even if you don't hear the sound of music distinctly. If *that is all* art is, Nettlau's biography is certainly not. The biography of Nettlau is *crystal clear in all details*.

A further criticism, probably well-intended, is that there are too many notes and quotes on each page. This is precisely where his biography aspires to science, and is a proof of science. It is not that Nettlau cites and makes references for reasons of pedantry, since it weighs in those quotes and annotations the probable value of the information and the definitive meaning of the words and expressions reproduced to reinforce his own understanding and storytelling. Anyone can make quotations and appear to be well founded: "The Devil can quote the Bible." Nettlau's quotations and comments in his works helps precisely to focus on the details, as a camera lens would, not to make the readers believe that his information is completely accurate in every detail and respect, beyond dispute or rebuke.

The last great objection to Nettlau's biography is that he is "too predisposed in Bakunin's favor, and that he tries to excuse the weaknesses of intellect and errors of action of the great revolutionary." While Nettlau may personally consider that Bakunin is one of the greatest men, it cannot be told from the book that he is trying to whitewash Bakunin at any point or present him as an atheist angel. That would be far from the object of the exact, scientific, and dispassionate biographer who Nettlau is, renowned for such traits. When he seems to defend or really defends Bakunin, it is only to show how the interpreters of Bakunin's actions and words have deliberately suppressed facts and expressed or falsified truths or unconsciously misinterpreted facts and circumstances. Nettlau frequently leaves certain facts about Bakunin unelucidated and even unexplained, although he can contradict those who made statements based on misunderstandings or extremely common prejudices. Nettlau pays precisely "his tribute to the devil," whether to Bakunin or his detractors. Scientific research cannot forgive anyone, big or small, who makes mistakes. Is it prejudice, defense, or simple refusal or affirmation when errors are revealed *through evidence* and are well examined against arguments? Critics of Nettlau would like him to also make unsupported and ill-founded information like they do. Nettlau does not allow such weaknesses to slip into his books. Naturally, his biography increases in volume, and if he revised his Bakunin manuscript today, with the additional facts compiled since he published the hectographic edition in three volumes, it would surely increase in size, precisely because the petulant and prejudiced writers on Bakunin have since then spread much more false information about the great Russian libertarian. He could also rearrange and correct much of the information from the original edition, precisely to improve and make it *more* accurate in the light of newer material, and would probably add how he thought differently in the past, and why he thought thus, and why he changed the sentences or the pages. Nettlau never needs to be critical of himself as a dispassionate researcher, writer, and conscientious and scrupulous scientist should be, whether Marxist or Bakunian. One-sidedness is always a weakness and requires the writer to support information with falsehoods. Nettlau is not one who argues as a lawyer, because *he is above the judges.*

The recent works of Max Nettlau are products of his inquiries into Bakunin and about anarchism. They are historical works about anarchism. For example: *Der Vorfrühling der Anarchie* and *Anarchism from Proudhon to Kropotkin.* They are written in the same style of exact and scrupulous inquiry that fills his biography of Bakunin. They are the most complete and most valuable works on the evolution of anarchist thought. If a permanent book on History should be written, these books are models and objective lessons in the writing of rigorous and scientific history. In them, all the facts fit, they *are* fitted, exactly one into another, adjusted as a box or a carpentry object without leaving a gap or a crack. In this *art* of writing, Dr. Nettlau is the first, unsurpassed by none.

It can be objected that histories should not be arid, and those of Nettlau are. But can history serve any useful or even interesting purpose when it is written just for rhetoric, and without taking the trouble or care to avoid useless words and inconsistencies? Can someone who wants complete knowledge and complete instruction complain that such a story is *totally* dry? The stories, like the biography of Bakunin *compiled* by Nettlau, are sources of information, almost regency books in ordinary style. They are encyclopedias about the issues discussed.

The art of juxtaposing facts in a synthetic and harmonic way is dialectical, and Nettlau has perfected this art. All juxtaposition of thesis and antithesis is not synthetic.

Nettlau's books are *not tendentious*, as he simply enumerates and elucidates as an objective and wise thinker and, therefore, they are dialectical. He never looks for points of defense or attack, defense of his topic or attack on his object or subject. This is probably what makes his books *seem* dry. But a scientific and disciplined book can never be written in any other way. If science is dry, then readers and editors should look for novels and stories and metaphysical and mystical works, not scientific works on real subjects. The proverb says: "The facts are more surprising than the novel," and this applies exactly to Nettlau's investigative style and, instead of making his books arid or fantastic, lends them the color of the realistic novel when discussing current events, characters, and figures.

The thinking style of Nettlau and the art of separating facts from fiction, of determining the essential and the accidental, of assigning the exact relationships of each fact to all the others, is what makes Nettlau's works exemplary books in the science of writing rigorous histories in an artistic style, methodologically and systematically.

"Max Nettlau como biógrafo y como historiador,"
La Revista Blanca, 13:328 (May 3, 1935), 410–412.

29. Ethics and "Isms"

M. P. T. Acharya

ETHICS OF MARXISM! WITH ALL great respect towards Com. Spratt in *New Age* maoras, I wish to roll out the question of Ethics in -isms, including Marxism.[1] We are accustomed to hear of Ethics of Hinduism, of Islam, Christianity, Judaism, and parliamentarism.

Is this ethics any "-ism" or any "ism" ethics? Is ethics the whole or part of any "-ism" or "-ism" part or whole of ethics? If any ism coincides exactly with ethics, we can call that "-ism" ethics. In that case, the ethics of that ism is a happy term. Otherwise we may then call it also the "ethics of exploitation."

Economic System

The term "ethics" of any ism implies that the ism is the whole and ethics is a part of it, a phase of it. The ism is supreme, and governs the ethics. It is not that ethics governs that ism. If any ism claims ethics, it is subjective ethics, from its own viewpoint. Example: Islamic ethics allows of slavery and polygamy, and attributes virtue to them. Think how many slaves and women find bread from owners! Otherwise they would be starving and perishing. In a tribe, where work is little found and women are too many, the argument of Islam holds good, as affirmation and justification of "its ethics." Who can gainsay that: But it is Islam, not free-men's ethics.

---

1. Philip Spratt (1902–1971), a British intellectual and early member of the Communist Party of India.

The economic conditions generate a particular mentality and this mentality is predisposed to affirm and justify the conditions and the psychology that codifies "its ethics." It is crystallized, fatalist "ethics" of those economic circumstances but not free ethics. Any ism or system can be justified if its particular ethics is accepted or any particular ethics can be justified if its economic system is accepted. In either case, it is acceptance of the economic system as good and moral, ethical. But by that acceptance we come round to the acceptance of the economic system, not ethics, free ethics, but particular ethics and its system. It is not ethics but the system that we accept, the economic system to which ethics is only attributed. The ethics of that system is a pleonasm, since the part is affirmed by the whole system.

What Is Ethics

By ethics, we mean or must mean what is acceptable to all without exception and good and conducive to their well-being and therefore moral. Such ethics have not been, unfortunately, formulated by any system, could not be formulated by any economic system known till now. We have only particular systems and particularist ethics, but no ethics acceptable to all and under every clime and in every hand. Of course, the particularist psychology implanted, inborn in us under particular, peculiar circumstances in every country, in every walk of life, in every stratum of existing society, is predisposed to accept particularist ethics and particular economic systems, and that makes the definition of ethics as well-nigh impossible. It is subjective predilection that is fostered as ethics: Capitalist exploitation is capitalist ethics.

What I mean to say is that ethics must be above all forms of exploitation, exclude all possibility of exploitation in the economic field, society. We have no such system formulated, and therefore we have a very vast variety of exploitation ethics but no possibility of ethics. Each one offers a new ethics but all include, carry with them some form of exploitation of man by man. By ethics, we must mean the suppression of exploitation of man by man, whatever that ism may be. But what is preached is one or another ism and "its ethics." When I show the economic nature of ethics, I shall show how the fundamentals of exploitation are not touched by Marxism even, not even by anarchists. The old fundamentals of exploitation are given a new basis in every new system—so far as known. Since peoples are accustomed to exploitation as inevitable, they catch to another exploitation as new, radical, revolutionary, and even scientific and emancipatory. The furrows of man's brain seem to be made only to accept exploitation and not to suppress it, make it impossible. Thus all past revolutions as ethical preachments have been failures so far as avoidance of exploitation is concerned. This history of mankind has been the history of defeat.

Only some new ethics or economic system, whatever it may be, so it is believed, will make for better, freer life with or without exploitation.

Ethics is chiefly concerned with economic exploitation. Otherwise, the ancient religions, preachments would be all right ethics. For what does it matter if exploitation goes on and ethics are preached? Ethics then would not be affected by actual exploitation—it would remain, as it remains, in texts. What matters? We can rest there satisfied, consoled, comforted that at least in books and in print there is ethics to ponder over when desired.

Wanted: Living Ethics

But when we want to find new ethics we think of finding living ethics—not dead ethics in books—i.e., a possibility of living without doing harm to others in material matters. We want a system wherein men can live together and go apart without any evil done on the material plane. If people do not agree, they can be sure of existence even when separating and none need convert and coerce others under economic compulsion to live and work against their inclinations, wishes, or will. Of course, the short cut to refute this statement is to say that it is impossible, idealist, utopian, and crazy, but that leads necessarily to negation of all ethics. No need to discuss or find ethics then, for it cannot be found and it cannot exist except in a state of hallucination. Then these parts, and particular ethics, do not exist and need not be discussed at all.

Ethics is against all exploitation of man by man: Otherwise, there can be also an ethics of imperialism, of stealing, maiming, and murder. Why not? In fact we have such ethics galore. These ethics are an attempt at justification of exploitation and cruelty. "The survival of the fittest," the "virtues of war" and "eye for an eye" in which the cunning weak overcomes the legitimate strong. These are all ethics of course if we admit that there is no way out of exploitation and cruelty, covert and overt. That is not the ethics we are going to deal with. We can say at the outset that there can be no ethics unless the root causes of exploitation on the economic, material field are burnt-out and extirpated. From this viewpoint, we shall show how little, even gradually, Marxism or anarchism are fitted to extirpate the root causes of exploitation.

That capitalism is an unethical system because its basis is exploitation and perpetuation of exploitation is no secret, even to capitalists. We even go so far as to say that an exploitation system, even if its ethics are accepted, cannot be perpetuated, since exploitation means trying to sell all goods to people without giving them money enough, which is the basis of capitalism, i.e., private ownership. Capitalism tried to perpetuate itself and "can" only do so by putting all out of the line of buyers. So capitalist ethics are automatically leading to the death of capitalism. No word need be wasted to labor this point. "Capitalists have made capitalism bankrupt," said a pearl broker to me in Paris.

Now the question is of socialism. If socialism is ethics, I have no objection to accept it. Then ethics is socialist and scientific whatever else it may also mean or be called. But the trouble comes, when anything is called socialism and scientific. Marxians call their ism scientific socialism and even ethical—or rather—therefore ethical. A certain German professor founded a party of ethical socialism, as he claimed based upon Marxism, accepting everything Marxian and including even vegetarianism and he collected a very enthusiastic following. They were conducting a daily in Berlin. This professor argued that Marxism is right but Marxians are not ethical. A curious combination, Marxians of all shades will call this a combination of pure vegetarianism and politics.

If Socialism is ethical and Marxism is scientific socialism, why this intense of Marxism as scientific socialism and ethical? Ethics alone would do. But we know that many varieties of Marxists—how many varieties and kaleidoscope changes are there among Marxists—would laugh at ethics as at Gandhism. For they do not put ethics above Marxism and Socialism, even science above Marxism.

But the only variety of socialism well known is the Marxian, just because the predilections for this ism is carried in us owing to the cultivation of unscientific, unethical, and an unsocialist mind by capitalism and anything that carries these elements and is called scientific, socialist, and Marxian will at once attack our brains in our struggle to get over or overcome our miseries.

A socialism must be first scientific in the sense that it is workable economically without exploitation, and that is also ethics. Firstly, it must be "economical"—i.e., match production and consumption exactly. But Marxian socialism has not yet put us out of the trade and currency mentality. If it did, it would not be according to Karl Marx or Lenin or Stalin. In fact, Marxian extremists like Trotsky even do not think that socialism can get along without these capitalist features. At least for generations, they say, although these are exactly what are making Marxism, its socialism, impossible. What is capitalism? It is investment—rather advancement of money—to take more money. Having used money in the process of production, it cannot count on returns—except to acquire more money through sale—without advancing also this money to be taken. If it did, capitalism would be bankrupt. This taking more money than given is not only unethical, because it is exploitation, but being unscientific it is also impossible having too long continued. Thus its ethics and exploitation are at an end together.

Capitalism is waste owing to too many producers competing and ruining each other in the same line. So far, Marxism tries to be scientific by eliminating competitors and wasters. But this science is only within the trade limits. The Marxians of every variety try to match production, exactly like capitalists, within the capitalist basis. Firstly, that is impossible, because none can be sure that one would buy this thing and not another. While there may be "under-consumption" and therefore overproduction in some things, there may be shortage and extreme demand in others even in Marxian plan. Apart from this, the cause of exploitation is not abolished in the Marxian state plan. For the Marxian State also advances money in the process of production and must take more than it gives in order to make its plan work. For example, it must make the buyers pay the State maintenance expenses without advancing that money to those who took part in the production process. However much wages these received, they must contribute toward the expenses of the State, otherwise all the State plan would crash. Finally, the State and ownership is in the hand of one party and that party cannot afford to give up the State, so that its functionaries in the State have to be fed and clothed properly in order to enable them to direct. This party is the employing class and lives by contributions out of the purchasing power of the workers it employs, i.e., by reducing the value of money it gives with one hand, by taking the contri-bution in the form of higher prices with the other in selling. Thus the workers are not yet freed from "surplus profit," exploitation. It is also as unscientific, i.e., unworkable, let alone unethical, as cap-italism in fundament, whatever may be the degree of exploitation claimed as law. If this is socialism, it is only a different degree of capitalism, nothing fundamentally, scientifically different. In fact, socialism as understood through Marxism is the highest, up-to-date, even decrepit form of capitalism. It may lead to socialist attempt by its own breakdown owing to its unscientific structure but only after its breakdown, not by its maintenance. It cannot lead to socialist society voluntarily but against its own perpetuation. "It will come all the same" is the only consolation.

Now to try to establish this system is not only impossible but cannot be ethical, however impossible and unethical, because unscientific and unsocialist, other systems may be. The question here is not if other systems are exploitation systems and therefore unscientific and unethical, but whether Marxism does not align itself with them, and is equally condemnable as other unscientific, unsocialist, unethical, nay unworkable systems that it condemns as "unfit." To talk of Marxism as scientific, socialist, and ethical is wasted effort.

The Mahratta (June 11 & June 18, 1937), 11, 3.

30. A Letter from India

M. Acharya

WHAT WORRIES ME IS THE FUTURE of Spain. But somehow I conclude that no state can be established on the debris left even if Negrin or Franco wins. Hence I hope for the defeat of both, whichever wins first.

I am afraid our Anarchist friends are not prepared for reconstruction. I had confessed the fear to someone from here. I had told Souchy in Berlin that reconstruction is hereafter impossible on any exchange, currency, and trade basis even if one desired it, if all desired.[1] I still warn them. I had written a plan as early as 1927 in the German Syndicalist Monthly, which was translated in the *La Protesta* of Buenos Aires and *L'en dehors* of Armand, under the title "Trusts and Democracy."[2] I feel certain that it still holds good if reconstruction is desired, has to come. Because I am quite out of traditions, I see clearly. Making water run uphill won't work.

I feel, the defeat of the warring and conspiring governments is certain for many reasons. The last currency—the Franc—is off the rails. France will have to fight a civil war as in Spain. It will spread to Belgium and even England. That will naturally affect already bankrupt dictatorships including Russia. I expect general civil war in Europe and even the U.S.A. Spain is the battlefield of all dictatorships

---

1. Augustin Souchy (1892–1984) was a German anarchist, member of the IAMB, secretary of the IWMA, and editor of the FAUD's papers *Der Syndikalist* and *Die Internationale*, traveled to Spain during the civil war and was active in the CNT. See also the introduction.

2. E. Armand (Lucien-Ernest Juin, 1872–1962) was a French anarchist, editor of *L'en dehors* and *L'Unique*. See also Chapter 13 and the introduction.

with democracy—politically—switched in. The field for Spanish anarchists will be free and open. But mental preparation is wanting even
in Spain for planned reconstruction. It may therefore even lead to
chaos. I know they are older in thought than myself but a newcomer
may see some points, for want of habit. I am myself pained to tell this.

In India, people are all expectant about Spain but the world
agencies boost only Franco or Negrin—Fascism or Bolshevism or
hypocrisy called Democracy. Anyway, sympathies are with radicals.
I have to meet a lot of opposition till the British Press lets out truths.
I used to get CNT bulletins but they have ceased to come in, despite
Souchy having assured their mailing to me.

I think the split in the IAMB is natural owing to conflicts between economic and philosophic thought.[3] Economics must become
philosophic—not the reverse. In India too, there is a conflict between
political philosophies and economic thought. This country is the most
rotten ripe for chaos, for it is poorer than any other including Spain and
Russia. We are not going to have any government here, chaos or not.
No possibility of founding one. But mental atavism persists in thinking
one has to go through newer forms of government, as in 1917 people
thought in and outside Russia that beyond democracy nothing was
possible there. Here in India it will be worse, just for want of mental
preparation and complete breakdown of all known economics. People
are talking as from a mad world, learning from Europe that once was.
The dead of Europe are speaking through Indians. The Chinese believe that the minds of the living are being ruled by the dead. It is true.
For mankind is just trying to run the institutions made by the dead,
and therefore the minds of the dead constructors are working through
those who want to run the institutions. I might say some Anarchists'
minds are being run by the dead through the channels of exchange
and barter—even currency—which they want to see continued. Only
they won't be able to work them after capitalists have bankrupted them
there or owing to their uneconomic nature. Beware of your head! I

---

3. The International Anti-Militarist Bureau (IAMB) was founded by Bart de Ligt in
1921, and a splinter group, the War Resisters' International, was founded a year later.

say even to anarchists as to the Capitalists and Bolshevists. They may laugh at me but they will learn. I think I see much better from this distance than those on the spot—without any exaggeration and pride. All this chaos—even of mind—is due the fundamental unworkability of every exchange system on which all civilizations are based. Yet we want to confuse it, is it not atavism? Exchange means two owners at least and the beginning of exploitation. Even a family would disperse if based on exchange. Scientific distribution is in the family system. We want only a world family without compartments. That would be perfect science. I hope our Spanish comrades would see this point.

As regards "anti-militarist government," it is forced upon them by Franco.[4] Better to have fought and lost than not to have fought at all. This war process is necessary to make anarchist revolution ripe when the war shall have forced all to the equal, Democracy in the anarchist sense would sprout, never to be smothered. A horrible process, no doubt. But "peace" would have been horrible also, and produced the same results. People would have died "by inches," by suppressed agonies. Now at least there is hope. Long live Spain for showing to the world that all is not lost yet. The mental depression has been broken by Spain throughout the world.

Those who were tired of Democracy, Fascism, and Bolshevism have found there is something else to try, that the last word has not been said already.

Spain has lifted mankind out of the slough of thought: something new is still possible in the world and is coming. The defeat of Franco and Negrin would open up vast vistas for Man!

Bolshevism will die with Capitalism, as mentally it is bound with it, as "economic capitalism." The world crisis will drown Bolshevism in its maelstrom. That is the significance of the executions of all old Bolshevists in Russia. They deserved it long ago. It is the revenge for Kronstadt.

Man! A Journal of the Anarchist Ideal and Movement,
3:11 (November, 1937), 3.

---

4. Original footnote: *Man! dissents from this view.* –Editor.

31. Is War Inevitable? Psychological Desire Without Material Basis

M. P. T. Acharya

BABU BHAGAVAN DAS M. L. A. has issued a manifesto calling upon the scientists of the world "to unite" to prevent another Armageddon breaking out and to abolish unemployment.[1]

As regards the first object, Babu Bhagavan Das has started on the supposition that another world war is in sight. The point is whether the supposition is justified and upon that will depend the probability of world war.

World War Not Possible

It is true that large armament preparations are going on—larger than before 1914. It is also true that Italy has annexed Abyssinia and Germany Austria while Japan is trying to swallow up China.

But there are arguments why a world war is impossible in spite of large-scale war preparations on all hands. The history of last year and this year shows that while bankrupt countries like Italy and Germany are prepared to swallow up any country, the big powers are just looking on helplessly and recognize every *fait accompli*. That must be proof enough. That a large-scale war is becoming more and more difficult. It is not a war when an up-to-date armed Power swallows up distant or near helpless countries. War is possible when equally powerful nations enter into a conflict.

---

1. Bhagavan Das (1869–1958) was an Indian theosophist, who advocated non-violence and supported Gandhi.

The rest is banditism and exactly banditism is being tolerated by the big Guardians of world peace.

Why do they look on? It is cheaper to manufacture armaments than to enter into a war. While it may cost £1,000,000,000 in five years to pile up armaments, that sum would be spent in no time if a world war has to be let loose.

Surely the *armaments* are finally waste, since there is no chance to enter into further commitments on account of war. The armaments only give help to a part of the unemployed. That also seems to be the motive behind armament programs proposed to be carried out. Big Powers are simply raising money in order to block a part of treasury deficits, which otherwise might lead to state bankruptcy. After all, accounts can be manipulated.

Yet armament programs are useless when there is no war definitely in sight. And the Governments know every war and armaments are absolutely ruinous to the State—mere complete breakdown of civilization.

Armament Race Useless

There is another reason why an armament race is useless. The armaments made today will be *antiquated in a few years*, since every Government tries to steal the secrets of others and improve upon them. In four or five years, the present arms are likely to be useless for war even if the secrets are completely preserved. The arms are likely to become useless for other reasons. The experimental use of the arms is likely to wear them out. The number of shots forced or the length of distance run are likely to wear out parts and even age-out the whole machines and keeping them without use is likely to rust them. It is therefore impossible to see where the use of these engines will come except in the exercise of men.

A war is not likely for other reasons. Before the last war, the nations, i.e., Governments had collected fat, which they expended in four years. Today all the Governments and the nations are in trade and *treasury deposit*. To make war without substantial sums is out of the question even for desperates like Hitler and Mussolini.

A war can be carried on further only when currency is stable. But *all currencies are walking on crutches* and there is no sign of their recovery. If a war is declared by anyone, even the little trade now being carried on will become impossible for the belligerent nations. War nations cannot export but must continuously import and part with gold that is burning candles at both ends.

Gold is put away already by even the richer nations and the currencies are going down even without war. If war is declared by anyone, the currency of that nation will not be touched by any other. Thus the war becomes merely a *psychological desire without any material basis*. The psychology cannot create the material basis. All the reasons mentioned above point not only to the improbability but also impossibility of war for a long time.

The Mahratta (April 15, 1938), 5.

32. Letter from India

M. Acharya

Bombay, March 1946

Miss Muriel Lester has just published a book on *Ghandi, World Citizen* (Kitab Mahal Publishers, Allahabad).[1] Miss Lester is a member of the International Fellowship of Reconciliation, Gandhi's guest in London during the Round Table Conferences, and was received several times at his home here. She knows him well. Reported as a pacifist, she was a suspect, and was interned for two weeks on the island of Trinidad, in the West Indies, and then released. She has written several books, mainly on India and the Far East, and written an autobiography. Her style is anecdotal, which is why her work on Gandhi teems with unknown anecdotes about him, and it is illustrated with hitherto unknown photographs.

Her work consists of two parts, each of which is about a hundred pages long; in the first, she deals with the ideas formulated by Gandhi in support of his doctrine of non-violence: truth, honesty, education, women, machinery, unimportant people, prohibition, the British Empire, and prayer. All this is interesting, written with childish enthusiasm, and the chronology recounts all the important facts of Gandhi's activities. For both Gandhists and their opponents, this book is useful and interesting to browse.

---

1. Muriel Lester (1883–1968) was a British pacifist campaigner and a close ally of Gandhi.

It seems to me that Miss Lester belongs to the Quakers, who, for religious reasons, are against murder and have been conscientious objectors during the two world wars. However, in England, they are considered powerful businessmen, subsisting on the dividends procured by industries, some of which are war industries. Their position is therefore contradictory, as no one can doubt their enthusiasm for pacifism and the pacifists, but it seems that this enthusiasm is idealistic, more than realistic and practical. Gandhi is obviously "their man," because he too is very contradictory, believing in the state and the armaments (and consequently in their manufacture and the financial means for their manufacture), and at the same time he asks each and everyone to put down their guns and give up on violence. It is doubtful that pacifism is realized in this way. Finance involves war, and pacifism based on financial support leads to ruin and even to war.

Gandhi's pacifism will prove untenable in conflict, civil wars, and others, despite the fact that he imagines having become a master of the technique of pacifism, by the ideas he disseminates, thanks to the martyrs who have added faith to his methods, and from which he has gathered glory. But he is far from it. He borrowed a few pages from Thoreau and Tolstoy, mixing their views with popular Indian conceptions of peace and "ahimsa." The trouble is that the opponents of Gandhi attack him as much as pacifism (as if he had the monopoly). This allows him to pose as the only man who can lead the world to non-violence—this world that groans under the weight of wars and violence—and to thus become famous. The reality is that pacifism is essentially just in itself; even those who want to annihilate the human race want peace, at least for themselves. However, Gandhi has nothing to offer because he is ill equipped to teach pacifism. The anarchists and Tolstoyans of the West have fundamental ideas about pacifism that Gandhi does not want to know of in any way. Gandhi practices pacifism in the manner of a man who would use a plaster to cure blood diseases! That the skin is rubbed and the blood poisoning will disappear! Quite simply, his quackery will kill the patient. Or he asks the patient to bring him herbs that do not exist, and then promises that he will heal them.

The Tolstoyans admire Gandhi, who, for the first time, applied Tolstoy's methods on a vast scale, but not for Tolstoyan purposes, that is to say societally, revolutionary, and economically. Thus, the Tolstoyans do not believe that peace is possible as long as the large landed property, the sense of property in general, and the caste system remains or is left untouched. Gandhi is the champion of these traditional institutions. Gandhi calls for a national state, with an army, and non-violence for the people. He is not a pacifist, while passing for a non-violent saint. One cannot personally be a saint and at the same time admit violence in others. Where is one's right to denounce violence? Gandhi distinguishes between established violence and potential violence, but this does not destroy the root of violence. He shouted "non-violence" at the top of his voice, and this word triumphantly sounded in the air, and that's all he is indebted to, while others perjured themselves and stopped believing that non-violence will ever be realized. Not touching the root of violence. Gandhi has no reason to lament his persistence, since he sided with established violence against potential violence, that is, the transfer of violence from one hand to another. Whatever he does or says, he is an agent of violence. The result of his ostentatious non-violent preaching will be that no one will believe in non-violence anymore, and that with each hand raising against the other, there will be more violence. We do not make fun of the public with impunity, without the most serious consequences resulting from it. This is where the Gandhist cult of non-violence will end. All the charlatans and the boasters of pacifism will see in him the greatest man produced by the earth—the Mahatma. At the same time, the English imperialists currently consider it their only support.

Gandhi exposes this argument that life is illogical, and that logic is not necessary to promote non-violence. It ignores reasoning and relies on the beauty of feelings for the realization of non-violence. But without the logic of reasoning, we waste our time, because it is only through this logic that we can reach the root of the evil. Like Krishnamurti, Gandhi lives in a poetic world, beyond the materialistic baseness of the human environment.[2] He thinks, as would "a mechanism of non-violence." His adversaries are prey to baseness and make fun of the foolishness of non-violence. But the followers of Gandhi come out of the ranks of the materialists, and they use him to hide their vilest interests. Nevertheless, he makes them believe that they are accomplishing his oeuvre. The greatness of all sincere men seems to be the fact that false and ambitious men who propagate or tolerate their ideas surround them. Gandhi works in the interest of all of those who aspire to power around him, even if it is against pacifism and non-violence. If it were otherwise, they would curse and boycott him instead of paying tribute to their ideas and giving up some of their profits—an investment designed to secure future gains. Without them, how could he carry out his propaganda? He only laughs at their misdeeds! But taken personally, it is violent men who are his best supporters. You see that Gandhi's Pacifism indeed has consequences! ...

Let Gandhi learn pacifism before teaching it to others! Pacifist quackery is more dangerous than the open defense of violence, about which no one is mistaken and which everyone disgusts—but pacifist quackery results in everyone losing faith in non-violence.

"Lettre de l'Inde," *L'Unique*, 11 (June, 1946), 13–14.

---

2. Jiddu Krishnamurti (1895–1986) was an Indian philosopher and writer.

33. Anarchy:
From Philosophy to Economics

M. P. T. Acharya

IN 1934, E. ARMAND WROTE in *L'en dehors* that in the event of another revolution in Spain, there should be no trace of business, money, and the state, to begin with a pure program. One of the least expressive paragraphs of this article was included in the work of the late de Ligt's *Conquest of Violence.*[1]

After this war, even if there are a couple of powerful states left, there is every chance that all states, businesses, and capital will go bankrupt. Although powerful states such as Russia, England, and the United States attempt to do their utmost to preserve business, states, and money capital, there is no likelihood, in my view, that they will succeed in their claims, whether in other countries or in their own. Business and monetary capital are the bearers of all States, and no one can survive without them. But the characteristic of monetary capital is that the people have to live without buying. All States urge and force the people to "tighten their belts" in order to preserve the stability of monetary capital and to prosper in foreign trade. It is also a fact that monetary capital cannot maintain its stability without the export of surplus products. Thus the interests of consumers and monetary capital are in opposition. Since there are only two countries that can buy, and others that cannot buy at all, business will decline

---

1. E. Armand (Lucien-Ernest Juin, 1872–1962) was a French anarchist, editor of *L'en dehors* and *L'Unique*; Bart de Ligt (1883–1938) was a Dutch anarcho-pacifist, greatly inspired by Gandhi, author of *The Conquest of Violence* (1937).

for the former. This means that businesses will become increasingly smaller for these countries. The great capitalist countries are threatened with economic chaos, because the impoverished nations cannot buy in order to keep their monetary capital stable with the help of foreign surplus-trade. Lately in England, despite the government's efforts to greatly increase exports, import is more considerable. EXPORT OR PERISH, is the dilemma of even the most powerful states. But the important thing is to know who is going to pay those two countries for their EXPORT SURPLUS, once the others are ruined by the war. The greater the capital invested, the greater the need to obtain EXPORT SURPLUS. Otherwise there will be chaos in the money capital. Once the war has ruined numerous countries, they cannot help the two powerful states by buying their export surplus, so they will suffer serious problems, even if strikes and internal disturbances do not erupt. The only path of salvation for the powerful states would be that they could export to other planets. The earth is too small to accommodate all leftover products. The only countries that can buy from each other are England and the United States. But each of them strives to have EXPORT SURPLUS to avoid the ruin of monetary capital. And both wish to export in order to have their industries in operation and their workers employed, and if their industries could not obtain profits abroad, then they could not keep the monetary capital nor its workers stable. This means that other countries have to buy from them so that they can survive. The other countries must provide raw materials to these two states, but they must do so with deficit in foreign trade, which means that such monetary capital cannot remain stable. These countries must make EXPORT SURPLUS, if they want to keep their monetary capital stable, which is exactly what they could not do, even if they were allowed to. So the great capitalist countries would also ruin those who would be their clients. They speak of resuscitating the international exchange of goods, but do not try to exchange them, unless the other countries do not pay their surplus commodities in monetary capital. Most countries have to buy more from those two states than to sell to them. Only thus can these two countries export their material surplus. Since the impoverished countries have to receive financial aid from the two great states, it is evident that they cannot buy more from them than what they sell to them. That would make the financial aid of the two large states useless for them and for others, since financial aid is another kind of business, giving less money than is received, because of interests and other conditions. Even England itself is obliged to buy more goods from the United States in exchange for the loan received. This means that England, in addition to paying its interests to the United States, gives it the profit of its purchases. The economic system that we know only tries to extract money either by borrowing or by selling merchandise. If it were not so, it could not be sustained. The countries that have money to lend and invest it in production have the greatest need to win, especially because they have so many industries and capital. This can happen within two years and, in the event of an immediate war, once this one is over. At this time there will be no possibility of the triumph of Bolshevism in any country, or in other words, the triumph of the Marxist proprietor state. Because the Marxist state has to develop according to the principles of the capitalist state, in order to obtain the necessary SURPLUS VALUE. The Marxist state is a profit state. It works with the established difference between prices and wages, obtained by a system of employment and sale. Only their foundations are narrower than those of private capital, since there is no waste in it. Waste comes from the unproductive workers of the state, that is to say the bureaucracy, the army, the police, the spies, etc., that is, the party that owns the state. But the state advances money for these unproductive "workers," and tries to recover as much as possible from the products sold to the real workers. Productive workers maintain the state by their purchasing power. Thus the state must make useless expenditures, so that the workers produce, or have to reduce the production, giving rise to unemployment. Exactly as in the capitalist system of waste. What was possible in Russia in 1917 is now not possible for impoverished countries. The Bolsheviks harvested the remains of Tsarism, but after this war nothing useful remains. Those who expect an owner-state after this war are not guessing right. For this time, it is not possible to have an owner-state anywhere. The Russian proprietor-state was enabled by the credit received from abroad. But this time there will be no possible credit for any state, because they will all go into stagnation and will not have the means to lend.

The work organized by the anarchists is about to take place, not because they have created the favorable conditions, but because the economic methods of the Bolsheviks and capitalists have made any other solution impossible. There is no other way for the people of all countries to conduct work without business, monetary capital, and the state. The anarchists must prepare themselves mentally to organize the production among the masses, and to propagate among others the way to do it, since there is no other expeditious way to conduct work. This solution can occur in two or five years, once the dealers have to stop production, realizing that there is no way to make profits, or SURPLUS VALUE, to keep the state machine moving. Five years is a very short time to prepare the mentality of the people.

The origin of capitalist business is exchange, but this cannot be done without profit or SURPLUS VALUE. For if one of the parties that exchanged gave or received as much as the other party, production would have no purpose. A man changes his X value products into cost, and he must receive X value, because if he receives less, he cannot sustain himself. One of the participants in the exchange has to pay for the maintenance of the other participant, because otherwise production would have no value. So what one participant pays extra when he buys, he needs to pay to the one who sells, creating a chain of exploitation—EXCHANGE LEADS TO EXPLOITATION: everyone has to produce cheaply, or make others pay more than they invest in their products. Without which the system could not hold together.

Moreover, from a Communist point of view, each exchange means different masters: master of work, of goods, of money. The idea of exchange is necessary for the owner-state or for private employers. But social anarchism or proprietary communism is the negation of exchange. But we have already explained that exchange is antisocial and requires exploitation, a chain of exploiters who use the needs of others to satisfy their own. But the main objection against exchange is that it is anti-economic and will lead to failure. So communist anarchists, partisans of social possession, and economists opposed to exchange, agree on the same principles of a scientific and practicable economy. However, we should not explain anarchism from an economic-scientific point of view. We should prove that scientific economics cannot be carried out without anarchism, and that the unscientific economy leads to anarchy, making it the only way out. So anarchy and scientific economics are identical, and one cannot exist without the other. We should explain scientific economics first and then anarchy to those who are not anarchists. There are two complementary ways of explaining this to the public: in the first place, the present economy, even the Marxist economy, will collapse because of its inability to make the people buy, not to mention the tyranny and violence it needs to maintain its system. This economy is negative, AND THEREFORE THE OPPOSITE SYSTEM WILL NECES-SARILY EXIST, which is a logical consequence of the first [i.e., the negative economy], and that new system HAS TO SUSTAIN ITSELF WITHOUT ANY EXCHANGE AND THEREFORE WITHOUT ANY MONETARY CAPITAL, BUSINESS, OR STATE.

A family provides for all its members, without any trade between them, what they can produce or obtain, even if they have to work out of the home for money to procure what they do not produce. If the father becomes a banker, the first son a trader, the second a man-ufacturer, and the other a wage-earner, the family will disintegrate, and all the members will become unemployed and go bankrupt. The same thing happens in society. The objection to exploitation is that it is uneconomical and incapable of organizing work; but it is also inhumane and immoral. There is no doubt that in the present the family is patriarchal, but the economy of a family is not commercial. That is why it is in a position to provide what is necessary for its members—as much as circumstances permit—when they are work-ing away from home to earn money. Likewise in society. There can be no trade in the family without the family disintegrating.

The use of exchange leads to the need to find and maintain a means of exchange to exploit (make others pay more than the cost of goods) to those who come to exchange their money. Each exchange of currency for commodity is for the sake of having currency, otherwise the seller cannot pay those who sell him, since everybody demands more than the real cost of products in order to continue with this system. But as I have pointed out, this exchange is only a necessary means for a non-communist society, not for social possession. Since a state cannot exist without exchange, even the owner state is not social communism. In addition, the means become the end: A certain quantity of goods produced at a certain cost does not represent its value in use, but that of the currency. Exchange of goods is currency exchange, much like bank operations. So the object of commodity production is to get more money for less money. Anything that looks for more currency for less currency is useful production. The means becomes the end.

As long as there is a "need" for means of exchange, nothing useful can be expected for society. The real needs of the members of society cannot even be calculated. Anyone looking for more currency for less currency is useful for production. If a nefarious service seeks more money, it is still a useful service. If damaged goods produce more money, their production is more convenient than the production of merchandise in good condition. If luxury goods generate more money than necessary goods, the production of the latter has no purpose. In addition, exchange creates business. Business cannot be planned. No one knows exactly what is certain to be bought, how much and from who. So it is almost impossible to calculate whether the production should be more or less.

Given that what makes more money is useful, a classification of unnecessary, useful, and luxurious products is impossible, because nobody knows what people might want to buy or reject according to the whims of the moment. It is a matter of luck that some products are sold and others are not. These are problems for a chaotic capitalist or Bolshevik society, but not for an anarchist society. BUYING AND SELLING SHOULD HAVE NO PLACE IN ANARCHISM, otherwise it would not be a scientific economy. NOTHING TO SELL would be the reason for anarchism. In addition, buying and selling would require wages and prices, and exploitation would start all over again, if it were possible at all to continue after the chaos. An anarchist plan must calculate what are the most urgent needs of all members of society, which needs to come second in urgency, which are desirable but not essential and, lastly, which of those are luxury needs. The plan for production must be made in this order. We already know that a certain amount of food, clothing, and accommodation is essential for everyone. Education and health for all are also necessary. Some entertainment is also needed. Transportation facilities, but not ownership of cars and airplanes, are a must for all who produce and work. Certain provisions are necessary to transport those who enjoy themselves, but with due prudence. Transport must be economized, because it is needed for work, distribution, and enjoyment. DO NOT MAKE ANYTHING USELESS to avoid waste of work and material. We cannot have the freedom to amass wealth for some to the detriment of others, as in capitalist or Bolshevik society. That would diminish freedom. Such a plan would yield more results than the theoretical freedoms of chaos. In theory, everyone CAN have cars in a capitalist society, but many die for lack of food. There is freedom to own a car, but most cannot afford it. But in an anarchist society, everyone has the same opportunity to USE a car for their own pleasure, but at the right time of the shift. It is natural that this freedom of tyrants and exploiters cannot be accepted in an anarchist society with a scientific economy? These are some considerations planned by anarchists, also called scientific social possession.

Bombay, India.

"Anarquia: De la Filosofia a la Economia,"
Tierra y Libertad, 3:56 (November, 1946), 2.

31. Labour Splits in India

M. P. T. Acharya

(This article is sent to us by our Bombay comrade, M. P. T. Acharya. For reasons of space, we have had to condense it slightly.)

THERE ARE ALREADY SEVERAL KINDS of trade unions in India. There are the older non-political unions; the Communist-controlled trade unions; and the Royist trade unions called the "Indian Federation of Labour," started during the war with the aid of a government subsidy to act as an adjunct to the war machine.[1] (There is also the oldest "National Railwaymen's Union," which is composed of white and semi-white engine drivers.) Recently, the Muslim League tried to start purely Mussulman unions.[2]

These unions are all acting against one another, although they pretend to help labor "unite." Sometimes the first three unite, or only two, while the other remain "neutral." Fortunately, the All-India Trade Union Congress to which the first two belong at present is a loosely affiliated body, though the Communists try to get the upper hand in it. Formerly, the Trade Union movement went hand in hand with the Indian National Congress, but during the war, the Communists went against the Congress on account

---

1. Mahendra Nath Roy (M. N. Roy, 1887–1954) was an Indian revolutionary and Communist, founder of the Mexican Communist Party, co-founder of the CPI, and founder of the Indian Federation of Labour in 1941, after a split from the AITUC.
2. Muhammad Ali Jinnah (1876–1948) founded the All India Muslim League in 1913 and served as leader until his death.

of its non-collaborationist attitude when Russia was attacked by Hitler. (Till then, they were "against the Imperialist War"—like the National Congress.)

Since the National Congress assumed ministries in the various provinces first, and later in the capital of Delhi, the Communists and Nationalists have grown more bitter against each other. The Nationalist Government, with the ex-Socialist Jawaharlal Nehru at its head, is playing a capitalist role, which exactly suits the Stalinists. V. Patel, Nehru's Home Minister, is an avowed tool of the capitalists—the mill owners of Ahmadabad presented him with half-a-million rupees for "his services to his country"![3]

Since the end of the war, owing to the rapid increase of living costs, there has been an epidemic of strikes. When labor is in trouble it is a good field for the Stalinists, who are not really the friends of labor—for they also want to keep workers as wage slaves. But their politics in favor of Stalin (called "Communism") is furthered by fishing in troubled waters. Communists are in favor of every strike—provided it furthers their party. Thus, the workers are tossed between Communists and capitalists in every country. Both talk of giving better wages to the workers!

Solidarity Without Class Consciousness

Between these two extreme millstones, the workers are also ground up by other political parties. There are the Congress Socialist and the Royists. The Muslim Leaguers are trying to form separate unions like the Catholic unions in Germany. But the workers who are in trouble are not so organized—*i.e.*, disciplined—as in Europe. They go on strike when it suits them and return to work when they cannot hold out any longer. That is one of the advantages of being illiterate and leaderless! They have no politics. Since they are continually in

---

3. Vallabhbhai Patel (also known as Sardar Patel, 1875–1950) served as the first Home Minister and Deputy Prime Minister of India (1947–1950) in Jawarharlal Nehru's government.

trouble, they must go on strike. Often enough they go on strike for the dismissal of one of their colleagues. They simply demand higher wages and walk out or sit down. Or they refuse to work because one of them has been insulted by a "higher-up."

All this shows a certain sense of solidarity, without class-consciousness, which is a very rare thing to find even in "well organized and disciplined" literate members of European and American trade unions.

It is, indeed, very difficult to "discipline", *i.e.*, muzzle Indian workers—that is the complaint of both the labor leaders and the capitalists! The labor leaders only pretend to go with the workers, and then try to sabotage the strikes. That is what they are doing! But again the workers come out. They do not know the niceties of negotiating roguery on the part of their leaders and the capitalists. They are straight out! Immediate in action! When the workers learn to read and are fed with misleading print, their minds will be unhinged as in pre-Nazi Germany and now in Europe. In fact, both capitalists and labor leaders want the workers to be literate in their common interest of keeping them down—doped with their literature. Hope is that both won't be able to educate them. The most unscrupulous class of workers are those who are able to read and want to be leaders. They are not only muddled by reading, but also become traitors in order to climb higher in the hierarchy of leadership—any leadership!

Measures Against Strikes

Since the Governments could not prevent strikes, they introduced compulsory arbitration by law—declaring any works to be a "public utility." But since even this did not prevent strikes, the labor leaders—who are in favor of compulsory arbitration even while they are protesting that "it was only Fascist arbitration"—could not prevent strikes either, they had to go along with the workers. So the Nationalists in the Government had to find other ways of meeting the situation.

The only remaining way was to found a rival organization of workers against all these, an organization that will accept compulsory arbitration. To machine gun the workers would only strengthen the Communists in the unions, and all other so-called Socialists who are in opposition to the Nationalists. The Government are therefore themselves starting a so-called "Indian National Trade Union Congress."

Meanwhile, they are trying to organize Fascist, company, and blackleg unions, and also perhaps bribery to some, for some workers will assuredly be paid to become stool pigeons in factories, or to create trouble among workers by trying to disrupt other unions. We have no sympathy for any of these unions, for they are all made to keep workers down by making them fight among themselves, and they are all in favor of the wage system, which makes this possible.

V. Patel said that this is no rival union, but only to unite workers "in their own interests." His argument was that the Communists were trying to create trouble and make production impossible; this makes the workers' lot more difficult than it already is, because the strikes, which they foment, make for lessened production.

But it is quite false that increased production makes for improved conditions. We had tremendous production before the war in all countries, at least for a time but that did not produce any improvement in any country, but only unemployment in all countries. Yet they are talking of improvement in the lot of the workers under the wage system through increased production. Either history never teaches anything, or they are blind to history! The stock argument in all countries against wage increases is that unless there is more production industry cannot bear increased wages. But even with increased production there was unemployment growing in all countries. Now they want—even labor leaders want—to increase production as if that would solve any problem, even the sales problem. Either ignorance or roguery seems to be the strength, not only of the capitalists but also of the labor leaders. The latter are surely more than ignorant—if they are not rogues, they are idiots. Neither capitalism nor Bolshevism can solve the consumption problem within the wage system; neither can sell the goods produced, however few or great they may be. So long as the workers hang on the promises of labor leaders and Governments (however red they may be) that there is a solution within the wages system, even for maintaining the wage system, they will all go unemployed or eat still less, if anything.

The only new kind of union that is worth having is one for running industry without prices or wages—after expropriation. Unless that is the object of the unions, the minds of workers will not be prepared to take possession of all things in order to run industry in their own interests. Trade Unions for maintaining the wage system are useless; they cannot improve trade upon which wages are based.

Anarchist Literature

But for the first time in Indian history, anarchist literature is being printed. Of course, more are imported than being printed. Till now, *God and the State* by Bakunin has appeared and also one pamphlet by R. Rocker: *Socialism and the State*. But *Anarcho-Syndicalism* by Rocker is to appear soon. These publications are put on the market not by any trade union or anarchist organization—no such organization exists, but by private enterprise. Whether labor leaders will learn anything from these books is very doubtful, for their leadership will be gone without the wage-system. Most likely, they will be against the spread of anarchist ideas and will join with capitalists against such publications, for fear their jobs will be lost. The labor leaders will try to ridicule such publications as crazy and impracticable, although in their heart of hearts they may rejoice if such publications will be prohibited by the nationalist-Fascists. But without an anarchist movement, this country will go Fascist and go to the dogs—in spite of the labor leaders trying to adapt themselves to capitalist-Fascism, which is the wage system. The labor leaders in India and elsewhere (along with their fellow travelers the capitalists and Fascists) will only invite the wrath of workers for having led them into a blind alley by trying to smother anarchist thought, which shows them the way out. Either society or state will arise out of the present chaos all over the world, and the state also requires society to prey upon. Most likely mankind will be decimated by the state before it goes down. In that case, there will be no government possible in India after this nationalist government, which seeks British brutish protection. The labor leaders will have themselves to thank when the workmen get wild in their tortures and remove them instead of following them. This country is in a wilder state than any other and any bloodshed might take place here.

Freedom: Anarchist Fortnightly (May 31, 1947), 5.

35. What Is Anarchism?

M. P. T. Acharya

ARCHY MEANS GOVERNMENT, RULE, STATE—Anarchy means non-rule, non-government, non-state. The Anarchists want non-rule, non-government, non-state. They want a non-governed, non-ruled, non-state society. Here, anarchism is the antithesis, the opposite of all other -isms. It negates fundamentally the necessity of all states, whatever their form. While in other -isms they try to find a synthesis between state and society, the anarchists believe, consider, and think that the state is the enemy of society, i.e., the state will suppress the society or the society will have to suppress the state. That means the two cannot co-exist. They therefore negate the theory of the state being the collective will of the governed, whether it is the liberal or democratic state, or the absolutist and dictatorial state, whatever the extreme form, i.e., whether the fascist or Marxist state. All states are dictatorial—preliminarily or ultimately. No constitution can be established except by violence. The most democratic constitutions had a violent rebellion before them to eliminate the previous rulers and states, and under that violence, new constitutions were formulated and established. Therefore the claim that constitutions are established by the free will of the people is incorrect.

If the states—or any states—were non-violent, where is the necessity for armies, police, and jails? The last arguments of all states are the army, police, and jails. Every constitution is protected by army, police, and jails. As much as autocracies! No state can exist without these.

There is no constitution that says that no army, police, and jails should be used. In fact, in an emergency all constitutions allow states to defend themselves from danger. What is emergency is a matter of interpretation by states and parliaments. When, as is generally done under constitutions of the freest kind, an emergency is proclaimed to exist, all constitutions are suspended, and the army, police, and jails come to defend the state and constitution. Peter Kropotkin, once a prince and later an anarchist, declared in his "An Appeal to the Young," what is the use of constitutions when martial law can be declared in defense of the state? When the rebels make trouble, the constitutions are shelved and the state is managed and defended by violence in the name of the will of the people. States thus create civil wars, even constitutional states. When the different parties and interests agree to rule together, there is a constitution, when they fall out, there is civil war and suspension of the constitution. The states born of violence cannot defend themselves without violence. Thus a non-violent state does not, cannot exist. All states in essence are violence, concentrated violence over society—whatever their forms and shades, just as much as autocratic absolutist kings are. To speak of non-violent society and state in the same breath is mutually contradictory. Non-violent society can therefore come into being only with the abolition or "withering away" of states of every kind. Therefore to produce a non-violent society, the anarchists work consciously, instead of leaving it (as Marxians do under the excuse of a "transition stage") to time and chance. All states refuse to wither away and try to perpetuate themselves as long as possible. The anarchists are therefore the only ones who want to abolish violence over and within society. They want that to be done deliberately. There will be eternal war between state and society and finally the state will not wither away but will be suppressed—that is the anarchist thesis. The object of evolution is for the society to get on without a state and rule from without. The anarchists want everyone to help evolution to that end, consciously and deliberately.

The anarchists maintain all governments are established and maintained only by a minority. Even under constitutions, states are violence by a minority over the vast majority, whether the states and constitutions are accepted voluntarily or enforced with the help of violence. No state can be conducted by all. Only a minority will be allowed to bear arms, even if the majority is allowed to vote. Only a minority will be allowed to manage the state. It cannot be done by a majority by, or after, delegating powers voluntarily, or after deception and compulsion. The anarchists want everyone to be rulers in their own right. They do not believe that there can be separation of interests between the representatives and represented. The representatives will serve their own interests even at the expense of the represented. Thus deception and force will prevail. The represented will be finally suppressed by their representatives. The representatives cannot be identical with the represented. Hence proxy-government is not self-government by the people. In order to have self-government by the people, each has to represent himself directly. That can be done through no state, however radical. *The anarchists mean by non-state (anarchy), government of society by society, by all members of society.* That cannot be done by a representative government, which can only be centralist. Government is always centralism—finally despotism of the center. Even the most "federalist" or "decentralized" government, like the Swiss, is in the last resort centralist and therefore despotic and cannot be of the people and by the people, and therefore for the people. Centralist democracy is a contradiction in terms. Either centralism or democracy is possible; mixing both ideas, which are as poles apart, is nonsense. No government can afford to be decentralist and federalist: The autonomy of the parts is an illusion. In most essential matters, even the most "decentralist" government like the Swiss is centralist, it decides as it suits the state best even if it means the curtailment of the liberties and violating, overriding the interests of the autonomous parts. On any essential question, the central state is for itself. Decentralization and federalism means absence of government, which means centralism. So non-government is both decentralization and federalism—the essential condition of both these. Decentralism and federalism will destroy centralism or centralism will destroy both. There can be no compromise between the two principles, which are antitheses. The anarchists go to the logical limit. The anarchists not only want decentralism of regions into local units but also distribution of power, decentralism of power, the making of every one in each locality his own master and representative. The power finally is vested into each individual. Of course, they recognize the necessity for delegation of power, but conditionally and *in the locality*—where alone the representatives can be under the watchful eyes of all.

Every government can be only by a section of the society against all the rest. There can be no people's government possible, except under anarchy. People (society) or government but not people's (or social and socialist) government. The anarchists, when they insist on non-governed society, mean government of the people, by the people, for the people—directly by the people themselves without any intermediary. Society ruling itself, not ruled by a party over itself, which can only be done with violence.

Every governmental "society" is divided into the rulers and the ruled. There are classes among such a society, the largest classes being those who are for the government or against the government. The government can only be in defense of itself in spite of a class supporting it. The class represented by a government is not all defended equally by that government. The nearest and most satisfied by the government is its bureaucracy: government is bureaucracy, can only be bureaucratic. In the Marxian so-called class-state, the bureaucracy of the party comes before all workers, for they are the mainstay of the state and government. There cannot be even a class state, for all the class cannot conduct the state after delegation of its powers. Especially as every state is centralist, i.e., despotic. There are gradations of class as there is gradation of income in every class. With such gradations, there is and can be no solidarity and identity of interests, even in one class. The so-called neutrality and justice of the state is but the neutrality of the money toward the quarreling cats. There will be no cheese left for the quarrelers who go before the state for justice. The state will manage its own affairs first and foremost at the expense of the "class brothers." The state is above those whose interests it is supposed to protect and defend, it is outside the pale of its own class. Thus the dictatorship of the proletariat through the state of the advance guard (communist) party becomes inevitably the dictatorship over all the proletariat. The party state cannot represent even the interests of the members of the party, which supports it. The state is independent and over the party.

The state of whatever form and name cannot be otherwise, since it can only be run by a bureaucratic, microscopic minority and must rule. The state is the part, but society means whole. Even a class means whole—all members of the class. The theory of the state metaphysicians is that the part, which is made to represent the whole, is identical in interests with the whole, is even the whole. But a part can never be equal to or identical with the whole. It can only be separate from the whole, independent of the whole in the name and under pretext of being delegates of the whole. The whole will go under the part whether this is erected or not, whether it assumed its role of a delegate by force or fraud. No government can be identical in interests with the people, even with that of the class it pretends to champion, even if these accept and elect it. People or state, class or state—not both together. The people or the class must serve their own interests without the intermediary of anybody, *all representation is illusion*. But that cannot be done through elections and constitutions, which delegate authority to a distant body. Hence the anarchists want only local elections where the delegates will be under the electors' control and direction. Distant delegates cannot be controlled. Hence they want no state and no centralism, which can only be distant. So far they are realists. All others hallucinationists.

The anarchists want freedom, democracy, and socialism. But they consider—nay, are convinced, these cannot be obtained or maintained under state protection or direction. The states are therefore the enemies of freedom, democracy, and socialism, for in the last resort they are despotic and only for bureaucracy. There can be no government, which is not bureaucratic, i.e., bureaucracy and government are interchangeable terms. To fight bureaucracies and keep governments is hopeless, since governments breed bureaucracies, red-tapism, red tape itself. People alone, if decentralized administration under local control and management is established, can conduct affairs without bureaucratism, because all things will be above board and under the eyes of the local people at all times. What is in their interests and what is not can be detected, corrected, and decided at once.

The theory of capitalist and Marxian states is that a state adjusts and distributes freedom to all equally and justly. But freedom cannot be rationed except by killing it. Sitting in different cells under the distribution of freedom is the death of freedom. *Freedom consists in free association*, if it has to be living. Association does not mean that the cell inmates are ordered by the state to group together in the courtyard under its rules. Alone no man is free. The state freedom is but freedom as in jails. There can be no liberty with state. State is enemy of liberty, except for its bureaucracy. No matter what state it is. State and freedom are incompatible, especially when the state has to be maintained with the help of the army, police, and jails. A free state has never existed and will never exist. Hence democracy is illusion under states, in spite of all voting rights conferred. There can be uniformity of slavery in the name of democracy under states. The minority will dictate to the majority at the point of bayonets in the name of democracy and freedom. (In some countries, not going to polls is a cognizable offense!)

Socialism is social ownership and management, i.e., ownership and management by society and people. Since states cannot be identical with, i.e., be the same as people, the state being an organ of the bureaucracy—a minority, social ownership is negation of state ownership and vice versa. We can have either state ownership or social ownership and management. But it is supposed that state ownership is in fact social ownership and management. It is Gandhiji's trusteeship theory in another form, the part that is government represents the whole and therefore is the same as the whole, hence is identical with the whole society! Pure logical nonsense. The socialist anarchists who form the majority of the anarchist movement are therefore both against private and state ownership and management. There are individualist, associationist, and group anarchists who do not believe in socialism, i.e., ownership by the society as a whole. There are also anarchists who are individualist capitalists, and they are even for one man or group Bolshevism. They want their own or their group interests above all others' interests, even if against others' interests. But the vast majority of anarchists are for socialism, either as pure anarchists, anarcho-communists, or as anarcho-syndicalists (trade unionists' ownership and management). They are all at one about states and state ownership and management—against them as negation and suppression of socialism, i.e., of social ownership. The states being run by minorities and infinitesimal minorities, state ownership is no improvement but even worsening of private monopoly, for in private monopoly or ownership, there will be still competition between individuals and groups, whose rivalry to ruin each other may give to others some loopholes of liberty from time to time, but under a monopolistic economic system, all will be crushed into a uniform mass of slaves for the service and benefit of the bureaucracy that is independent and armed with all means to suppress all. The anarchists claim that state ownership cannot lead to socialism, since the so-called socialist state will prevent the society from owning anything. (Whether it will benefit the slaves materially is another question and on this point, the anarchists think it can only reduce the standard of living of all in order to maintain the state, as the state reaps by its monopoly the surplus value of profits as much as it can). Anyway the combination of political (i.e. state, army, police, and jailing) power with economic monopoly will end in absolute despotism of a clique. It will be absolute centralism. The anarchists are more against state ownership than even the capitalists. They are more inimical to Bolshevism than the capitalists are. The capitalists have at least a common platform with the Bolsheviks on the state issue—and therefore both the capitalists and Bolsheviks are the deadly enemies of anarchists. *The capitalists are individual or group Bolsheviks while the Marxians are collective capitalists.* The anarchists are against both forms of capitalism. Only the capitalists and Bolsheviks agree that Bolshevism is socialism, which the anarchists deny. They call Bolshevism the worst form of capitalism. Bolshevism is monolithic capitalism managed by a few monopolists. All the rest are their slaves who can be killed outright if they are useless for the state and its monopolistic parasitic economics. No elections and Soviets change this fact.

Every liberal and democrat is a bit of anarchist, for he does not want the complete mastery of his life by the state machine. The anarchists agree with Jefferson that the best government is one that governs least.[1] But they claim that the logic of it is that non-government is the best form of "government": *Society itself as government*, government of society by society.

As regards laws, on the necessity of which both Bolsheviks and anti-Bolshevik capitalists agree, the anarchists believe like Lenin: laws without force or violence to apply them are no laws, are ridiculous. Only Lenin said that *to create a force or violence to maintain laws and enforce them*, exactly like capitalists. But the anarchists say that because laws have to be enforced with violence, laws are not instruments of non-violence, and not non-violent, and if force has to be applied to maintain laws, what is the use of all laws? Force alone is enough to maintain the state. In fact, all constitutions and laws are but veils over force and violence behind them. And force consists in armies, police, and jails, the last line of defense of the states, their constitutions, and laws. But these are necessary for a divided society, to maintain it divided. Lenin observed that just as there are class laws in capitalist countries, there must be class laws in Russia: just as they suppress workers in capitalist countries, the Bolshevik state must suppress capitalists. He was logical from the state-mania standpoint, which he maintained. Only that is not calculated to abolish the class structure of society even under the proletarian state: in Russia, there are two classes, the ruling party, which employs proletarians, and the ruled who have to work for wages. In Russia also, owing to the state monopoly of all things, in spite of the claim for social ownership, there are laws against theft (of course, of state-property!). The state

---

1. Acharya, via Henry David Thoreau's opening line of "Civil Disobedience," wrongly attributes this quote to Thomas Jefferson.

is the owner, the rest are wage slaves. Where is social ownership, except as proxy-ownership? Political power is proxy-power and state power is proxy ownership. In both cases, the proxies are the real ones in power and the real owners. That is where a "representative system" leads to. *There can be no social ownership with a political state, hence there can be no social state, as socialist states are supposed to be.* All states are parasitic and anti-social: only the ownership changes for worse. Hence the anarchists refuse both states and state-ownership. They want ownership *by all the society*. A part cannot own anything for the whole society, politically or economically. It will own all things for its own benefit to the neglect of others, suppressing them to keep the benefits to itself. The means will become the object to the part called state.

The anarchists do not want confiscation, which means taking over by the state. They stand for expropriation, which means in their view collectively taking over the land, soil, and means of production. They do not want that only a class should expropriate, for that would mean making another class the master: they want all the society to expropriate all things. The anarchists want the immediate abolition of all classes while the so-called socialists and Marxians believe in gradual abolition of classes during a transition period. There can be no transition between capitalism and socialism, for these are opposites without a bridge between them. The one or the other is the only possibility. Once the owners are expropriated by the society, none is a capitalist or monopolist. The class distinctions are thus at once abolished. The Marxians are reformist capitalists compared to the anarchists.

Anarchists are pacifists, not necessarily socially but internationally. The anarchists refuse both wars and civil war. If necessary, the anarchists prefer civil wars to external wars. But their ideal and object is to make both wars and civil wars impossible. They believe that states are causes of wars and civil wars and the armies are meant to suppress people at home and make wars abroad. Hence they are against armies, however radical or red. There can be no social armies since armies are always part of the people trained against the rest. Arms can only be monopolies of a small, microscopic section of the people. Moreover, armies and arms are a burden upon the people, and therefore parasitic. They recognize that no states can be maintained without armies, police, and prisons, and therefore they are against all these, and the states. To abolish armies and violence all states must be abolished and made impossible, however red and "socialist" they may call themselves. To talk of peace and at the same time to maintain states—even Bolshevik states, is to do incompatible things. Even to abolish civil wars, states must be abolished. For states are inevitably the instruments of rule by one group of persons against and over the rest. So long as states remain, they must continue parasitism and therefore exploit and impoverish people and they thus create the necessity for rebellions and civil wars. As consistent and logical pacifists, the anarchists refuse to serve in wars. But if civil war is forced upon them and they can get arms, they are not averse to using them, in defense of their lives and ideals, i.e., to eliminate the causes of civil wars and wars. The anarchists, unlike the Bolsheviks, are averse to establishing another state in place of the old. They had believed before 1917 that the Marxians had the same object as they, but after the experience and experiment of the Marxian revolution in Russia, which they thought would lead to the suppression of the new state, they have abandoned all hope of Marxians abolishing states. Like Lenin before the last war, the anarchists were also against both sides in wars, since both sides were capitalists, but now they are against all wars, between one or more capitalist states and between socialist and capitalist states. The anarchists refuse to recognize territorial frontiers and therefore they have no fatherland, which they should defend. Frontiers means states and since they want no states, frontiers do not exist for them. Only undivided mankind exists for them, undivided as a whole and also as classes.

Somehow the idea of anarchy and anarchism is associated with chaos and violence—so that the two words are interchanged: anarchy means chaos. But to the anarchists, anarchy means only order without violence, unenforced order. All state orders are enforced orders, order enforced over chaos. Lift the state and its order, there will be chaos that was kept hidden. The anarchists are as much against chaos as those who pretend to be against chaos and therefore justify and maintain the states, any kind of state. They say that chaos cannot be abolished by states, but only *kept suppressed*, hence they require armies, police, and prisons with or without constitutions. Keeping chaos suppressed means not preventing chaos—the order that is imposed has only suppressed open chaos. The anarchists try to prepare the minds of people how they can live without chaos and without states. For there is no question of imposing anarchy upon the people as the Bolsheviks, capitalists, and fascists try to do "in order to prevent chaos," as they think. For the anarchists do not try to impose any state nor to establish any armies, prisons, and police at the expense of people. The minds of people being addicted to states, the people are likely, nay bound to welcome a new state in place of the old or hated one. The anarchists tell all that a new state can only make the conditions worse. But the old states cannot also be maintained, hence chaos. The anarchists want to tell that if people wanted no violence from above, they should organize themselves without violence, to prevent a new violence being imposed by others. The only way to prevent a new violence being imposed is to organize themselves without any state! That is anarchy. But the minds of men have a predilection for slavery and therefore they accept or help in the imposition of a new state after the old one is destroyed. That is why they suffer more and more after every revolution. Anarchists are not responsible for chaos if it comes, but states are responsible. The anarchists are against killing or imprisoning even one man or woman. They want no killing in the name of any idea including their own and no prison for anyone. Hence they neither want wars nor civil wars and take part in the latter only as a defense measure. Or because they could not remain neutral owing to both sections in civil wars treating them as their enemies, which of course they are. They refuse to take part in any so-called "revolutionary or society government"—for them, there can be no revolutionary government or socialist government even if it calls itself "communist"! There is either revolution or government, not both—since both cannot be combined. We have already pointed out that a socialist or communist government is a contradiction in terms, and therefore the anarchists refuse even socialist and communist government as false and illusory. They are as much against the socialist and communist governments as against the capitalist ones. They consider that every government that takes the place of an older one will do worse. Will be more dictatorial or more lying and cunning and cruel and deceptive. The remedy for one state is not for another but the abolition of all states.

The anarchists argue that all states must necessarily be static, i.e., must prevent progress. All states are therefore reactionary apart from being dictatorial. The society alone can be dynamic and the states want to prevent social dynamism. Otherwise, there would be no justification for the states. It is claimed by all states that they have furthered progress. Either it is a lie, or it is true, that is in spite of their statism and reaction, because they could not prevent it. The society is continually marching forward, but the states in order to keep their power are acting as breaks upon society, till at last a new revolution becomes necessary or a break-down of the state is inevitable. There is no virtue in any state in the sense that it helps social dynamism. In proof of this, every constitution says: Thus far and no further! When a state is established, every action or development calculated to upset it becomes revolution and "treason to the people," i.e., to itself, however inevitable, justified, and necessary such actions or developments may be and are. That is because the state, which means "standing," cannot afford to be dynamic with society. It is generally supposed that laws create changes! But laws are but seals put upon facts. No law comes till the people have taken the law as it were into their own hands—for the argument of governments is that the people are not ready for it and will consider it too radical. If laws create changes in progressive direction, monarchies must have been abolished by their own laws and republics must have made socialist laws and so called socialist governments must make laws abolishing their own states. No. They prevent and, if necessary, bloodily suppress every change in the direction of progress, for if progress came their states will become unnecessary. Monarchies and republics were first established by force and bloody fights and they can be abolished only by force, unless they die of inanition, i.e., economic breakdown. They will never make republican, Socialist, or Bolshevik and anarchist progress but each will prevent the next step whatever the consequence may be. Somebody or something must pull them down before progress is possible, for progress means losing the power and means of existence for statesmen. After every so-called revolution leading to the establishment of a state, there was a reaction. Revolutionaries were "purged" by revolutions, because the purged wanted what the states could not have or give. That is the consequence of revolutions for new states, which means new reactions. The anarchists want a social revolution, not a revolution for state formation: they want the society to own all things instead of giving them to a state however radical or revolutionary it may call itself. They believe that salvation and solution are only in social ownership of all things. They not only refuse to take part in state power, but want to prevent the rise of any "political power" for any or all the groups who want to capture the state and its force. Therefore they are against all political parties, which want to capture power together or separately and therefore against all parties and partisanship. Political and state power can only be at the expense of the people, to deceive and exploit and suppress the people. For politics is parasitism. Even so-called revolutionary and communist politics. They do not claim that one state is better than another and therefore must be supported against its enemies. So far as anarchy, i.e., non-violent order is concerned, all states are equally united against it. There can be no better and worse among them so far as anarchy is concerned.

It is true that the anarchists had been requested toward the end of the Spanish civil war to send a representative into the Catalonian government and they sent one. But the representative was not willing to join in collective responsibility, for it would be against anarchist objection to all states. The anarchists were placed in the same position as the democratic and left wing parties of Spain by the civil war made by Franco, and the anarchists were as much in danger as the democrats and left wing politicians. As Franco could not be fought except with weapons, the anarchists had to take up arms and help the republican armies composed of democrats, socialists, and communists who wanted to maintain states. Otherwise, the anarchists had to give up the fight against armed Franco! Of course, the anarchist troops tried to fight as separate units of the army, which the other parties did not like, and under the name of unified command they coerced the anarchists to submit to non-anarchist command. The anarchists submitted to it owing to the common danger to all. The communists who had most influence with the republican government, and finally became masters, decimated the anarchist troops and members, as they were unwilling to submit to total centralism. In this act, they did as Franco would have liked. The anarchists practiced what is called (in India) responsive co-operation with fatal results to themselves and with the defeat of the left wing politicians also. The anarchists were decimated both by Franco in front and communists from behind. Next time they hope to be more careful and prepared.

The charge of violence against anarchists is due to several attempts made before the last war against the lives of ruling presidents and kings by those claiming to be anarchists. Nobody denies this. But terrorism is not peculiar to anarchists. It was practiced by nationalists of various countries, by the social revolutionaries of Russia and even by Nazis and monarchists who all wanted states of their own and therefore could not be expected to take lives of statesmen. In a desperate state, all parties and many groups are likely to resort to terrorism, for no other activity is allowed to them. If people are prevented from making open propaganda, they will make propaganda by action, by terrorism. But since the last war, the anarchists had opportunity to propagate their views, even though at great risk, and therefore they abandoned terrorism. Most of the terrorists were not even anarchists although called by the vile press such, and some may have mistakenly taken themselves to be anarchists. All that does not prove that anarchism thrives by terrorism and terrorism is its only propaganda method. Many bandits and robbers were called by the vile press terrorists and anarchists who wanted chaos or only thought that their actions were "anarchist." The Bolsheviks who wanted a strong state also practiced bank robberies to fill party coffers. Some bank robbers might have had accidentally some anarchist acquaintances but that does not make them anarchists or all anarchists (or their bandit acquaintances) alike and the same. Moreover, some individualists who claim to be anarchists because they do not want any state may feel justified if they resorted to terrorism. But anarchists do not want terrorism either by the state or by individuals and parties, which are usually organized, and even justified by states against their opponents. Anarchism and terrorism are two different things; terrorism is prevalent among non- and anti-anarchists. States consider "the ends justify the means"—the anarchists don't. But some anarchists may be mistaken some time, which is no proof against all anarchists or anarchism.

In fact, I have met one terrorist nationalist who called himself "anarchist" taking cue from the denunciation of the police and papers. When I asked him, if he did not want any state, he protested: No, we must have a strong national state! If that is anarchism, the anarchists are not for it.

Since the object of the anarchists is the overthrow of all state, armies, police, and jails, which are possible only with the help of arms, their object is destruction of all arms and refusal to bear arms. They are absolute pacifists and humanists. Arms corrupt and blunt the mind—that is the anarchist standpoint. Hence they refuse to have any chance to use or make arms. Anarchism is the only way in which arms can be made and will be made superfluous. All other conditions of society will necessitate and facilitate making arms, and using them, for they are rulerships of a part of society over the whole made to suppress revolt. The states are with the Bolsheviks and fascists in justifying use of arms.

The anarchists want to see anarchist society established not with the help of arms and soldiers but by social solidarity. As they do not want to see a state established by themselves or others over and against the society, they cannot and do not require the use of arms. They know that those who use arms against all others will establish their rule, state, and dictatorship over all others, which they want to prevent being done in order to make anarchist society possible.

The anarchists appeal to social solidarity and social strike against all states and armies. The anarchist society can be established only by direct action on the economic field by all, or by most people. They call for strikes, boycott, civil disobedience, social strikes, or the general strike to make states impossible. The trouble is that other want only partial strikes and boycotts for partial objects or political strikes and against some state in favor of another. So long as there is no social solidarity, therefore no social strike, there will be no society and any set of armed men will be able to rule all. So long as people believe in governments, they will be victims of all governments; the people's will being paralyzed by the idea of governments. Only they will change one government after another and will be prey to all of them. The anarchists say to make a strike, even a general strike or social strike, only to change governments is suicidal. Of course, a general or even a partial strike and boycott may weaken to some extent some of the governments. They are in sympathy will all strikes because it demonstrates the will to resist, but that is not enough to abolish tyranny or exploitation. Finally the strike will subside. A total strike to abolish all states must be the final object of mankind. Otherwise, life will become worse and worse for all.

Every armed revolution will fail to emancipate mankind from thralldom, economic or political, for a worse government will take the place of a bad one, just with the help of armed men. Only society can emancipate itself from all governments and miseries. What is the use of government if there was social solidarity? The society can do all the functions, which governments have arrogated to themselves. In fact the anarchists' object is to take away the functions of governments—especially the useful functions by the society, not by themselves. If the society has to protect itself, why establish a government and ask it to protect it against malefactors? It can do it itself by delegating some to do it. Once Gandhiji said: why appeal to municipalities or governments to have the lamps lighted? A few persons can walk along and light the lamps. That is social self-help. Similarly every service can be organized by the society itself and organized under its own control. That is what anarchism and anarchists mean. The anarchists do not want rights of society surrendered to any set of rulers. That is crime against all states and state-makers. Naturally that cannot be done except in a decentralized and localized manner. States are the enemies of decentralization and local self-organization, no matter what state. That is why the anarchists are against all states, whatever the form.

The anarchists argue, since all production is based on raw materials and work, where does the state come in production or services? The society can organize itself to do all these without parasitism by the state. It can do better than the parasitic state. It can organize all social services and employ everyone. Why not? The anarchists are not against centralized planning of production but against centralized methods of distribution by delegating "authorities." The anarchists, while they are against "rule" (rulership), believe only in agreement as the solution. Localities agree what is the best method or plan of production and distribution and how best the products and services should be distributed. That will be quite enough to set about working and distribution of work, goods, and services. No complicated contracts like constitutions and its paraphernalia like oaths and elections are necessary for the essential services to be performed. All have to see what is the best for oneself under the circumstances. Contracts like constitutions can only be enforced, taking advantage of and even creating bad conditions. *Free men will never make contracts.* For the circumstances may change and one of the parties in the contract will get no benefit by improved work. Moreover contract presupposes master and slave, so that the party in need may be coerced into a disadvantageous contract. The idea of social contract leads to rulers and ruled. For there must be a third party to enforce the contract, whatever the disadvantages to one and advantages to the other party. Hence the states arise as arbiters as of necessity. If something is in one's interest, all will agree if the same advantages accrue to all. People must learn by doing, i.e., serve themselves in combination with all instead of leaving it to some delegate as "authority" and abide by his decisions, whether it will be disadvantageous or not to all. *Anarchist society is an education itself to all,* for all act and serve themselves instead of leaving responsibility to some and taking orders. It instills responsibility in everyone—for he may suffer if he is not careful and intelligent in the choice. States makes people irresponsible to themselves and others. What does it matter if others suffer, provided I am safe and the state protects me better than others? That is slave mentality. People can be bought to do anything, however odious and nefarious. Under anarchy, such things will become impossible, for each is master of his own destiny and has equal rights with all. The motto of anarchism is each for all and all for each, and an injury to one is an injury to all! That is at least what they strive for. Beyond this, there is no object.

Of course anarchists, like Marxians and capitalists, differ as to the method of achieving their objects of social welfare. In fact, economic theories of anarchism have been different and not fully developed. That is why most people could not be convinced that anarchism "would work." But that is not proof that other systems will work, although they have been maintained by force and fraud till they broke down or were overthrown. There is every certainty of other systems breaking down on account of state and parasitism. Hence anarchism can work economically.

Proudhon elaborated a theory of mutualism and a People's Bank to make people independent of the state. Later, Peter Kropotkin gave an economic basis for anarchism in his three books *Fields, Factories, and Workshops*, *Mutual Aid*, and *The Conquest of Bread*. Kropotkin was the founder of anarcho-syndicalist (trade union) economics. The anarchists believe in a liberal kind of communism, instead of the rigid Marxian state kind. The liberal communism starts with local councils, which are linked together to supply all the needs of all local communes mutually. The idea of anarchist communism is that all things wherever found and produced are common property of all local councils, although they may be locally held and managed. The local councils themselves are just the administrators of the local electors. These councils agree and arrange production and distribution of all things produced everywhere for the greatest benefit of everyone everywhere. Of course a central statistical office is required and a central technical planning council to advise how best and where to produce what is required by all as of necessity and as desired. The highest possible benefit and production should be achieved for and by all. The local councils will take the proportionate share according to populations who contribute work, i.e., go to work and distribute as the local electors determine. It is all done as a matter of agreement, not by decree or laws. Such an agreement can be achieved locally according to the technical possibilities of production and distribution. Of course all this has not been attempted anywhere and not even definitely discussed and settled. That is the drawback of anarchist thought till now. But one thing is certain, that when all other systems are wrong and therefore not workable, the opposite of them all must be right and possible to work, that is anarchism, especially anarchic (social) communism. State communism is not socialism, even according to Marx, Lenin, and Stalin. It is claimed only as a "transition stage." Communism is possible only when the State of the Bolsheviks "withers away." That is Lenin's theory. *That means communism is beyond state, not earlier.* That is, after the state withers away or is abolished. State and capitalism cannot be separated. If capitalism is bad and unworkable, the anarchism and communism alone can be right and workable, and good. That is the logic, not saying that it is both capitalist and socialist and communist. Shutting eyes to logic will not straighten things, will not make the impossible work.

Not that anarchism is not workable but that men do not want anarchism since they want states. If capitalism and Bolshevism are bad, then the enemy of both—anarchism—must be workable, good, and desirable. Then they say shutting their eyes and mind, Bolshevism is only a passing stage and some day communism will come. That is shutting one's eyes and mind against "solution"! Either we wait for solution or we make the solution! The one is fatalism and the other free will. Anarchists believe in conscious acting in favor of what is inevitable. They have no transition stage—except social strike and social solidarity against states—as offered by capitalists and Bolsheviks. But people seem to want a state as a transition or bridge and to wait, and suffer! That is not the fault of the anarchists. They do not intend to rule by violence and therefore do not want to capture but smash political power and power seekers. They want power only to the total society. The anarchist ethics is: instead of ruling men, men should administer things. But that cannot be done with the help of any state, for all states are bound to be parasitic. People want to help parasitism, submit to it instead of overthrowing it; only they want change of parasitism called revolutions. But no revolution will succeed till all acquire bread, room, and clothing. The revolutionary governments only supply these to those who serve them to maintain their power, taking advantage of the necessities of life. That will produce parasitic states. If the people took hold of the necessaries of life (expropriated) and made use of them for all, instead of letting the revolutionaries take and monopolize them (confiscate) and distribute them according to their desire to get supporters for their state, then production without parasitism can proceed. Until that is done there can be no emancipation of man from the tyranny of states. Hence the anarchists call upon workers to expropriate the works and use them for the benefit of all. The bread problem is the first revolutionary problem, both for the anarchists and the state-makers. Without this—i.e., without social solidarity to prevent bread from going into the hands of state-makers, there will be either chaos or states. There can be no political action—*either* politics *or* action! Action is only in economics.

Consistently with their anti-state and anti-authoritarian attitude, the anarchists (who call themselves also libertarian or free socialists) stand against politics and political parties, making propaganda against parliaments and elections to that centralist authoritarian body. Their theory is, according to Michel Bakunin, once a noble of Russia who helped formulate anarchist principles, that "Politics is the theology of the State" (in his *God and the State*). Politics and political parties dissipate and divert mental and other activities away from the main issue, which is economic well-being.

They want to set up and capture "political power" in the state as an essential condition of economic well-being of the people. But the means become the objects so that the state well-being becomes the first and last consideration of politicians and statesmen to the neglect of economic well-being. Therefore the anarchists warn the people against becoming involved in politics, state form, and political parties against their own interests. Economic betterment can only be brought about by direct action on the economic field by the peoples themselves, not by voting for any or all parties who want to have a say or power in the state. The general or social strike must pave the way for social (economic) revolution with the object of an anarchist society being established. Only then will there be freedom, democracy, and socialism. All the rest is illusion and dissipation of energies in trying to realize a chimera. There is going to be *either a state or socialism* and not both. A socialist state is a myth! The people alone can emancipate themselves, not through any politicians, state, or statesmen. *Office corrupts men.* Especially under centralism and authoritarianism. The problem of abolishing tyranny, corruption, and deception is not so simple as authoritarian statesmen and politicians suggest. "*State is source of crime and corruption*," Aristide Briand said in the Chamber of Deputies, of course before he became a statesman, premier, and patriot.[2] It is no use establishing a state, any state, and then complaining against evils, tyranny, corruption, and deception: the anarchists are realists, matter-of-fact, and therefore refuse to have anything to do with political parties and states and their machinations—except of course to combat them. They refuse military service and propagate against bearing arms. (A broken rifle is their symbol). They are unconditionally for every rebellion against states, whatever state it may be. But they do not support the objects of a revolution if it is to establish a new state in place of the old. States make people irresponsible, for they take away the rights of people (freedom) to manage their own affairs. They become

2. Aristide Briand (1862–1932) served as Prime Minister of France eleven times between 1909 and 1929.

mercenaries of the state, doing whatever is ordered and paid for. To make the people responsible to themselves for their own well-being, they must be made to act for themselves. Nobody can serve the interests of another as oneself. But he must have an opportunity for serving himself and that can only be done in an anarchist society: where he can create his own well-being with the well-being of all. Society must be dynamic. Hence no states.

The organs of the anarchists are their anarcho-syndicalist (free, libertarian, or anti-authoritarian) trade unions, which are also organized on a decentralized plan—for the overthrow and prevention of states. They are organized for eventual social or general strike, which should lead to the anarchist social revolution. These anarcho-syndicalist unions are stronger in Central and South American countries than in more advanced ones, except perhaps in Sweden and U.S.A., and especially among seamen. In England there never was and is not any anarcho-syndicalist organization, although there were anarchist propagandist centers. In France, once all trade unions were more or less anarcho-syndicalist; in fact, it was the mother of syndicalist trade unions. In Italy, before Mussolini's ascension to power, the most powerful trade unions were the anarcho-syndicalist unions with their large co-operative societies. In Germany, there was a growing syndicalist movement and intellectually anarchism was preached by Germans even in Kaiser's time (they called themselves, appropriately, Localists); till Hitler came to power, the anarcho-syndicalist trade union international headquarters was in Berlin, the first world congress of that organization having founded there in December 1922 as against the Third International. Later on it was transferred to Barcelona, as the biggest anarcho-syndicalist trade unions (with over 2 million members) were in Spain and the Catalan Republic was more favorable to the anarchists and anarcho-syndicalists. As in Russia so in Spain, Marxism was a superimposed organization, i.e., not native to those countries.

The First International founded by Karl Marx and later joined by M. Bakunin till its end in 1872 (with Bakunin's death) *defined socialism as the abolition of the wage system.*[3] For wage system is the means of exploitation upon which all states, however radical or communist, are based. The wage system is the cause of division in society as classes: the employing class and the employed. The state as employer is also a wage-system and an exploiting and oppressive system. It is authoritarian and corrupt. Hence the anarchists stick to the definition of socialism given by the First International, which was called the "International Workingmen's Association," which is also the name of the anarcho-syndicalist international. The anarchist principle of distribution is: to each according to his necessities and from each according to his abilities. Equality does not mean equal wages or comforts for all, but equality of treatment for people under the same conditions: as for example when one is ill or invalid. For example when milk is scarce, equality does not mean equal distribution of milk for all, able, invalid, or ill, or infant, but supply for and to the invalid, ill, and infant.

The anarchists do not believe that one is mentally proletarian by birth or one is mentally capitalist by birth. For there are many capitalists who are and will be for social revolution even in the anarchist sense, while many proletarians are and will be capitalist or petty bourgeois and Marxian by mentality. If therefore the capitalists are expropriated by society, it would be wrong to ill-treat them for their being formerly capitalists: once expropriated, they are practically proletarians and must be treated as such till they become dangerous to the social order. The anarchists do not believe in punishment but only watchfulness and molding social surroundings. Mind cannot work outside social surroundings.

There are religious anarchists and communists like Tolstoyans and Doukhobors (both Russian) who also stand against private ownership, state, and arms-bearing and want to return to primitive Christianity. The anarchists who are atheists have nothing against them, provided in secular matters they do not bring in religion. Religion is a private affair as much as atheism. If sometimes, as in Spain, anarchists converted convents into anarchist universities

---

3. Bakunin died in 1876 not 1872, as Acharya claims.

where atheism is taught, it is not because they were against religion or Christianity but against the Church, which was corrupt, tyrannical, and fanatical against all else, especially in Spain. The Church stood on the side of Franco!

It may be mentioned that anarchist books by Kropotkin were translated into Japanese and Chinese long before the last war and some of the Japanese scientists were anarchist propagandists and were executed by the Imperial government as early as 1908. Only in other Asiatic countries, anarchism was not known till now. Some of Kropotkin's works were translated into Gujarati and published by the Navjivan Press about twenty years ago, but nobody seems to have studied them as anarchist texts. It appears Kropotkin's *Fields, Factories and Workshops* was published in Hindi by B. S. Pathik some time after the last war.

An *Anarchist Encyclopedia* was published in four volumes in France in Paris before the last war, edited by Sébastien Faure. The works of Bakunin in six volumes in French have not been translated into English till now, except his "God and the State." The first anarchist publications in India will be *Socialism and the State* and *Anarcho-Syndicalism* by R. Rocker in English first, then in other languages of India, published by the Indian Institute of Sociology, Bombay. A Marathi and a Gujarati edition of *What is Mutualism?* by Swartz have appeared from the same Institute.[4]

Whither India?: Socio-Politico Analyses, ed. by Iqbal Singh and Raja Rao (Baroda: Padmaja Publications, 1948), 117–140.

---

4. Clarence Lee Swartz, *What is Mutualism* (1927).

36. A Libertarian Voice from India

M. P. T. Acharya

M. P. T. ACHARYA, FROM BOMBAY, India, writes to us. He is a high expositor of libertarian ideals. "Don Nadie," pseudonym of a comrade based in the United States, has translated some texts from English to Spanish for publication. We cannot publish them in full in *Inquietud*, since it only contains brief articles. Consequently, we will be satisfied with publishing the most salient and substantial paragraphs. We publish in this issue a commentary on the representative of the Government of India's performance at the United Nations Assembly. And, in the next issue, we will publish the essentials of an interesting work by Acharya on a basic anti-statist issue.

"Don't Run So Fast, Mrs. Pandit"

Mrs. Pandit is a representative of the Government of India at the United Nations Assembly.[1] She is well educated in diplomatic ways. She affirms what she does not believe, like all her colleagues. In a session at the United Nations, she said: "We are for Peace. We will devote all our resources and energies to the abolition of every cause of War."

Did Mrs. Pandit mean that the Government of India, which she represents, is ready to lay down the principle of the abolition of all governments, which are the real obstacles to the existence of peace?

---

1. Vijaya Lakshmi Pandit (1900–1990) was an Indian diplomat and politician, sister of Jawaharlal Nehru, and headed the Indian delegation to the UN Assembly.

In truth, we believe that no representative of any government can say this publicly, because they do not believe so. Governments are the greatest obstacle to peace and harmony among peoples, and when they talk a lot about peace it is because they are starting to mobilize the causes of war and want to hide their cunning maneuvers.

The good Lady of V. Pandit, after such radical affirmations for peace, did not even challenge the right of veto, of the three great governments, so much defended by the Soviet state. And that deliberate omission of the representative of the Indian government will serve the policy of Communism well, but it will not benefit the cause of peace at all.

If we wish, Mrs. Pandit, to suppress the causes of war, we must sacrifice the social class system, reduce the misery of the masses, and eventually abolish money, business, and the state.

But this is not the work of governments, but the work of peoples. No government will act against itself, stopping in its tracks, and removing itself from its dominant role in society.

The statesmen and diplomats are the most eloquent propagandists of peace, while they covertly act toward war. Consequently, to the misfortune of humanity, governments will not favor peace, whether in India, or elsewhere.

"Voz Libertaria en la India," *Inquietud*, 2:42
(April, 1948), 1.

37. Libertarian Thought in India: Why the Food Problem Cannot Be Solved

M. P. T. Acharya

THE FOOD PROBLEM HAS NO solution. No government can act as a direct distributor, without profit and with equity, for the benefit of the people. The high command of the Indian National Congress believes they can do what European governments do not even dare to attempt, based on their self-belief that they are honest and even "holy." But sanctity and honesty are not enough when the system does not allow for economic miracles. In addition, a government functions to make men sick, and holiness and honesty disappear, leaving no trace.

The Indian National Congress plays politics with the promise of equal distribution of food to the children of the people. They promise what they can never, ever, do. It is true that they gained adherents by ensuring that they would set high wages for the producers, but at the same time also offered large dividends to the capitalists. It is perfectly clear that they will not be able to benefit workers and employers at the same time. No government has eradicated the misery of the workers' lives. Not even the Communist government in Russia was able to guarantee salaries and wages large enough for the workers to survive. Also, in government hands, the system of making immovable, by law and decree, prices and wages fails. It is well known that the Roman emperor Diocletian dictated that prices and wages should remain fixed throughout the Empire. The results were negative, despite his imperial authority. Prices rose and wages fell, day after day. The statesmen, the politicians, and the economists do not learn anything from history. They believe themselves capable of accomplishing the impossible.

It is useless to make promises within the existing economic order. As long as the people do not control the direct distribution of the products they create with their work, the system of wages and prices that the rulers run will continue to kill millions of people by starvation. The urgent needs of the people are not satisfied with promises. The identity of government and people is a myth.

The state is nourished at the expense of the people and is a factor of hunger and slavery even if directed by "saints." No one avoids the influence of the power they exert, and they all become tyrants on their reigning thrones.

Government and people cannot harmoniously coexist in terms of freedom, fraternity, and justice. There can be no "non-violent" government, as the people of India believe. Governments do not produce wealth, they consume it. Consequently they create a permanent violent conflict, because they are sustained at the expense of the producers. "Holiness" and government cannot live together, ever. Even the "saints," once seated in the governmental high seats, will lose their "sanctity," as history teaches us; and what was impossible throughout time elsewhere is not going to happen in India now.

What will happen to the government of the Indian National Congress is more or less the same that happened under the rule of the English. The "saints" of Congress will adopt the "slogan" of all other governments: "law and order, first and foremost." Those who complain, who protest, because hunger inhumanely decimates the people, will be repressed and violently punished. And those men who went to British jails for disobedience will go to the prisons of Congress, for the same reasons.

"El Pensamiento Libertario en la India," *Inquietud*,
2:43 (May, 1948), 3; reprinted in *Tierra y Libertad*,
5:91 (September, 1948), 3.

38. Money & Moral Values

M. P. T. Acharya

An examination of the Gandhian economic theory of replacing the factory system by a return to handicraft with an introduction of "moral values" into the money system.

Gandhians (like Dr. J. C. Kumarappa), socialists, communists, capitalists, and governments of every variety may say that production is what will solve the consuming problem.[1] As if production has anything to do with the system under which consuming is "arranged." Whether it is the state—of whatever form—that produces (states never produce but may organize production!), whether individual or group (company) capitalists produce, whether the socialist or communist parties think that they can produce and distribute, consumption is a thing that they cannot arrange.

Varieties of Nonsense

All these groups, ideologies, parties, or organizations accept certain measures of organizing production as necessary. In fact, they all have something in common. On that point they do not want to change anything. The state, individual, or group capitalists, or socialist, and communists parties, as well as Gandhians want production to be carried on as now by buying things required for production and paying

---

1. J. C. Kumarappa (1892–1960) was a close associate of Gandhi, and developed rural economic theories based on Gandhism.

for labor in the same manner as now. But if they produce whatever they can, the people who have to pay all the expenses and organization (offices and government), cannot pay for them, for they will not have received the amount of money that they are required to pay to maintain the offices or government, and even for the material required for production, for they earn only salaries and wages. The prices being labor costs, material costs, and organization charges, those who received salaries and wages cannot pay for all these and therefore cannot buy up the goods at prices that will include all these expenses. For we know that handwork cannot be purchased by those who produce it. The same applies to machine goods. It is only when those outside production buy up the goods that expenses can be met. For wages and salaries are only parts of the prices and the total expenses cannot be recovered out of wages and salaries. But all these so-called economists think that the part can pay for the whole, *an absurdity that is common to all*. It is with this absurdity that they are all approaching the so-called economic problem. It can be said safely that they will not solve the problem of distribution and consumption whatever and however much they may produce, even however little they may produce. For distribution cannot take place at all on this production basis, for before the distribution can take place the producers and their organization must be paid their full price. These so-called producers control production for their own benefit and cannot permit of any other result. So it is a waste of time and energy because it is talking in the air, without consideration of the conditions. And this neglect of conditions, fundamental conditions, is common to all of them. The whole civilization and mankind may go down, but there can be no distribution and consumption under these conditions, which they have all accepted and want to maintain. But they have platform and paper and can shout without thinking in the least. They are even able to live for shouting or by shouting like that. No other voice can be raised or heard in the midst of their din, which is called "economics." They are all trying to square the circle and they promise they can do so. They quarrel only on non-essentials and drag others who are starving into their quarrels.

Recently, Dr. J. C. Kumarappa, the great exponent of Gandhian economics said that "Gandhism is aimed at eschewing violence and dishonesty from daily life and at making people self-sufficient in regard to the primary needs." Dr. Kumarappa explained "the present day money economy made them lose sight of the real value of things as distinguished from their commercial value. Money was not a safe way of valuing articles."

Moral Value of Goods

He said that Mahatma's self-sufficiency program founded upon moral values would, if implemented, raise the moral consciousness and lower money considerations and material values. Now, we must ask, apart from questioning moral values and raising moral consciousness, whether Dr. Kumarappa wants no money to be used in the production process? No, he does not say so definitely. He simply wants to *lower* money considerations. Does he mean that whatever may be the money price of goods, he would let those in need have the goods? That he does not say either. In fact, goods are not material value but moral value! Does he mean goods are not to be produced for material needs and satisfaction but only for the moral value and satisfaction obtained in producing them? That would mean "production for production's sake." I suppose, Dr. Kumarappa does not mean to go on piling up goods without distribution just for the sake of moral values contained in them. Even an absurd man cannot say that. Surely he would want to distribute the goods. How will he do it? Just give it away! That would be nice. But then the goods will have no money value but only use value. Is it what Dr. Kumarappa wants? But since he does not say so, we must have a clear answer from him. All right, supposing for the moment that Dr. Kumarappa wants goods to be produced for use and not for sale—shall all, whether those who live only by preaching something for production, get the goods alike—free? Then there would be no difference between producers and parasites. Is that moral consciousness? That also would require elucidation from Dr. Kumarappa.

No Money but Payment

How would Dr. Kumarappa organize producing goods? He would not simply confiscate the materials and equipment needed for producing goods. Does he want only labor to be confiscated? Make work compulsory without any payment? I do not suppose so. Therefore, Dr. Kumarappa, supposing he organizes production and not merely preach about the moral beauties of production, will pay some kind of money for raw materials and equipment, land, houses, and transport, and also some wages to those who work and organize production. Or can he do this without any of these requirements? Those who sell raw materials must also live and therefore must earn, and so Dr. Kumarappa must pay more than what the raw materials cost them to produce, must pay them profits. Those who supply equipment must also live, must earn more than they paid for them and have profits. Dr. Kumarappa will not deny them these. Then he will either have to purchase or rent house and land or he must buy them outright without loss to their owners and even with some profit or he must pay rent continually. All these must be paid in some kind of money. Then he will have to pay the technicians, employees, and laborers with some money at least. Thus there will be money payment throughout. Having put in the money, he cannot distribute the products without consideration of any money. Rather he will have to recover the whole cost or expense during the distribution—with something to pay himself. Now, the total cost of all the goods produced will amount to X-money and this must be recovered with something more than X. Otherwise, Dr. Kumarappa cannot buy anything and must go without food. Unless someone makes charity out of their earnings to feed, clothe, and house him and provide for all other necessaries out of their portion of earnings.

Distinction Without Difference

In the organization of production, there are those who directly produce and those who do necessary work for production and distribution, e.g., technicians, organizers, and employees. All these must pay the total cost of the goods produced. The total costs include the price of raw materials, equipment, land, houses, transport, and all office charges, such as stationery. But these men have received only their wages and salaries. How can the whole products be bought up by them, especially as they work only in one branch of production, say handloom, and with their wages, they have to buy also other necessaries produced by other branches, where others get paid in the same way and whose payments must also be recovered by the other branches with all expenses on materials, equipment, houses, lands, and transport, as well as technicians, organizers, and employees, and producers? Dr. Kumarappa and other economist theorists suppose it is being done and therefore can be done. If that *were* being done, there would be no overproduction and reduced consumption in any part of the world, i.e., consumption and employment, crisis.

Wages and Profits of Handiwork

Dr. Kumarappa's hand production must also recover all the costs just as factories have to recover all the costs, whether factories produce plenty in a short time and handlooms produce small quantities in a long period or not. Having put money into the production, the total money has to be recovered both by handloom and factory production. So fundamentally, there is not much difference between the economics of handwork and machine work. For both, goods are money, whether the buyers are few or many. Economically, both are money economics. Dr. Kumarappa attributing moral consciousness to handloom production does not change facts.

Words Without Things

Not to get out of the difficulty, Dr. Kumarappa argues that "money economy based on centralized industries had encroached on the primary requirements of the people, made them starve, and brought about ill-health. The present food scarcity is in no small measure due to such encroachment." Now, words can be jumbled up anyway without relation to things. But Kumarappa's money can be no more moral than the factory owner's money. Both will have to make the buyers pay all the expenses, whether the buyers are few or many and every production unit will have to make the buyers pay all its expenses.

Gandhian economics can no more be magic than factory economics—both will sell less than they produce in the normal course of things or must sell at higher prices in order to make both ends meet. Otherwise they cannot recover the costs. These relations are not changed by hand or machine or more or less production. The problem remains the same for both. And it cannot be resolved within the limits of the problem. Unless the limits, i.e., the conditions, are broken, the problem will remain unsolved. Unless you can get the help of God to make the impossible work in arithmetic. Dr. Kumarappa may call God to his help. But God may not agree to help him. It is curious how a man who had American education in economics could talk as he does. I suppose in India arithmetic can be set at naught with Gandhiji's help.

Part Must Pay the Whole

The only way the total costs can be recovered after producing by hand or machine is by selling a part—a great part of the products— to persons who have not earned by contributing useful work in the production of the goods. They must belong to those who do not form part of the production of the goods. They alone can contribute toward filling the deficit. They must be outsiders in the case of industry (factory industry), there must be foreign buyers or those who can earn by parasitism at home. It is also true that those who buy Khaddar are not those who produce it, but those who earn by other means, for Khaddar is too dear for its producers, owing to the long time it takes to produce it.[2] So it will be with every other handwork.

---

2. Khaddar (or Kaddar) is an Indian homespun cotton cloth.

Don't Eat but Produce

Dr. Kumarappa thinks centralized factory production is responsible for penury. But the fact is the money and payment system, which makes prices far higher than the real costs whether production is carried on by hand or machine, puts goods out of reach of producers who work for wages. If there were no mills producing cloth, most people would to go naked, for the Khaddar cloth is too dear for the wage-earner, even for Khaddar wage-earners. The mills exploit this situation and make money. The cheaper the goods, the more people can afford to buy them. That can only be done by machinery, although the poor who buy have to pay far higher prices than it cost to produce by machinery. Thus the poor are exploited by machinery, but still they have been able to buy something which handwork could not supply. Even in the U.S.A. where workers earn far more, durable goods cannot be bought by workers, for their prices are beyond their reach. Hence much business is done there with spurious goods. For example, linen shirtfronts and collars are expensive. And they cost a lot to keep laundered. So many firms supply substitutes that are far cheaper and that could be bought at any time. For example, paper shirtfronts and collars, which look like linen. These do not require to be laundered and can be thrown away when they become dirty. Wage and salary earners cannot afford to buy durable goods anywhere. Hence a whole industry supplies these people only and makes huge profits out of them. So long as there is demand, real or artificial, people will try to buy and therefore there will be firms, which will make such goods as they can buy. Mr. Kumarappa would rather that people went naked in the cold than buy mill cloth. That is called economics, Gandhian and moral. Mr. Kumarappa can afford to buy Khaddar or is supplied free but others not.

Choice Between Immoralities

So long as money, prices, and wages obtain, those who want to get money will manufacture anything that will sell, and the people have a choice only between buying spurious, harmful, or useless goods and not buying at all. Some things, good things, they cannot buy at all. So long as the wage system—which means *lease of existence from hour to hour*—continues they cannot afford to buy what they want, for their wages limit their choice and prevents them from buying even the most necessary things. Does Kumarappa try to abolish the wage system? No, his economics like capitalist and factory and state economy requires the wage-system, although the system will prevent even the little quantity of goods produced from being sold. In the wage system, it is not the quantity of goods, which is decisive, but the ability to recover all the money put into production from the sale of a part of the goods produced. Producers cannot purchase all the goods and they can only be employed when *non-producers* buy them. Of course, those who engage others to produce are alone considered producers, the actual producers being considered "workers." Mr. Kumarappa's Gandhian handwork economy does not also intend to abolish "workers," i.e., those who are hired for wages by others, be it a "society." Only hunger can drive people to be "workers" for they will not benefit by this "technical arrangement" in production. They cannot be interested in production, because the benefits are all in favor of non-producers. Mr. Kumarappa should start abolishing this "technical arrangement" in production—abolishing the wage, payment, price, and selling system, before he can make production and consumption normal. We quite agree that others continue or want to start immoral production, but that does not make the Gandhian method of production less immoral. For it is based on the same system though with handwork in place of millwork. It is also a wage system. The wage will stop production because it cannot sell all the goods, whether the goods are produced by hand or by machine. It cannot be worked, even by irresponsible Bolsheviks and socialists, because they pay for the goods, have to sell them, and recover the expenses—and *pay themselves*.

Freedom: Anarchist Fortnightly, 9:27 (December 24, 1948 & January 7, 1949), 4, 4. Originally published in *Kaiser-i-Hind* (November 24 & 30, 1948).

39. Life of the Workers in India

M. P. T. Acharya

Continuing our series of studies on the economic and social situation in various foreign countries, we are now entering India. This is an example which is full of meaning for men struggling in so-called "colonial" or "backward" countries. Having been recently officially "liberated" from British imperialism, India turned to excessive industrialization and statehood. What fate is left for the worker in the new state? This is what our correspondent M. P. T. Acharya describes in a long letter from Bombay, from which we extract and translate the main passages below.

There is no anarchist movement in India—only for the last two years a propaganda group. Hitherto, as a result of the British control of India, all parties and groups considered that social issues could only be resolved after the departure of the foreign imperialists. Now that this is done, social issues are emerging, first and foremost the problem of landowners and industrialists. Unfortunately, all parties play politics and think they can solve problems by (state) political methods.

At the present time, there are eight parties in India that claim to be "socialists," and which call for state control over industry. They start where trade unionism started during the past century. Most of these parties are Marxist or close to Marxism. The Congress and the so-called socialists want—they say—to arrive at "socialism" by Gandhian methods, and methods that appeal to the state. But the state is now in the hands of industrialists given that the state pushes for the industrialization of the country. The capitalists declare that they are unwilling to make investments for the good of the state, and the state is obliged to make concessions to the industrialists at the expense of the workers and the consumers. The Indian government and industry are appealing to foreign capitalists, especially to the Americans, whereas up to now the nationalists have been against any intervention by foreign capital.

Trade Union Rivalries

The unions actively fight for a monopoly. The anti-Bolshevik groups now desert the old All-India Trade Union Congress (AITUC), which was practically neutral until recently, and the others are in the hands of the reds. At first the government organized a so-called All India National TUC and seized a number of unions. This was relatively easy by promising the recognition of these unions and their protection by the government. Thus, in the beginning, the Bombay Labor Minister, Mr. Nanda, was the union's general secretary.[1] It was he who pushed for the formation of new unions. Meanwhile, the Socialist Party of India began to organize several unions under its control. Last year in Bombay, the Party organized a one-day strike, which was also attended by the Red Unions and even the National Trade Union, although the Socialist Party is against these two unions. Some time ago, the Socialists asked all independent unions to form an organization against communist-controlled unions and the government. All gathered on non-political bases, but some unions controlled by the Revolutionary Communist Party (Trotskyist) refused to participate, arguing that the new federation would be under the control of the Socialist Party. As a result, they formed a separate organization. Thus union efforts led to four groups of unions.

The law allows only one union per plant, the one with the most members. Last year, the government enacted laws to make strikes difficult. Negotiations, conciliations, and arbitrations must

---

1. Gulzarilal Nanda (1898–1998) served as Labor Minister of the Bombay Government (1946–1950), and interim Prime Minister for thirteen days after Jawaharlal Nehru died in 1964.

necessarily take place before a strike can be declared. Despite this, strikes are frequent. The government declares them illegal and imprisons some union leaders and some workers. Sometimes, even before strike action begins, the government stops union leaders who are suspected of sympathizing with strike action. Through numerous emergency laws, a man can be arrested and detained without trial; and even when the courts release a defendant, the defendant may be arrested again and kept in prison on an administrative basis (stating that he has a "dangerous character," for example). Recently some provinces have enacted laws allowing the authorities to also crack down on any person (friend, parent) complicit with a "dangerous character." No one—no wife, no husband—can give asylum or assistance to a "dangerous character," and to do so is to risk being imprisoned in turn. On the other hand, the government can declare any work essential work, in which case a strike becomes illegal in the corresponding sector.

The Workers' Reaction

Fortunately, Indian workers do not know how to read, do not know the intricacies of the law, and they go on strike for a yes or a no; to protest against the dismissal of a worker or a foreman who acted rudely. In one factory, they went on strike because a worker had been transferred from one shop to another. These men are not easy to handle and the union leaders themselves do not succeed. One manages to deceive them momentarily, but in general they quickly discover that they are mystified.

In Europe, workers are influenced by written propaganda from a party or the trade union bureaucracy. It is not so here. People do not have the patience to read a whole page when they already know. What forces them to go to work is famine prevailing at home. The economic situation of the workers is bad (because of high prices and low wages), so anyone can ask them to go on strike. The teachers themselves went on strike in entire provinces. Their students joined them. As a result, the police beat them when they marched in protest.

Last February, 40,000 teachers resigned from one province. All this under a national government. In the old days, workers could think that misery was the fault of a foreign government. But at present the economic conditions are worse than before, and the government, which spends huge sums of money on the army, bureaucracy, and in various ways, claims that it cannot pay the workers any more. Also, these are all prey for communism and fascism. The Communists push for demands—although, if they were in power, they would not treat the unhappy workers any better than the current leaders.

Political Parties

Communist leaders stay in hiding, but they are arrested in large numbers. Besides, the government indistinctly treats any person who dares to make any criticism as communist. It stops others as pro-fascist Hindus. It stops both Muslim troublemakers and communists or anti-Hindu Muslims. It is sad to note that it is precisely a government that claims to be faithful to Gandhi's principles of truth and non-violence that does so.

No syndicalist newspaper in India accepts that I write about the situation as I understand it, because all are propaganda journals, and they do not allow one to rise against the system of wage labor and against the state—they are two Siamese brothers—because all want to integrate into the system. One of my articles was published by a Trotskyist weekly, but this journal was suppressed shortly afterward and the officials expelled. The latter also attacked the communists, the government, and the capitalists. Here the Trotskyites march with the nationalists against the Communists—because they know what to expect if one day the communists come to power. The Trotskyite group known as the Marxist-Leninist Bolshevik Party recently merged with the Socialists of the British Labour Party tendency.

"La Vie des Travailleurs aux Indes," *Etudes Anarchistes*, 5 (December, 1949), 3–4.

10. Voice of India

M. P. T. Acharya

World Pacifist Conference

It is strange that a pacifist conference should be held behind closed doors, as if pacifism was a conspiracy or a *coup d'état*. Journalists themselves were not admitted, and press releases were only given in short sentences like governments do it.

The assembled pacifists were individualist conscientious objectors, ignoring mass pacifism and antimilitarism. They refrained from asking the people to refuse to bear arms and to refuse, on a large scale, to go to war. Why would they prevent governments from sending men to war since they are themselves loyal to governments? That is why this pacifism is worthless, since it affects only a few individuals who are refractory due to personal or religious convictions.

The question of trade was discussed. The pacifists at the conference declared themselves against its "regimentation." But can it be admitted that commerce can work without exploitation if profit is retained and if exploitation and profit are not abolished? Profit and exploitation, whether for the benefit of the state or individuals, make it impossible for most people to be pacifists!

The president of this world pacifist conference—whose speech I enclose—Dr. Rajendra Prasad, is an old friend and collaborator of Gandhi. He is still president of the War Resisters' International. He became minister when Indians took control of the affairs of the country. He then resigned, presided over the ruling Congress party, and then the Constituent Assembly. In a month he will probably be president of the so-called "Indian Republic"![1]

In its December 25, 1949 issue, the newspaper *The People* (Delhi) asked if Dr. Rajendra Prasad can still be called, and indeed call himself, a war-resister and a pacifist when as President of the Indian Republic he will be called upon to command the armed forces in chief. He will have to sign a declaration of war if the country were to be attacked. He will have to make sanctions, and will have to justify shootings and hangings, to continue them "efficiently," that is to say without pity, in the case of a rebellion or a war, because trade, the state, and property—private or state—must be protected and defended!

While one of the old and better Gandhists went to the war camp, all the Gandhists now support the national state of India, although the latter can only be the supplier of cannon fodder for the benefit of foreign governments. What can the Indian army do, when it absorbs, meanwhile, 60% of the nation's revenue in collaboration with the police forces, who are always willing to tame the people.

If there were no conscription in India, there would be hundreds of millions of people who would not be fed, armed, or dressed for battle. In many areas, university students are forcibly subjected to military training. There is a corps of men and women for internal security, not to mention a women's police, and a territorial army. Men who declare themselves to be "Gandhists," and who praise Gandhi because he allowed them to seize power, have created all these formations. These Gandhists have completely abandoned the pacifist camp and are organizing vast forces to oppress and dominate the people in subordination and misery for the benefit of an increasingly strong state. The new constitution, under the pretense of "rights to independence," takes away civil liberties, and is worse than the previous British imperialist constitution.

---

1. Rajendra Prasad (1884–1963) served as the first President of India (January 1950–May 1962).

Dr. Rajendra Prasad made a point of absolving himself by asking foreign delegates not to judge severely what was done against the Gandhist principles, because Gandhi is no longer there to guide them, and because Indians are pacifists at heart. The same can be said of all people, because they are not the ones who organize the killings but the governments.

Under the allegation that our weakness is the cause of all that we suffer in this country, and that if Gandhi was still alive he would have shown us a way we could dispense with an army, he provides an excuse for what he and his government are doing right now. If Gandhi was still alive and he advocated dissolving the army, these followers would have declared him mad and probably thrown him into prison as dangerous.

The fact that he was murdered is probably a great chance for him, as it prevents him from being disowned by his own supporters, who are already establishing a hidden fascism in India.

(Special correspondent for *N.P.* in India)

"Voix de l'Inde," *Les Nouvelles Pacifistes*, 2:7
(March 1, 1950), 3.

11. The End of an Era: Echoes of Free India

M. P. T. Acharya

THE MINISTERS OF INDIA, like those in the rest of the world, say daily that they will raise the standard of living of the masses by increasing production. Easier said than done. The hungry masses will be forced to produce more, but from there to raise the standard of living and consumption is a vain dream. The truth is that they do not produce for consumption, but to enrich the owner. The fundamental basis of bourgeois—or state—economy is not to increase consumption, but profits. People are employed for the purpose of making a profit, and it needs to be exacted from the current day laborers first. The future day laborers do not make profits to the owner, since they have to be employees and receive salaries first. If more day laborers are to be employed, those who are already working must provide the profits that will create the new jobs. Those to be employed do not make a profit yet.

Invest to Win

Production—including Bolshevik or Gandhian production—is based on investment. When one invests money, it is with the object and certainty of making a profit. Capitalists do not invest money based on mere calculations, but only when they are certain to make a profit. The number of day laborers—those who earn their living in the factories—is very small and cannot bring enough profits to start new investments. Those who can pay the profits of manufactured goods are—with the exception of textiles, matches, and sugar—those who pay taxes, and these do not exceed four million in India. It is not enough to create new industries or to raise the standard of living or the purchasing power of the lower class. For industry requires the purchasing power of those who already have purchasing power and who can pay the profits. Talking about increasing the purchasing power of the majority through industry is an idiocy or mockery of people.

Native and Foreign Capital Will not Improve the Situation

Our government tries to induce the capitalists of India and abroad to invest their capital here, offering all kinds of attractions. But the traders—manufacturers, stockists, or bankers—have a mind of their own. These traders invest in insurance and do not risk their capital in companies that do not offer the security of large profits. Although Pandit Nehru offers investors ample freedom of action, they are not determined to invest their capital because they do not see the certainty of making a profit. The population that has purchasing power in India is very small, and investors could only exploit the material resources—natural and human—if they had markets abroad. They will not be able to invest their capital without a guarantee from the government, and if it were granted, they would present high bills as losses, and not having produced anything, the government would have to pay those bills without obtaining any benefit.

What is Produced for Profits is not for Consumption

Even if the government offered to pay for the losses, the industrialists would not venture their capital here, for the government could not repay the losses, because it was already in debt. They do not need to manufacture anything, since the government has to pay for the losses anyway.

Whether they invest local or foreign capital, it will be impossible to raise the standard of living of the masses, since investment would be done with the exclusive purpose of making money and not giving it away. It's about getting more money out of the business than you put in. Therefore, the opposite being impossible, it would be foolish to invest money.

Our bosses, and even the economists and Gandhians, believe that we produce for distribution and consumption—despite the investment. But the greater the investment, the greater the gain. Producing goods does not mean making a profit: profits are obtained from sales. If there is no possibility of sale, it will not be possible to obtain profits, and therefore the investment will not be necessary—even in the case of a Bolshevik or Gandhian state—since it is impossible to produce more than at present. Investment does not generate profits, as these are obtained by reducing consumption. That's right, even under a Bolshevik or Gandhian government. If there is no profit under the investment economy, production will not be necessary.

Production with Investment is to Reduce Consumption

Those who invest capital do not give profits to their employees (state or private) in advance for them to buy the goods. They are simply told to look for money elsewhere to obtain the goods. What each group of traders does is take the profits of those who made the money by producing for others—the same money that is then distributed to their employees by others. Gandhians, Bolsheviks, and private capitalists give the name "economic and scientific system" to this chaos. There is nothing scientific about this.

Even if you invest more, there will be less consumption, and it would be necessary to sell abroad. After they say "produce or perish," they will have to add: "Export or perish." Even in England, a heavily industrialized country, the socialist government says to people: "Tighten your belt a little more."

Raising the Standard of Living by Reducing Consumption

Our economy has to be maintained, according to these "experts," by producing more and consuming less. What do we want the production for then? They say that without raising the standard of living there will be no business. Business presupposes that there is already a high standard of living; otherwise you cannot make a profit from production, since no one can make a profit from hungry people.

Socialists and communists around the world speak the language of private capitalists. The Gandhians who preach the Sarvodaya and a society without classes are saying the same thing. However, it is already proven that investment reduces consumption and then paralyzes production altogether. And at that point we should recognize that this economic system has failed and needs to be discarded. And if this system is a fundamental failure, the logical thing is that we start a system without investment and without profits: produce to consume.

The Difference Between Two Half Dozens and a Dozen

This situation cannot be improved by harmonizing with this unjust system, as Marxists and Gandhians suggest: we have to produce for consumption. There is no middle ground: producing in accordance with needs and consumption leads us to a human economy and to goodness.

The economy, human or antihuman, has nothing to do with political machineries, because the latter operate under the economy. And no force, no matter how great, can keep an anti-human economy alive. But brute force is used for this purpose, and it is intended to show that two and two are five—by violence—it is as absurd as forcing the water of a river to run upward. And this is what the capitalists, the Gandhians, and the Marxists are trying to do.

The Past is Not Inevitable in the Future

A human economy cannot be maintained through investment and the wage system. And because it has been done in the past, it does not mean that it can be done again in the future. Economic investment requires foreign markets that do not exist. The fact is that there is a lot of money in the hands of U.S. bankers. It does not mean that all Americans are potential buyers. And that happens in all countries where there are a few rich and many poor. This economic system exists while it is capable of exploiting people at home and abroad. Then it perishes. Because each country tries to sell a lot to other countries and to buy little from them. This route leads to bankruptcy for all.

Both Die of the Same Evil

The system of investment is not only bad for the masses of all countries, but it is also bad for traders, since they perish as traders—that is why they are afraid to invest money.

If we could have an economic system without investment, humanity would not be doomed. But since life is impossible under this system of theft and plunder, we must create a more humane system, one where the means of production are at the service of distribution and consumption. Nothing else will save the human species. Neither the proprietor state, lord of everything, nor Gandhism.

Bombay, India.

"El Fin de Una Era: Ecos Libres de la India,"
Tierra y Libertad, 8:113 (July, 1950), 2.

12. Trade Unions in India— Pillars of Capitalism

M. P. T. Acharya

THE BRITISH LABOUR PARTY and the American Federation of Labor have nearly succeeded in roping in the Indian socialist trade unions. They have established a so-called Free Trade Union Committee in the best hotel here in charge of Mr. L. G. Deverall, and have issued several pamphlets.[1] (Unless one sits in the best hotel, nobody will believe it is the Free Trade Union.) They go about like YMCA missionaries telling us nice things—that the Free Trade Union International is free from government control, although they freely support their governments, just like the Indian National Trade Unions, sponsored by the government here. Whether they are controlled or not, their policy is that of their governments. The Socialist Party Unions are opposed to the Indian National T.U.C., but they hobnob with the A.F. of L. and the British Labour Party, since both of them pretend to be against capitalism. The whole question is one of swelling membership and misusing labor unions for government and war purposes. The chief unions that will benefit by their connections and activities will be the munitions, transport, and essential services unions. They will get some bonuses to make them feel like "aristocrats of labor."

Of course, the object of trade unions is not to abolish capitalism but get the best out of it for certain, state-essential categories of workers, keeping them wage slaves. All grand trade unions are

---

1. Richard L. G. Deverall (1911–1980) was the Asia representative of the AFL's Trade Union Committee from 1949 until 1952.

out to maintain the wage system, both here and anywhere, for otherwise the leaders and organizers will have no role to play. They do not want workers' ownership of works, but only to play a secondary role to capitalism, state or private. No wonder trade unions have only been able to keep workers subordinated to the exigencies of capitalism and war and state throughout history, not to emancipate them from these as the whole class struggle of centuries thought it would do. Accepting the wage system is subordinating oneself to wage slavery. Today trade unions are absolutely at the mercy of capitalism, workers are kept slaves of capitalism both by private employers and states, which in Russia are the same as the Communist Party. If capital—state or private—cannot make profit, the workers will have to go without eating even when working, e.g., as in Russia. Trade unions are interested in capitalist profit, in order to maintain the unions, although of a part of workers. They are agencies of capitalism, employment agencies. This they call "free trade unions"—freedom to bargain. Bargain you may, but may not get anything, except for the most essential—essential to state and capitalism—workers, to keep down all the rest.

There is really no choice between the four groups of trade unions in India, because they all work merely for better wages, and not for the abolition of the wage system. In fact, they all want to prevent the downfall of the wage system. Of course they won't get better wages, except for that small section of workers, which the government wants to use against the others. The wage system can only be maintained so long as export is maintained. Since Russia, for example, is not an export country, the workers can only be sent to labor camps to die giving the last ounce of strength and work without payment. Without foreign markets, the workers will be thrown out of employment since the wages they receive will not buy all the products at their prices, which includes taxes, rent, interest, and profits. The trade unions are a conspiracy between the union leaders and the capitalists and state to plunder foreign buyers.

I was told long ago, by Albert Baumeister, once of the I.L.O., that German trade unions furnished strike funds to am Italian textile workers' strike, not because they sympathized with them (although that was the open reason given!) but because German textile workers did not want the competition of Italian textiles on foreign markets and dislocation of Italian textile mills would help the export of German textiles.[2] In this both the German unions and government could go together. Similar things were practiced by British labor unions against Indian textile capital: they sent funds in support of striking Indian textile workers. The more strikes in another country, the unions as well as manufacturing capitalists in exporting countries will be safe. All roguery! The workers are pawns of rogues. Mr. Furtwängler, a German labor leader, had written a book on India in which he said that Indian textile workers, as well as Chinese and Japanese, are a menace to the textile industry of Europe and America because their labor is cheap and sweated.[3] That is a pure capitalist business proposition. When I pointed this out to him, he was angry. The logic of it is that the workers in India and China and Japan must be encouraged to strike and fight for higher wages, as if out of brotherhood, but really to make it more easy for European and American textile workers and capitalists to sell abroad. Did they mean that capitalism should be abolished both in Asia and Europe or at least in Asia or in Europe? Not at all. If capitalism is abolished, trade unions and their bossdom are finished.

We also know that when the IWMA (International Working Men's Association—the anarcho-syndicalist international) asked for sympathy and solidarity strikes to support some strikers, the reformist trade unions always said that it must be referred to the headquarters that later on said it did not want, even did not like to support with money. For by sympathy and solidarity strikes they did not want to dislocate "national business"! No wonder we have

---

2. Albert Baumeister (1882–1953) was a German trade unionist.

3. Franz Josef Furtwängler (1894–1965) was a German trade unionist, Foreign Secretary of the Allgemeiner Deutsche Gewerkschaftsbund (a confederation of German trade unions), and took great interest in Indian labor and independence. He and Karl Schrader, head of the German Textile Workers Association, described their trip in *Das Werktätige Indien* (1928).

more international and less brotherhood. The mentality of party and labor leaders is capitalist and national, even international in the capitalist sense. Business first! For without business, they will have no role to play. They will become simple producing workers, will have to degrade themselves into nonentities. So I am not interested at all in trade unions, which do not want to overthrow capitalism and the wage-system but want to maintain them, let them go to hell with capitalism.

Freedom: Anarchist Fortnightly (September 16, 1950), 3.

13. An Indian Looks at "Independence"

M. P. T. Acharya

SIRDAR PATEL GAVE UP CHEROOTS and drinks to organize the revolt of the peasants of Bardoli.[1]

As a lieutenant of Gandhiji, he went to prison several times (1st class).

As a result of all this, he has become the uncrowned Emperor of India—a good change from barristership to emperorship—the cost of his sacrifice.

Now he—the man, the only man, who knows Gandhiji's mind (Gandhi was the father of the nation and Sirdar Patel has become the grandfather of the nation), goes about like an emperor and speaks like an emperor. He addresses the Navy in Dhoti as white emperors did in former times, "inspects" the guard of honor and ratings with the white commander of the navy paying respects to him.

Nothing has changed under republic except the skin and dress.

Now, if I planned, I would go about it like this:

(1) 340 million people require so much food per day each, hence so much food is required for the whole year for all the people.

(2) Then calculate how much land is required to produce each kind of food and where they are available.

---

1. "Sirdar" (or "Sardar") Vallabhbhai Patel (1875–1950) was a barrister and the first Deputy Prime Minister of India.

(3) Then, what kind of materials, implements, and animals are required to produce the different kinds of food to make the total.

(4) Then find out where and how much of the materials, implements, and animals are available.

(5) How much food and fodder are available to keep these men and animals alive.

(6) Collect them to produce all the food required for all.

(7) If, say 40%, or even 50 or 60%, of the people can produce all the food required for all the people, then the rest of the population can be fed and put to work—to produce other things, to transport everything, to give education, medical aid, and sanitation, to provide clothing and housing, and even entertainment, to all people all over the country.

But the trouble now is that everything has to be bought and paid for, and it would require more money than we have—or even can print. All things are in the hands of persons who have to be paid these prices. Otherwise nothing can be had for "national economy." But that is what our planners are trying to do, and cannot do, can never do.

Their plans are stillborn.

Freedom: The Anarchist Weekly (October 28, 1950), 3.

11. Savarkar: A Criticism

M. P. T. Acharya

Bombay, India
November 17, 1950

Dear Guy Aldred, I see that you call V. D. Savarkar the father of the Indian National Movement. While it is true that Gandhi joined the national movement later than Savarkar, it is not true that Savarkar was the father of the Indian national or Indian independence movement. It was B. G. Tilak who was the father of the independence movement, although he worked on propagandist and political lines.[1] Savarkar worked on the terroristic lines and preached violence to overthrow British rule. But it is Gandhi who put the national and independence movement on a *mass basis*, although only after 1919, which gave channels to terrorists to work openly. In fact, it was Gandhi who made the masses disobey the government in their millions. Of course, the national movement was founded by the Congress with Bradlaugh, Hume, and Naoroji—30 years after the failure of the Indian revolution, which was monarchist, but it asked for self-government and home-rule, and scarcely Dominion status.[2] Under those circumstances more could not be expected. Mrs. Besant was the one even before Gandhi to put the Home Rule movement

---

1. Bal Gangadhar Tilak (1856–1920) was an early Indian nationalist, an advocate of violence and terrorism, and part of the so-called "extremist" wing of the INC.

2. Charles Bradlaugh (1833–1891) was not a founding member of the INC; Allan Octavian Hume (1829–1912) founded the INC with Dadabhai Naoroji (1825–1917) and others in 1885.

on a mass basis, for in 1915 she organized village, district, and provincial home rule committees.[3] Gandhi made Congress organize itself on those lines.

I am no less an admirer of Savarkar's work in these days than you are, in fact I was associated with him in London. I also have every respect for him for his having suffered fifteen years in the Andamans.[4] But probably because he spent most of his youth in the Andamans, his mind has not grown. His greatest mistake after his release from internment in Ratnagiri was his association with the Hindu Mahasabha instead of standing aloof from Congress and the Hindu Mahasabha, and conducting his own independence movement. He could not have become a great figure in the Congress, and so it seems he chose to be leader of the Hindu Mahasabha. Savarkar thus became a party man instead of staying independent of all parties. The first wrong step leads to all the rest.

While India was agitated with social and economic questions, Savarkar stood for the religious and racial basis of the Hindu Mahasabha movement. Of course, many of the Hindu Mahasabhites do not believe in Savarkar's Hinduism, because he does not believe in the caste and untouchability (Pariah) system nor is he insistent on the prohibition of cow-killing. The orthodox Hindu Mahasabhites believe in all this. Recently, as you published in the letter of Om Kahol, a general-secretary of the Hindu Mahasabha was boycotted for having married a South African lady who became a convert to Hinduism. Moreover, Jinnah's propaganda for Pakistan made Savarkar and the Hindu Mahasabha a purely Hindu religious movement, which aspired to capture the state. In his London days, Savarkar had collaborated with many Muslims, like the present governor of Orissa, Mr. Asaf Ali.[5] He

---

3. Annie Besant (1847–1933), a close associate of Bradlaugh, she was the leader of the Theosophical Society, joined the INC, and spearheaded the Indian Home Rule movement during the First World War.

4. In 1911, Savarkar was given two sentences of imprisonment for life in the penal colony on the Andaman Islands, but was moved to a jail in the Ratnagiri district in 1921 and interned there until January 1924.

5. Asaf Ali (1888–1953) was briefly associated with India House in London and

has praised in his *The Indian War of Independence* Emperor Bahadur Shah and Azim Khan. That Jinnah wanted a separate Muslims state—since 1937, although formerly he was a Congressman and nationalist in spite of being president of the Muslim League, does not justify Savarkar in putting religion before politics. By doing so, he was indirectly helping Jinnah's fanaticism. Moreover Savarkar and his Sabha were in league with Arya Samaj, which believes in converting all India to Hinduism, although its Hinduism is hated by orthodox Hindus as heterodox, since Hinduism does not admit of conversion. Even now the Hindu Mahasabha has no social questions. Of course, like all parties in India, the Mahasabha pretends to want to raise the standard of living of the masses and even to establish Socialism (of some kind!) in order to catch votes, but nothing has changed in the Hindu Mahasabha.

Recently the Mahasabha pretended to admit non-Hindus into its fold, but only to put them forward as candidates for general elections where in parliament non-Hindus have to vote according to Hindu Mahasabha decisions. It is pure humbug. Nobody will be deceived by it.

The Hindu Mahasabha takes sides with Brahmin landlords whose lives were endangered and property destroyed when Gandhi was murdered. If it were not for the preventive arrests of the Hindu Mahasabhites, there would have been a massacre of them.

What an end for a man who sacrificed his youth: he has ended politically nowhere. Others are much blacker reactionaries than Savarkar. I mean those who conduct the Hindu Mahasabha. Savarkar is now old and too decrepit to do anything.

Your foreign readers may not know these facts, for which reason I write this comment on your writing.

Yours fraternally,
M. P. T. Acharya

The Word, 12:2 (December, 1950), 23–24.

---

probably met Acharya there as well as at the Egyptian National Congress meeting in Brussels in September 1910.

15. How Long Can Capitalism Survive?

M. P. T. Acharya

KARL MARX WAS WRONG IN expecting the collapse of capitalism around 1848. Kropotkin was wrong in looking for widespread social revolution about 1905. But I have a strong belief that a general disintegration of capitalism is near—much nearer than the most pessimistic adherent of the capitalist system can imagine. That collapse can come about in one or another of two ways: either without a war or after a war.

If governments postpone a war hoping that capitalism, sick and tottering, will recover, they miscalculate. If the war does not come soon, it will be impossible to carry on a war later, for capitalism will have fallen in pieces by that time instead of regaining its strength. There are two ways of going down and out for capitalism: with war or without war. In either case, it is doomed.

If those who are optimistic about the continuance of capitalism are correct in their contention (and unfortunately such optimists are more numerous in labor camps than among the capitalists), then there can be no hope for the coming of Socialism and therefore no use of any of us preparing for Socialism. If Socialism will not come for a long time, why try to create it? It won't come if capitalism can last long. While capitalists are having nervous breakdowns worrying about their own system, it appears that the Socialists and Communists are the only optimists with regard to the continuance of capitalism.

Reasons for anticipating capitalism's early collapse are ready to hand. Capitalism is a wage system, even if Socialists carry it on and even if Communists want to carry it on. In fact, they are also capitalists, for they can maintain the states in which they live only with the help of the wage system. But the capitalists will bankrupt that system so thoroughly that even the Socialists will not be able to salvage it.

It is no longer 1917, which made possible the resuscitation of the wage-system and abortion of the Revolution in Russia. The economic chaos in Stalin's country and the want of food there are evidence that the wage-method is in its last throes in the Soviet Union. A monolithic economy is more difficult to carry on with the wage-system than even the divided private capitalist economy. Under private capitalism, the ruined capitalists act as shock absorbers in any economic crisis, but in a totalitarian or monolithic economy, the shock affects the whole set-up.

Whether in Russia or elsewhere the wage-system, because it can be conducted only under the aegis of the state, leads to reduction of consumption, for the masses have to pay a substantial portion of their earnings to maintain the state, and as the cost of such maintenance rises, they necessarily consume less and less. Added to this, it is out of the pockets of the workers that must come the money to pay for interest, rent, profits, and sales commissions involved in the operation of capitalistic industries. Thus the wage-system constantly throttles consumption of commodities. And capitalism inevitably will abolish itself by strangling consumption. So will state capitalism that is called Marxian Communism. If we do not believe that the wage system lives on its own fat, then there is no use for Socialism, for capitalism could continue for all time. That is what the Socialist and Communist Marxians hope for. Otherwise, their getting the state into their own hands will not be possible. Their hopes are based on their wishes.

While Marxism has been tried in various forms everywhere, the Anarchist theory, which is older than Marxism, has not yet been tested anywhere. Now, with the impending smash-up of the wage-system—made hopelessly bankrupt by the capitalists themselves, there is only one feasible possibility ahead. That is Anarchism. The time for testing Anarchist economics is nearer than ever.

If or when the capitalist collapse comes, mankind has before it only two alternatives—Anarchism or chaos. That is the perspective. It will depend on the Anarchists themselves how far they can put the human race on the road to Anarchist economics.

Capitalism appears fully entrenched—but only appears so. For it has no rival. But that does not prove that it can save itself, thanks to the wage-system and the steady reduction of commodity-consumption. Already its currency system has been wrecked; there is no chance of reviving the gold standard. Currencies in present use are fictitious. Yet the capitalists and their sponsors in the halls of government try to maintain the fiction by agreement.

Capitalism is money economics. It can continue by changing less money into more money; otherwise it is lost. The exchange of commodities is carried on only as a means of making less money into more money, both internally and in foreign trade. Now all countries are endeavoring to sell more and more goods abroad in order to earn more money with less money, because in internal trade sales will mean only the taking of more and more money from the wage-earners, thus reducing their power to purchase and consume. Internal trade alone cannot keep capitalism going. Now the capitalists of all nations are impelled to resort to the same trick, if they can do it: sell more to other countries and buy less from abroad. Otherwise, there will be less and less money internally. This means that more and more countries cannot buy or sell, and this will cut the ground from under capitalism and the wage system.

Today the world is nearer to a single capitalist economy than it ever was. That is the great difficulty and danger that capitalism faces. It is like the right hand trying to sell to the left hand and get profits—or the right trying to put some money into the left pocket in order to take out more money. It cannot be done. All the international economic and trade conferences called in these days are motivated by anxiety about this danger. But the conferees find themselves unable to agree, since each country wants to make the other countries pay profits that they cannot afford to pay.

Capitalism will be "tied up" whether Socialists are prepared for the situation or not. If it does not cease existing there can be no hope of Socialism coming and no use for it. Capitalism will collapse even without a general strike for social revolution. Otherwise, let us not think of Socialism at all. It would be only intellectual delectation without any practical use. Many Socialists appear to have the attitude that "it will come some day anyhow," so why worry about the situation? But capitalism will crash about their heads with a deafening roar. It will be too late then to think of Socialism.

Socialism and Anarchism are ahead of us, or chaos. Never mind how soon. If the great collapse is to come, it is up to Socialists and Anarchists to prepare for it, even if it should come next month or next week. But according to all present indications, we seem to welcome chaos rather than Socialism and Anarchism.

Anarchism and Anarchists must be ready with a scientifically workable plan. For Anarchists, Anarchism is synonymous with scientific economics. For such economics inevitably make anarchic (non-state) conditions essential. But we Anarchists must formulate a scientifically workable social economic plan which will be for the benefit of all—an economic blue-print that will be acceptable even to non-Anarchists who do not care for Anarchism. We must not offer that program as an Anarchist plan, but only as scientific social economics, which are easily understandable to all and which will benefit all persons equally. We must deduce Anarchism from scientific economics, and show that it is inseparable from scientific economics.

People generally are bound together more by bread than by freedom, although for Anarchists bread and freedom are identical. While freedom may have different meanings for different people, bread has the same meaning for all. Bread and economic well-being. Economics being material, there cannot be absolute freedom. How to make the best of economics for the well-being of all without exception is the only thing that can be attempted today. That is the limit of freedom. Outside of economic possibilities there can be no freedom.

Today people are bound to hear how they can assure their living from birth to death, though they do not care for freedom.

But they hope that the wage system will not be abolished. They are victims of everyone who promises higher wages, whether they really get a better income or not. Anarchists must say that we cannot live any longer by the wage system, whether we want it or not, for that system will eventually lead to economic collapse even if sponsored by Socialists or Communists. Therefore those who promise higher wages are quacks, humbugs, and deceivers.

We have no solution for the great existing economic problem within the wage-system, nor has anyone else. Only rogues assert that they have. Today there is no validity in any battle for improvement of wages, but only in striving for abolition of wages. All else is illusion and delusion. The syndicalists must not let themselves get entangled in the struggle for wage increases, if they want to prepare for social revolution. The days for such struggle are over. People now want to hold on to their jobs and to preserve whatever wages they can get; there are too many others waiting to take those jobs at even less wages if they are vacated. It is a waste of time to battle for higher wages. Either we abolish the wage-system or we go down with capitalism and Bolshevism. There is no third alternative.

Before us there is one huge, over-all question, and no partial questions. The wage struggle, trade union movements, agrarian problems, colonialism, present-day democracy, even the struggles against State Communism and Fascism, do not exist in the total problem confronting us. Those struggles will have their adherents, but they cannot help even themselves—for the whole capitalist system from the Fascist to the Bolshevik forms, based as they are on the wage-method, is cracking and is bound to crash. It is the special business of the Anarchists to point this out. If another global war comes, they cannot prevent it, and if a general economic crash has to come they cannot avert that either. Let others waste their time over the partial capitalist problems—and there *are* many individuals who squander their hours on partial problems. The chief concern of Anarchists is with the total problem: after the capitalistic collapse, which cannot be followed even by Bolshevism, what should people do? And how shall we make them understand what they should do?

Many voices still cry against exploitation by capitalism. But if capitalism collapses, no new exploitation through the wage-system will be possible. We may have banditry and murder on a large scale, but compelling people to work for wages will become impossible. That is how I envisage the future. We may all die of starvation but we will not be wage-slaves. Countless men and women are still willing to be wage-slaves, but will have no chance to be after capitalism falls.

The capitalists dig their own graves with the wage-system, whether the workers desire it or not, but that is no consolation to the millions of wage-slaves. In fact, they are afraid of the day when the capitalists will be gone. For they do not know how to live beyond that turning point. Here is rich opportunity for Anarchists to point the way—provided that they formulate a workable, scientific social, and economic program. It may already be too late to propagate such a plan, for we are nearer to chaos than to Socialism. But certainly an attempt should be made—to the exclusion of everything else.

Bombay, India

World Scene from the Libertarian Point of View
(Chicago: Free Society Group of Chicago, 1951), 52–56.

16. Our Indian Correspondent on the Stuffed Dove of Peace at the Indian Peace Convention

Marco Polo

SOON AFTER THE INDIAN CULTURAL CONFERENCE, came and went the so-called Peace Convention. Whether the Cultural Conference was Anglo-American in inspiration or not, as is alleged by the so-called Peace Convention and even some neutrals and outsiders of both conferences, the claim that the "Peace" conference was not inspired by the Communists is not proved. In fact, this "Peace Conference" was once held in Prague, which is within the Russian orbit. That in itself it enough to damn the organizers of the Peace Conference as champions of Stalin's regime. Of course, their argument will be, because it was not allowed to be held in London or Paris it had to be held in Soviet territory. But the so-called Cultural Conference would not be allowed to be held in the land of "Freedom," because no conference, which had the smell of neutrality, can be held in Russia or satellite countries. Hence the Czech Communist government allowed the so-called Peace Conference in its territory, which is sufficient proof to damn it as Bolshevik-inspired. It was reported that there was some opposition to communism by delegates in the Convention. It only shows that these so-called delegates were either ignoramuses and have been gulled, or the conference has nothing to do with Communism but was only meant to support *Stalinism*. That they proclaim peace does not make them less the agents of Stalinism. They may not themselves know it. I asked one Gandhian why he signed the peace pledge placed before him by an avowed communist. He having been gulled and being not willing to admit it, said: there was nothing in the wording of the pledge that I could object to!

Peace Humbug

When the Peace Pledge was issued in Stockholm, I received an air-letter from one of the organizations which participated in the so-called Stockholm Peace Conference saying that it was inspired by the Bolsheviks and the truth was discovered only after the issuance of the Pledge and so they held a conference to denounce it as a Bolshevik, Stalinist machination. When I gave the news to one of the biggest dailies in Bombay—they refused to publish it, saying it was not important. Yes, Reuter had not telegraphed it, hence the news had no value.

A friend of mine who had been asked to sign the pledge but refused to do so, saying he was against and outside all politics, tells me that his name has been included in some list issued in Delhi. Pure swindle! Many who had signed the pledge in Europe protested and withdrew.

Many of the organizations, which participated in the Stockholm Peace Conference originally, have now set up an office to denounce the Peace Pledge as a Bolshevik contrivance and its office (*Sveriges Fredsråd*) is situated at Jungfrugatan 30, Stockholm.[1] They must know better than our leaders and editors, being on the spot and being *au courant* from the beginning. But in the kingdom of the blind, the one-eyed man is the wisest! Two-eyed men are not wanted.

If quackery and humbug will achieve world peace, it will, as a result of peace conferences, official, quasi-official, demi-official, and officially inspired. The real makers of war conceal themselves behind these conferences—in the distance in government offices and they do all the intrigue, which makes the war inevitable.

Dr. Atal—a nephew of Pandit Nehru—recently returned from a 12-day tour as a government guest, of course, or as a conducted

---

1. The Swedish Peace Council (*Sveriges Fredsråd*) was established in 1946.

tourist in Russia and gave a flamboyant interview in London saying that the Russian people are thoroughly against the war.[2] Who says that the Russian people want war? For that matter, no people want war. Do the American or British or any other people want war? Dr. Atal means *only Russian people do not want war*. People do not want war, but that is different from saying that their governments are also against war.

Busy-Bodies of Peace

Who are these delegates to appeal to governments not to make war? Are the governments only waiting for their conferences to know what they should do! Are governments there to carry out their resolutions? They will do what they think they must do at any moment. Mr. Karanjia said cheaply that others are "Washington patriots," they can retort "You are Moscow patriots."[3] We need not take film actors who participated in the Convention seriously—they are only well directed!

Dr. Atal said bombastically that the peace movement—meaning Stalinism—has caught the imagination of the people and "nobody can stop it." They thought so on the platform before every war, but when the war came, they had to go in defense of their regimes or go into concentration camps. Neutrality in another war is impossible for any government. Even during the last war—Switzerland, Sweden, and Turkey had to help their powerful neighbors, for fear of being invaded and occupied. Picasso's Peace Dove—a dead symbol—will not make war impossible. It will remain a taxidermist's *stuffed bird, without life*.

The fact is peace cannot be made by governments. It is governments, which make wars. To appeal to one's own or foreign governments to keep peace is irresponsible advice. They can claim that they are heroes of peace when they support their own or foreign

---

2. Madan Atal (–1954), a nephew of Motilal Nehru, who also went to Spain in 1937.
3. Rustom Khurshedji Karanjia (1912–2008) was an Indian journalist and editor.

governments. If peace were wanted, governments would be made impossible in all countries. But the heroes of peace are *supporters of one government against others*.

Bombay

Freedom: The Anarchist Weekly, 12:18 (June 30, 1951), 3.

17. Confusion Between Communism and State Capitalism

M. P. T. Acharya

IN THE ARTICLE "IN REGARD TO COMMUNISM" and the correspondence between Com. S. A. Dange and Shri Vinoba Bhave, Shri Mashruwala and Bhave do not refer to real communism as such, but to other side-issues which have nothing to do with Communism, although referred to as such.[1] Neither Mashruwala nor Bhave nor Bharatan Kumarappa questions whether what the party calling itself Communist tries to force upon mankind is really real Communism. Even the Capitalists have taken for granted that what prevails in Russia is real Communism. It does not occur to them that it can be anything but Communism. They give the Bolsheviks the undeserved compliments of being Communists. They do not know that it is not Communism but Russian Bolshevism, which is a danger to the peace of the world. They quarrel about a word about the meaning and contents of which they have no idea at all.

Let me tell you—and any radical Marxian will confirm it—that what the Bolsheviks do in Russia and try to do elsewhere is just Capitalism of another type, and the quarrel between Capitalists and Bolsheviks is not about Communism but about the type of Capitalism

---

1. Acharya refers to Shri Kishorlal Mashruwala's article "In Regard to Communism," *Harijan*, 15:25 (August 18, 1951), and a correspondence between S. A. Dange and Vinoba Bhava in the same issue; Shripad Amrit Dange (1899–1991) was a founding member of the Communist Party of India (CPI); Vinoba Bhave (1895–1982) was an Indian advocate of non-violence, influenced by Gandhi and the Sarvodaya movement, with anarchist leanings; Mashruwala (1890–1952) was an associate of Gandhi and editor of *Harijan*.

which should prevail. Both have a common basis of thought, which is capitalistic. What the Capitalists are against is the Bolshevik attempt at doing away with divided private owners and setting up a state by their party as the sole owner. The mode of management is the same, namely, making the entire people wage-slaves, exactly as Capitalist owners do. The issue between them is not whether or not Capitalism should be totally abolished and Communism should be ushered in, but who should manage Capitalism. Both are opposed to Communism. Neither the Capitalists nor the Bolsheviks will argue about Communism. Yet Bolshevism is supposed to be Communism and the opposite of Capitalism! It is State Capitalism—Capitalism by the state,—owned and run by the Bolshevik party pretentiously calling itself Communist. All the three brands, Marxism, Leninism, or Stalinism are advocates of state ownership and state Capitalism, and they want it to be kept under the control of the Bolshevik party of Moscow throughout the world (Ask Tito, who claims also to be a Marxian and Leninist, about it).

Am I to understand Shris Bhave, Mashruwala, and Kumarappa have no quarrel about the Bolshevik Communism provided that the system is introduced peacefully and non-violently through the ballot-box and voluntary relinquishments—although it would be a new slavery instead of the old? Do they object only to the method of reaching the system of new slavery?

The Bolsheviks would have no objection to that method. But they think or know it cannot be brought about without force and fraud. Hence they do not believe in the ballot-box method or voluntary sacrifices. Hence they say: if you submit to our Capitalism voluntarily you are welcome; but if you do not do so willingly, we are not going to wait, you shall surrender, or be massacred. This is also the threat to workers, peasants, middle-classes, and employees, though it is addressed to them in a cunning and sugar-coated manner. As a matter of fact, they have also to submit to that slavery under their rule. If the Capitalists want to massacre these so-called Communists before they themselves are massacred, the Communists have no right to complain, for they want to do the same thing against them if possible. It is a war between two rival claimants of capital, one being the defender of private Capitalism, the other, the fighter for state Capitalism.

There can be no political Communism like the one the Bolsheviks want to establish. Communism means undivided society. But what the Bolsheviks and Marxians of all varieties want is the rulership of their parties over all. They may practice some sort of communism among themselves but they are rulers and employers living upon wage-slaves in the same way as capitalists. In real Communism, there can be neither employers nor employed. The employer-employee system is an essential feature of Capitalism. Its abandonment it acceptable neither to the Capitalists nor the Bolsheviks. Of course, the Bolsheviks say that ultimately they want to abolish the state, their rulership and relations as employer and employee. Yes, after establishing and perpetuating the wage system! The Capitalists may also take a leaf from the Bolsheviks and say they also want to abolish employer-employee relations some time, in its own time, when the time is ripe, and when all agree to do so through the ballot-box! They may also allege that there is a transition stage between the two, which must be passed through. That transition stage is our rulership. Both can say this without the least abashment, and both would be equally good Communists.

Com. Dange may be a sincere man but he is a fanatic of the Bolshevik party which stands for the hegemony of Moscow. Sincerity can do nothing against the fanaticism of a wrong idea, the wrong idea will become sincerity. One cannot argue with fanatics.

When Com. Dange and lesser Socialists say that they want to help the peasants to own land, they are telling things which they don't want and which they won't allow if they sat in government; for, they do not want peasant proprietorship but want state-ownership of land, collective and state farms where peasants will become virtually landlaborers for the state. It is the pride of Soviet Russia, their fatherland, that 99 percent of the land is nationalized and there are no individual peasants. It is not Marxism to divide land among peasants. I have myself heard it from the mouth of Lenin. He meant "neither private ownership, nor common ownership" but state ownership. But Communism is common ownership and not private ownership or state ownership. Private ownership is what Capitalists want. The Communists encourage private ownership of land among peasants in order to use them for their fight and not for the benefit of peasants. They know very well that it is not Communism. In newly acquired territories like East Germany, Czechoslovakia, Poland, and the Balkans, the Bolsheviks no doubt first distributed the land among the peasants, but soon started collectivizing them under state ownership, and establishing collective and state farms where the former peasants become only wage slaves. That is what they will do here. Peasants will be deprived of their lands by the state peacefully or violently.

Com. Dange sheds crocodile tears over the miseries of peasants. But under the rule of his party, and even under his own military governorship on behalf of Stalin, all these things will not be done even after feudalism and landlordism are abolished. By simply abolishing feudalism and landlordism the peasant will not be emancipated. In Eastern Europe, after the peasants were given land, they found they could not cultivate their properties, for want of enough means to start cultivation. So the governments asked them to collectivize lands if they wanted help from the state. As they could not live otherwise, even exist, they had to accept the proposal and work as contract laborers for the state. In Russia, the collectives are rack-rented by the state with the help of the tractors, which are lent to the collectives on exorbitant conditions. It is also another, modern kind of feudalism. The tractors are not owned by any collectives but are the monopoly of the state. They want to introduce this Socialism in India, and call it Communism. The state bureaucracy, army, and police cannot be run even by Communists except at the expense of the producing workers and it is Communism of parasites which they want to bring to India. One must be ashamed to call that Communism.

Communism cannot be established until the peasants take over all the land and instruments and run the lands collectively for their own benefit without any state to interfere with, or "protect" them.

Communism is all right if it were Communism, but to admire anything with a label of Communism will neither solve the problem nor make it Communism. It will be paying tribute to a false thing going under an ideal label. Communism cannot be established from the top by violence, not by cutting the Gordian knot, but only untying it diligently. Most likely we will have chaos rather than Bolshevism. Bolshevism alone will save Capitalism. May Com. Dange be happy!

Harijan (October 27, 1951), 298–299.

18. Letters to the Editor, *Thought* (1950–1952)

M. P. T. Acharya

Co-Operatives

Sir,—With reference to the report from Madras on Pseudo-Co-operation in your issue of July 14, every co-operation for business is but co-operation to plunder third parties. It is not co-operation for satisfying the needs of others. There is not much difference between a capitalist limited company or combine and a so-called co-operative society, since both are capitalist, i.e., made for profits to be taken out of others. Yet people talk of co-operatives being against capitalism, while they are only another form of capitalism and exploitation for profits. The famous British co-operatives, which handle a quarter of British business, are now only business concerns trading for profit.

Thought, 2:30 (August 4, 1950), 5.

Bogey of Revolution

Sir,—As one who has seen two revolutions in Europe—the German revolution and the Russian civil war in 1919—and also the Hitler palace revolution in 1933, I think I can be permitted to say something about your comments on the Bogey of Revolution. I was living in Europe from 1914 to 1935, from 1922 to 1935 in Germany.

A revolution presupposes hope by change. But today neither in India nor in Europe people expect any good by change. There may be political frays but no revolutions, such as the one that happened in

Russia. People are more enslaved to the bread problem than to ideas. In India, a revolution is even less desired than in Europe. Starving people have no mental stamina. They are preoccupied with today; tomorrow has no attraction for them.

We have seen that during the war, 3 million persons died of starvation in Bengal without any resistance. That may repeat itself elsewhere in India. Frustration creates mental paralysis. But banditism may grow.

Those who accuse the Nehru Government of fostering corruption and nepotism and thus of making the famine of food and clothes inevitable are self-righteous. Put any person or party in Nehru's place, the story will repeat itself. It is also a superstition to believe that the economic system can entirely be controlled. The Bolshevik or Totalitarian way may concentrate economic power in the hands of the party but it will never mean improvement in the economic situation of the people.

There is no all India leader as Nehru is. Of course Kripalaniji is well known but people cannot believe that a man like him will do much good in Government.[1] "Honesty may be a good policy but certainly not the best principle."

I think the only person likely to play the role of a dictator possible is Pandit Nehru, but he ought to know that dictatorships will mean increased corruption and worsening of the conditions. Even the Socialists, if they come to office, cannot play dictators. For if they do, they will lose foreign support, which will mean dislocation of their economic program.

There can be no change for the better politically or economically without recognizing that our economics is fundamentally wrong; it is based on the theory of society. The Socialists and the Communists cannot change that basis. Why then should the people want change? Even in Europe, people have come increasingly to believe that change does not necessarily mean increased security. They prefer food and shelter.

Thought, 4:2 (January 12, 1952), 6.

---

1. Jivatram Bhagwandas Kripalani (1888–1982) was a Gandhian socialist and presided over the Indian National Congress in 1947.

Lenin after the NEP

Sir,—It may interest your readers to know that I heard from Prof. M. Reisner, an old friend of Lenin and a Neurologist who visited him when the latter became ill after the introduction of the NEP in 1921.[2] Prof. Reisner says that Lenin had a shock as the consequences of NEP and his mind was so paralyzed that he looked blank and vacant-minded. Even the picture, which was published in the papers saying, "Com. Lenin is expected soon to resume his premiership" bore that out. Prof. Reisner told me that the picture was bad propaganda for it revealed a vacant look.

Before that at a party Congress meeting when Mme Kollontai complained against want of party and proletarian democracy Trotsky got up and threatened her with concentration camp.[3] She was the first workers' opposition movement. She was given an Ambassadorial job and sent out of the country. Later on, Trotsky himself became a victim of high-power dictatorship.

Lenin and Trotsky were themselves responsible for the subsequent course of the Revolution—they aborted the freedom, which was still available to some extent before 1921. The Kronstadt Rebellion of March 1921 was the end of the Revolution.

Thought, 4:3 (January 19, 1952), 6.

Madame Kollontai

Sir,—Mme Kollontai had written early in the Bolshevik Revolution a book called *The New Morality and the Working Class*, which was reviewed by a Swedish labor paper under the caption "Is it pornography?" In that book she complained that the working class had taken and followed bourgeois sex morals.

---

2. Mikhail Reisner (1868–1928) was a Russian scientist, doctor, and close ally of Lenin.

3. Alexandra Kollontai (1872–1952) was a Russian revolutionary, Menshevik turned Bolshevik, who championed women's issues, and became ambassador to Norway in 1923.

Mme Kollontai was the daughter of a General and quit her father's home in order to serve—as she thought—the working class through Marxism. She was a free woman. Her beloved Dybenko was executed during a purge in the Bolshevik Party.[4]

I had the privilege of being taken by Mme Balabanoff into Mme Kollontai's room in the Hotel National and being introduced to her, when the latter was the head of the women's section of the Communist International. Mme Balabanoff was the mentor of Lenin and Mussolini whom she later quit. Mme Kollontai told me that there was no more emancipation movement among the women in Russia proper but only in Muslim Russia. The Russian women think, she said, that with the success of the Bolshevik Revolution, emancipation is over and want to drink, dress, and dance.

She was a charming woman and very graceful and was simply dressed at the time I met her.

Thought, 4:14 (April 5, 1952), 6.

---

4. Pavel Dybenko (1889–1938), a Russian revolutionary, married Kollontai in 1917, and expelled from the Communist Party in 1918. He was executed during Stalin's purge in 1938.

19. Letter from India: Nehru and Korea

M. P. T. Acharya

PANDIT NEHRU SAID THAT WE can do nothing about the bombing of the Yalu Power Station in Korea.[1] Yalu is only an episode but why Yalu only? We can do nothing about the whole war in Korea, which is a civil war backed by big powers. Pandit Nehru protested against the bombing of the Yalu Power Station and called on both sides to cease fire. Pandit Nehru claimed that India had to be consulted as a member of U.N.O. before the bombing. But the U.S.A. acting in the name of U.N.O. did not even consult Britain. Even when U.N. troops went into Korea, U.N.O. had not authorized sending them there. The U.S. Government sent the troops and U.N.O. obligingly later on confirmed it on their behalf.

U.N.O. is U.S.

The U.N.O. cannot exist one day without the U.S.A. Nobody would contribute funds to a U.N.O. and act according to its decisions if the U.S.A. were not in it. Most of the Governments are helped to remain on the saddle in their own countries with the military and economic help of the U.S.A. If that help was not coming, all the so-called free world would be a prey to Bolshevism.

---

1. In June 1952, the United Nations carried out several bombings of power stations along the Yalu River in Korea.

Two Capitalisms

The war in Korea is but a fight in the battle between private capitalism and State Capitalism, which is raging all over the world. U.N.O. supports the private capitalist order while the Chinese and Russians support the State Capitalist order. The Koreans themselves are ranged against one another as partisans of state or private capitalism—the former going as communism, the latter as constitutional democracy. Both say they want freedom and unity of Korea.

Unity Under Dictator

Both say they want to unite Korea which means simply they want to bring both parts under state capitalism or private capitalism. Even if foreign champions of one or the other systems did not intervene or help in Korea, Korean fanatics of state and private capitalism will continue to fight each other, and decimate the people, in order to "unify the country" as they claim. *Unity in the Grave!* Now, of course, there will be no more Koreans left alive before Korea is unified by one or the other side. Both sides do not mean to unite, even to keep the two systems separately as before this war.

Both Are For Slavery!

It is good for India to protest when nothing can be done about it by India, and to ask both parties to cease fire and come to truce. But there is no chance at all for uniting Korea under their own rule. If Korea is given over to Syngman Rhee, he will have pro-Bolshevik enemies behind his lines.[2] But if it is delivered to Kim Ir Sen, the Koreans will be complete slaves, as in Russia.[3] Korea will be a vast forced labor camp. Constitutional democracy will be used for private capitalist exploitation and dictatorship under which only a

---

2. Syngman Rhee (1875–1965) was Head of State of the Provisional Government of the Republic of Korea and President of South Korea from 1948 to 1960.

3. Kim Ir Sen (Kim Il-sung, 1912–1994) was President of North Korea from 1948 to 1994.

few will be pleased while Bolshevism will make Korea a vast prison house in which only the Bolsheviks will be happy jail warders, as in Russia.

Constitution Façade for Dictators

Pandit Nehru wants to see Korea united and free but there can be only dictatorship, exploitation, and prison-freedom whether state or private capitalism is established in Korea either with the consent or without the consent of the Koreans. If that is unity and freedom, it does not matter which is freedom: both will be slavery. Only the Bolsheviks will profit by and exploit the constitutional democracy if it is really maintained. It will soon degenerate into fascist dictatorship and civil war.

Harmony Among Dictators!

This slogan "United Korea," "Free Korea," "Hands off Korea," whether of Bolsheviks or private capitalist friends of Korea is meaningless. Pandit Nehru is a naïve man to think there need be no conflict whether either Bolshevism or private capitalism is established.

Democracy is a façade for dictatorship while Bolshevism is naked dictatorship. Both stink in the nostrils. Both Kim Ir Sen and Syngman Rhee want their own dictatorships with foreign backing.

The Only Hope of Koreans

In Korea there is only a group of persons who are against Syngman Rhee—and Kim Ir Sen and their foreign helpers. They neither want foreign governments nor native governments. They want a *Korea free from government as the only solution.*

They were only 70,000 persons but they work among workers and peasants to wean them from all political parties who are out to establish governments. Early in the Korean War, we published their manifesto in these columns (*Freedom*, 28/10/50).

Their leader and six others were arrested by Syngman Rhee. They were sentenced to death and now pardoned.

Again they go among the people to wean them from war and civil war on behalf of native and foreign rulers. They are the only hope of unity in Korea except for a "unity" in which the Koreans will be extinct.

Freedom: The Anarchist Weekly, 13:37
(September 13, 1952), 3.

50. Indians in British Colonies

M. P. T. Acharya

THE SECOND REPORT OF SHRI G. Raghava Rao on the conditions in East Africa smacks very much of the tenor of British propaganda about the natives.[1] It even praises the British East African Government: "with the idea of helping the Africans toward raising the standard of living, the Government of Uganda has begun to assist Africans in purchasing ginneries and coffee curing factories from the Indian and Europeans owners." African poverty can be attributed to the African lethargy, illiteracy, and contentment with the minimum of "food and shelter." The British used similar arguments against Indians formerly. The British would like Africans to be energetic so that the final benefit will go to them. But the Africans find no incentive—as capitalists say—to work hard in order to provide ease to others. And they want to be independent cultivators, not employed for wages.

The Africans are paid less than the Indians who are in turn paid less than the Europeans. How can they have incentive to work hard? Indians are in a privileged position to work harder. Moreover, Indians have capital, which Africans have not—they can employ Africans to work for them. If Africans work cheaper than Indians, Indians would employ them instead of Indians.

In 1923 or so, I asked Mr. Kareem Jivanjee in a meeting of Indians in Berlin what he and other Indians were doing for

---

1. G. Raghava Rao, "Occupations of the Africans in East Africa," *The Economic Weekly*, 5:29 (July 18, 1953), 801–802.

Africans. The reply was that the Africans were primitive and illiterate and what could one do for them? He was their representative (appointed by Government) in the African Legislative Council. Mr. Jivanjee had gone to England to represent (defend) Indian interests at the Colonial Office, which was authorizing the East African Government to confiscate the highlands, but he had no word for Africans. But Mr. Jivanjee owned large portions of the highlands and was representing "Indian" interests. But Mr. Jivanjee himself said in the meeting that he was illiterate and had just learnt to sign his name on checks. Yet he was using the same language "primitive and illiterate" toward Africans, taking up a superior attitude toward them as the British took toward him and his compatriots. That he was illiterate did not prevent him from taking a contract for the construction of the Uganda Railway and executing it, because he could find the necessary capital.

Recently I read that when an Asiatic Union was formed in East Africa, all Aga Khanis joined it. But their leader did not countenance it because the Union was pro-African also, and he did not want them to get into trouble with the British Government, and all his followers quit the Asiatic Union.

Indians in East Africa, South Africa, and even Mauritius occupy a middle place—they feel superior to the natives and inferior to the Europeans. Till now, the British protected them in their superior position, and now they are setting the natives (rich ones and their poor and ignorant but fanatic followers) against Indians, saying Indians are bloodsuckers.

If the Africans force the British to quit, Indians will have to go away with them. As Indians are generally businessmen who sell foreign goods and export native produce, they will be considered as adjuncts of the British—allied with the British. Not only Indian businessmen but their Indian employees as well. That will be the result of Indians' "superior" position.

The late Mr. Kareem Jivanjee was deprived of all his property in the highlands, and from the position of an Indian Hugo Stinnes (vertical and horizontal trust magnate), he disappeared from the scene. Formerly he had owned shipping companies, saw mills, and import-export business by dim of hard labor.

Indians are the forerunners and agents of British trade and all foreign trade till they established themselves. They distribute all foreign goods supplied by British and other manufacturers and make money; later on, of course, they start industries, e.g., in Malaya and Burma.

Indian indentured laborers in South Africa started trade after the expiry of their term, and established themselves there. Now they are no longer wanted except as subhumans. Ditto in Malay, Ceylon, and Burma.

Sikhs cleared forests in Canada and settled down there, but they are no longer wanted. Not only Indians, but even Russian Tolstoyans who emigrated to Canada in the Tsarist days, cleared forests and made them habitable.

We cannot sit between two stools. Pandit Nehru advises Indians abroad to heroine one with the people. But the Indians in trouble there want protection from the Indian Government, which he cannot give.

63C, Walkeshwar Road

Bombay 6

July 20, 1953.

The Economic Weekly, 5:30 (July 25, 1953), 821–822.

Chronology of Events

1887	April 15	M. P. T. Acharya born in Madras, India
1889	July 20	Magda Nachman born in St. Petersburg, Russia
1907	Aug–Nov	Editor of *India*
1908	November	Departs for Europe; arrives in Paris and proceeds to London; stays at India House
1909	August 17	Departs for Morocco, with Sukh Sagar Dutt, to joins the Rifs against Spain
	September 22	Warrant for Acharya's arrest issued under Section 124A (Sedition) of the Indian Penal Code
	October 5	Returns to Paris
1910	Sept 21–23	Attends the Egyptian National Congress in Brussels, under the name "Bhayankaram"
	November	Departs for Berlin; proceeds to Munich
1911	November	Departs for Constantinople to establish contact with the Committee of Union and Progress
1912	July	Departs for New York City
1914	April	Joins the Yugantar Ashram, San Francisco, and translates for the Tamil edition of the *Ghadr*
1915	April	Joins von Hentig's mission to the Suez Canal to set up Indian National Volunteer Corps
1916	March	Joins the Young Hindustan Association of Constantinople
1917	May	Sets up the Indian National Committee with Virendranath Chattopadhyaya in Stockholm
	July	Indian National Committee meets the Dutch-Scandinavian Committee in Stockholm

	September	Acharya attends the third Zimmerwald Conference in Stockholm
1919	February	Acharya attends the International Socialist Congress, Berne
	May	Acharya joins Mahendra Pratap's delegation to meet Lenin in Moscow
	December	Acharya joins Suritz mission to Kabul, and sets up Indian Revolutionary Association with Abdur Rabb
1920	July–Aug	Attends Second Congress of the Communist International, Moscow
	August 7	Provisional All-India Central Revolutionary Committee (PAICRC) formed in Tashkent, Russia
	October	Communist Party of India (CPI) formed in Tashkent, Russia, with Acharya as chairman
	December	Acharya resigns from the CPI
1921	January	Expelled from the PAICRC
	June	Attends the Third Congress of the Communist International, Moscow
1922		Works for the American Relief Administration in Moscow
		Returns to Berlin with Magda Nachman
	Dec-Jan	Attends the International Working Men's Association (IWMA) conference in Berlin
1925	June	Warrant for his arrest issued under Regulation III of 1818 in case of arrival in India
1926	Jan–April	Acharya applies for a passport with the British Consul, Berlin; offered Emergency Certificate
1928	May	Agnes Smedley writes to the Indian National Congress for help on behalf of Acharya
1929	August	Applies for a passport with the British Consul, Berlin
1931	February	Applies for a passport with the British Consul, Berlin

	August	On the Executive Committee of the Indian Independence Union, Berlin, led by Chattopadhyaya
1934	February	Acharya granted passport for return to India; guarantee to not prosecute if he ends political activities
	April	Acharya and Nachman move to Switzerland to stay with Nachman's family in Zurich
	August	Acharya and Nachman move to Paris
1935	April	Acharya returns to Bombay; Nachman follows a year later
1937	July–Oct	"Reminiscences of a Revolutionary" published in *The Mahratta*
1945		Joins the Managing Committee of the Indian Institute of Sociology
1947		Joins the Managing Committee of the Libertarian Socialist Institute
1948	January	Acharya is diagnosed with tuberculosis
1951	February 12	Nachman dies in Bombay
1954	March 20	Acharya dies in Bombay

Index

A

Acharya, M. P. T: 1907-22, 4–8; 1923-27, 9–15; 1926-35, 14–20; 1935-1949, 20–9; 1950-54, 29–32; as anti-communist, 15; arrest warrant, 12–13; and communism, 8; critiques of, 14, 18; as denouncer, 19; and Gandhi, 1; illness, 27, 32; impact on anarchism, 3–4, 33–4; impact on India, 3, 33; and Kropotkin funeral, 8; literature to India, 13–14; money from Berkman fund, 32; as nationalist, 2–3; overview, 1; as pacifist, 17; and passport inquiries, 12–13, 16–17, 20; in poverty, 9, 27, 32–3; as rebel, 1–2; research into, 2–3; as revolutionary, 4; and Roy, 8; as steno-typist, 10, 12; supporting Muslims, 6; as translator, 10, 14, 19; turn to anarchism, 8, 11, 16–20; as tutor, 19

Acharya, Magda Nachman. *See* Nachman, Madga (wife)

Acharya, Mandayam Prativadi Bhayankaram Tirumal. *See* Acharya, M. P. T.

activity, 153–4

Advance Guard (magazine), 35

Afghanistan, 7, 8

Africa, 271–2

Aiyar, V. V. S, 5

Akahi peasant movement, 105

Aldred, Guy, 13, 22–3, 30

Alexander Berkman Aid Fund, 26, 32

Ali, Asaf, 10, 246–7, 246n5

All-India Trade Union Congress (AITUC), 185, 228, 239

American Federation of Labor (AFL), 239

Amin, Govind, 5

anarchism: Acharya impact on, 3–4; Acharya's manifesto, 45–6; appeal of, 31; of Bakunin, 60–1; and Balabanoff, 67–8; and chaos, 200–1; and communism, 16, 43–4; vs. communism, 26, 61, 197, 201–2; definitions of, 43–4, 191, 196–7, 200–1, 210, 213; differing theories of, 208; and Eastman, 60–1; and economic crisis, 130; and elections, 195; and exchange, 169, 183–4; and Gandhism, 29; goals of, 193, 195, 198, 203; influence on India, 3; literature, 11, 13–14, 19, 189, 214; as local economies, 109; money for, 26; and nationalism, 135–6; as only alternative, 16; as pacifist, 146–7, 175, 199–200, 205–6; in Paris, 5, 24; as powerful, 85; preparing for, 143, 251, 253; and production, 181; and scientific economics, 182, 184; and socialism, 43, 62, 63–5; as solution to capitalism crumbling, 145; in Spain, 160–9, 170, 203–4, 212, 213; and the State, 211; and terrorism, 204–5; testing, 249; as transition, 43, 117; and violence, 192; and wages, 252. *See also* Bakunin,

Anarchism from Proudhon to Kropotkin (Nettlau), 159

Anarchist Encyclopedia, 214

The Anarchists in London (Meltzer), 33

anarcho-communism, 124, 182, 208–9

Brazil, 110–11
Briand, Aristide, 211, 211n1
British Government: as bringing development, 36; Free Trade Union Committee, 239; pressure on Germany for deportation, 12–13; thoughts on Acharya, 12, 17; and violence, 103, 104. *See also* imperialism
Brockway, Fenner, 17
Brokaw, Warren Edwin, 123nn1–2, 213
Buddhism, 148–54
bureaucracy, 194–5
Burma, 148–9

C

Cama, Bhikaiji, 5, 7, 20
Canada, 273
capitalism: vs. Bolshevism, 268–9; Bolshevism as, 50, 61, 64, 180, 197–8, 254–5; celebrating workers' delegations, 56–7; as chaos, 128; and class struggle, 116; communism as, 83–4, 116–17; and co-operatives, 263; as decaying, 119, 248–53; Delaisi's ideas of, 93–6; and ethics, 162, 164, 165; and exchange, 111–12; and industrialization, 97; and investment, 227–8; Marxism as, 65, 180; and money, 100; and nationalism, 186; 1934 forecast, 145; and poor nations, 179; and trade unions, 119, 230–40; understanding socialism through, 64; workers in, 118–20. *See also* profits
capitalists, 213
Carpenter, Edward, 51
castes, 70–1, 137, 138, 246. *See also* Brahmins
centralism, 193–4, 197
Chakravarti, Chandra Kanta, 6
Chand, Feroze, 15

chaos, 128, 146–7, 169–70, 200–1, 250, 253
Chatto, 1, 5–7, 9–10, 11–12, 14–15, 19, 21
Chattopadhyaya, Virendranath. *See* Chatto
Cherney, John, 27
Chicherin, Georgy, 19, 53–4, 53n6
children, 55, 80
China, 50–2, 112
choice, 108
city and countryside exchange, 121–2
civil disobedience: as honored, 133–4; salt tax march, 131–2, 131n1; and solidarity, 206; teaching resistance, 18; and violence, 103
class, 38–9, 109–10, 194–5
class struggle, 56, 114, 115–16
CNT (Confederación Nacional del Trabajo), 169
collectives, 257
colonization, 1, 271–2. *See also* imperialism
Commission de Relations l'Internationale Anarchiste, 22
Committee of Union and Progress, 6
commodities, 96
communes, 77–82, 110–12
communication, 79–80, 84
communism: and anarchism, 43; vs. anarchism, 16, 61, 201–2; and Bolshevism, 209, 254, 256; as capitalism, 83–4, 116–17; and dictatorships, 194–5; and exchange theory, 125; in India, 55, 230 (*See also* Communist Party of India); and LAI, 15; red scare in India, 230; as selfish, 83; and true form, 42–4. *See also* Bolshevism; Marxism; socialism
Communist Party of India (CPI), 3, 4, 8, 15, 35n1, 36
constitutions, 45, 46–7, 74–5, 81, 191–2. *See also* the State

The International Anti-Militarist
Bureau (IAMB), 169, 169n3
International Socialist Congress, 7
International Working Men's
Association (IWMA), 3, 10–11,
14, 19, 241
internationalist approach, 4
internment camps, 71
investment, 234–8
Islam, 161
"Isms," 161–3, 191
Istanbul, 6
Italy, 212, 240–1
IWW, 15, 28

J

Jagirdars, 46, 46n2
jails, 191–2, 196, 229
Japan, 18, 214
jealousy, 89–91
"On Jealousy" (Acharya), 18
Jean, Jaurès, 5
Jensen, Albert, 22
Jinnah, Muhammad Ali, 246–7
Jivanjee, Kareem, 31, 271–3
Juin, Lucien-Ernest. *See* Armand, E.
justice, 194, 229

K

Kabul, 7, 8
Karakhan, Lev, 19, 52, 52n4, 53–4
Karanjia, Rustom Khurshedji, 261,
261n3
Karanth, K. Shivaram, 15
Karma, 150–1, 153
Keell, Thomas, 13, 14, 24
Kerensky, Alexander, 53
Khoikhoi people, 138–9
Kim, Ir Sen (Kim Il-sung), 268,
268n3, 269
Kollontai, Alexandra, 265–6, 265n3
Korea, 267–8, 267n1

Kripalani, Jivatram Bhagwandas, 264,
264n1
Krishnamurti, Jiddu, 176–7, 177n2
Krishnavarma, Shyamaji, 4–5
Kropotkin, Peter, 8, 26, 112, 192, 208
Kumarappa, J. C., 219, 219n1, 221–5,
255
Kuomintang party, 52n4

L

La Cite Chinoise (Simon), 51
La Revista Blanca (magazine), 20
La Voix du Travail (newspaper), 16
Labour Kisan Party of Hindustan, 15
Labriola, Antonio, 66
Lachmann, Benedict, 123, 123n1
land, 37, 71, 105, 256–7
landowners, 51
laws, 37–8, 198, 202
leaders, 56, 84–6, 114, 186–7,
189–90. *See also* dictatorships
League against Imperialism (LAI),
14–15
L'en dehors (newspaper), 18, 24, 32
Lenin, Vladimir, 7–8, 59, 198, 265
Leninism, 52–3
Les Nouvelles Pacifistes (newspaper), 24
Lester, Muriel, 174, 174n1
Letourneau, Charles, 51
*L'Évolution du commerce dans les diverses
races humaines* (Letourneau), 51
Li Shizeng, 20
liberals, 38, 56
Libertarian Book House, 22
Libertarian Socialist Institute (LSI),
22, 25–6, 28, 33. *See also* Indian
Institute of Sociology
libraries, 20, 22, 25–6, 28
Lind, O., 148
L'Internationale (Guillaume), 26
literacy, 186–7, 229, 272
local vs. country, 47
logic, 176

London, England, 5–6
London Indian Association, 15
Longuet, Jean, 7
Lord Irwin, 132, 132n3
Lotvala, Kusum, 21, 26
Lotvala, Nitisen Bhavan, 19
Lotvala, Ranchoddas Bhavan, 19, 21
Louvet, Louis, 24
love, 90–1
Lu Chien Bo, 22
L'Unique (newspaper), 24

M

Maccreagh, Gordon, 110–11
Madam Cama. *See* Cama, Bhikaiji
The Mahratta (newspaper), 4, 16, 21
Makhno, Nestor, 2
Makhnovism, 135
Marx, Karl, 59–60, 212, 248
The Marxian Way (newspaper), 23
Marxism: vs. anarcho-syndicalism,
    67–8; and bureaucracy, 194; as
    capitalist, 65, 166–7, 180; and
    ethics, 165–6; and exploitation,
    166; general criticism, 58–9; as
    postponing socialism, 64–5. *See
    also* Bolshevism; communism;
    socialism
Mashruwala, Shri Kishorlal, 29–30,
    253, 254, 254n1, 255
The Masses of India (journal), 15
Maximoff, Grigori, 11, 25, 25–6
Mazumdar, J., 33
Meltzer, Albert, 1, 25, 30, 32–3
Melville, Herman, 111
metaphysics, 58–62, 64, 77, 150–1
militarism, 72, 74–5, 85
minorities/majorities, 45–6, 192–3
money: and banks, 98; and capitalism
    decay, 250; controlling, 141;
    definition of, 127; and distribu-
    tion, 222; and ethics, 165; and
    exploitation, 107, 109; as insane,

129–30; and interest, 128–9;
    and Kumarappa's ideas, 221–4;
    and production, 48, 100–2, 183;
    stabilizing, 178–9; and trade
    unions, 107–8, 113; and war, 173;
    and work, 99, 111. *See also* banks;
    gold standard; inflation; taxes
monogamy, 90–1
monopolism, 93, 94, 114–15, 117,
    131n1, 197
morality, 221, 223–4
Morocco, 5
"Mother India" (Acharya), 17
Mukherji, Abani, 35, 35n1
Mumbai (Bombay), 20–1, 26
Muños, Vladimir, 2
Münzenberg, Willi, 14
Mussolini, Benito, 173
Mutualism (Acharya), 22
Myanmar (Burma), 148–9
Myasnikov, Gavril, 27

N

Nabokov, Vladimir, 9
Nachman, Magda (wife), 8, 9, 19, 20,
    24, 27, 31–2
Nambiar, A. C. N., 9, 11–12
Nanda, Gulzarilal, 228, 228n1
nationalism: Aldred warned of, 30;
    and anarchism, 205; as anarchist,
    135–6; and bourgeoisie, 72; and
    capitalism, 186; in China, 50–1;
    described, 134; of Gandhi, 131,
    134–5; as inclusive, 135; *The
    Mahratta* (newspaper), 21; as
    pacifist, 131. *See also* anti-colonial
    nationalism; Indian National
    Congress
nationalization, 37, 84
Native Americans, 110
Nazism, 19, 137
necessities/comforts, 47–8, 79–80,
    183, 184, 263–4

provocations, 105, 133–4
publishing industry, 155–6

Q

Quakers, 175

R

Rabb, Abdur, 7
Rabochii put' (newspaper), 11
race, 70–1, 137–9, 149
racism, 271–2
Radical Democratic Party (India), 23
Ram, Jagjivan, 28
Ramnath, Maia, 2, 22
Rana, S. R., 5
Rao, G. Raghava, 271
Rao, Madhav, 5
Rao, Raja, 28
Rappoport, Charles, 5
"In Regard to Communism"
(Mashruwala), 29, 254
Reisner, Mikhail, 265, 265n2
Relief Fund of the International
Working Men's Association
for Anarchists and Anarcho-
Syndicalists Imprisoned and
Exiled in Russia, 14
religion, 30–1, 38, 46, 47, 148–54,
213, 246
"Reminiscences of a Revolutionary"
(Acharya), 4, 21
representatives, 193, 195, 203
responsibility, 208
revolution, 51, 52, 146, 203, 263–4
Revolutionary Communist Party, 228
Reynolds, Reginald, 132, 132n3
Rhee, Syngman, 268, 268n2, 269–70
Rifaat, Mansour, 5, 10
Rifs, 5
risk, 119
Road to Freedom (newspaper), 17
Rocker, Rudolf, 8, 10, 11, 21, 26, 214

Roosevelt, Franklin D., 127, 127n1
Rowlatt Committee, 40, 40n5
Roy, M. N.: about, 35n1, 185n1;
and Acharya, 1, 8, 19, 23;
and Bolshevism, 37–8, 38–41;
contradictions, 35–7; and Indian
National Congress, 35, 40. *See also*
Indian Federation of Labour
Rubanovich, Ilya 5
Ruminov, Basil, 23
Russia, 7, 8, 212. *See also* Bolshevism

S

Sacco, Nicola, 87–8
Saklatvala, Shapurji, 55, 55n1
salt, 131, 131n1
Samoa, 109
Savarkar, Vinayak Damodar, 4, 30–1,
245, 246n4
"Savarkar: A Criticism" (Acharya), 30
Schapiro, Alexander, 10, 11, 16, 27
Schrader, Karl, 56–7, 56–7n2
science. *See* economics; metaphysics
Scotland Yard, 5
Sea Customs Act of 1878, 11
Second International, 7
Second World War, 21–2, 144. *See
also* war
self-rule, 193, 194, 198, 206–8
sexuality, 90–1
Shaw, Tom, 56–7, 56n3
Shiromani Gurdwara Parbandhak
Committee, 15
Sikhs, 15, 104, 273
silver, 144
Simon, G. Eugène, 51
Singh, Ajit, 5
Singh, Iqbal, 28
Sino-International Library, 20
slavery, 89–91
small businesses/producers, 98–102
Smedley, Agnes, 9, 11–12
social contracts, 207

trade unions: and capitalism, 119, 230–40; and credit notes, 101; elitism of, 113–14; and exchange, 124; Free Trade Union Committee, 239; government corruption, 188; government recognition, 55; leaders, 56–7, 114, 189–90; and money, 107–8, 113; and solidarity, 240–2; splits in India, 185–6, 228; and trusts, 93; and wages, 240. *See also* anarcho-syndicalism; syndicalism
transitions, 109, 116, 117, 199, 209–10, 256
Trent, Evelyn, 40
tribes, 70–1
Trotsky, Leon, 19, 265
Trotskyites, 230
Troyanovsky, Konstantin, 7
trusts, 61, 92–6
Tsvetaeva, Marina, 9
tuberculosis, 27, 32–3
Tugwell, Rexford, 127, 127n1, 129
Typee (Melville), 111

U

Uganda, 271, 272
United Nations (U.N.O), 215, 267–8
United States, 6, 112, 180, 213, 213n1, 225, 228
unity: and categories, 46; and constitutions, 45; forcing, 83; and Indian National Congress, 35; in Korea, 268–70; and militarism, 75; mutual production, 100; and privilege, 48; and trade unions, 114; traitors to, 44
University of Bombay, 26
Untermann, Ernst, 58–9, 59n3
upper classes, 38–9
Utopia, 8
Uzbekistan, 8

V

Vanzetti, Bartolomeo, 87–8
Vasantha (newspaper), 15
violence: and anarchism, 192; and civil disobedience, 132; and constitutions, 191; distinguishing, 72–3, 176; and laws, 198; prevention of, 133; and socialism, 74–6; and the State, 73, 103, 104, 192, 218
Voline (Vsevolod Mikhaïlovitch Eichenbaum), 27
Volunteer (newspaper), 15

W

wages/wage system: abolishment of, 47, 189, 252; in Africa, 271; and anarchism, 252; and Bolshevism, 37; and capitalism decay, 253; and class struggle, 114; and consumption, 225–6; and First International, 212–13; and prices, 140–1, 217–18; and production, 76, 92, 188; and socialism, 76; and Stalin's Russia, 249; and trade unions, 240. *See also* equitism system
war: and anarchism, 199; and capitalism, 248; civil, 192 (*See also* Spain); and Depression, 144; in Korea, 267–70, 267n1; and Prasad, 231–2; predictions, 168, 171–3; and Russians, 260–1; and the State, 215–16, 261–2. *See also* First World War; Second World War
What is Mutualism? (Swartz), 214
"What is Property?" (Proudhon), 22
White Waters and Black (Maccreagh), 110–11
Whither India? (Singh and Rao), 28
Witkop, Milly, 8
Witkop, Rose, 8

women, 89–91, 266
Wood, Edward Frederick Lindley, 132, 132n3
The Word (newspaper), 22–3, 30
work, 48, 79
workers: children as, 55; definition of, 118–20; life in India, 227–30; and literacy, 186–7, 229; and the State, 180; and trade unions, 113, 229
Workers' Councils, 38
The Workers' Dreadnought (newspaper), 11
Workers' Party (India), 56
World Pacifist Conference, 231
The World Scene from the Libertarian Point of View (Free Society Group), 25
Wyllie, William Hutt Curzon, 4–5

Y

Yajnik, Indulal, 19
Yamaga Taiji, 10, 22
Yelensky, Boris, 23, 25, 26–7, 32

Z

Zemindars, 46, 46n2
Zimmerwald-Kienthal movement, 66–7
Zinoviev, Grigory, 52, 52n4
Zurich, 20

AK Press is small, in terms of staff and resources, but we also manage to be one of the world's most productive anarchist publishing houses. We publish close to twenty books every year, and distribute thousands of other titles published by like-minded independent presses and projects from around the globe. We're entirely worker-run and democratically managed. We operate without a corporate structure—no boss, no managers, no bullshit.

The Friends of AK program is a way you can directly contribute to the continued existence of AK Press, and ensure that we're able to keep publishing books like this one! Friends pay $25 a month directly into our publishing account ($30 for Canada, $35 for international), and receive a copy of every book AK Press publishes for the duration of their membership! Friends also receive a discount on anything they order from our website or buy at a table: 50% on AK titles, and 20% on everything else. We have a Friends of AK ebook program as well: $15 a month gets you an electronic copy of every book we publish for the duration of your membership. You can even sponsor a very discounted membership for someone in prison.

Email FRIENDSOFAK@AKPRESS.ORG for more info, or visit the Friends of AK Press website: HTTPS://WWW.AKPRESS.ORG/FRIENDS.HTML.

There are always great book projects in the works—so sign up now to become a Friend of AK Press, and let the presses roll!